RAND McNALLY

Road Atlas 2018 EasyFinder®

CONTENTS

TRAVEL INFORMATION

Best of the Road® Trips 2-6
Our editor's five favorite road trips from our Best of the Road® collection.

Mileage Chart 7
Driving distances between 77 North American cities.

Mileage and Driving Times Map
inside back cover
Distances and driving times between over a hundred North American cities.

MAPS

Map legend inside front cover

United States overview map 8-9

U.S. states 10-109

Canada overview map 110-111

Canadian provinces 112-127

Mexico overview map and Puerto Rico 160

U.S. and Canadian cities 128-159

Photo Credits: p. 2 ©Michael Dwyer / Alamy, p. 3 ©digidreamgrafix / istockphoto, p. 4 ©Cindy Murray / istockphoto, p. 5 ©tonda / istockphoto, p. 6 ©Giorgio Fochesato / istockphoto.

 Published and printed in U.S.A.

For licensing information and copyright permissions, contact us at permissions@randmcnally.com

If you have a comment, suggestion, or even a compliment, please visit us at randmcnally.com/contact or write to:
Rand McNally Consumer Affairs
P.O. Box 7600
Chicago, Illinois 60680-9915

1 2 3 VE 18 17

SUSTAINABLE FORESTRY INITIATIVE · Certified Sourcing
www.sfiprogram.org
SFI-00993
This Label Applies to Text Stock Only

W9-BPL-614

State & Province Maps

United States

Alabama	10 - 11
Alaska	12 - 13
Arizona	14 - 15
Arkansas	16 - 17
California	18 - 21
Colorado	22 - 23
Connecticut	24 - 27
Delaware	28 - 29
Florida	30 - 31
Georgia	32 - 33
Hawaii	13
Idaho	34 - 35
Illinois	36 - 37
Indiana	38 - 39
Iowa	40 - 41
Kansas	42 - 43
Kentucky	44 - 47
Louisiana	48 - 49
Maine	50 - 51
Maryland	28 - 29
Massachusetts	24 - 27
Michigan	52 - 53
Minnesota	54 - 55
Mississippi	56 - 57
Missouri	58 - 59
Montana	60 - 61
Nebraska	62 - 63
Nevada	18 - 21
New Hampshire	64 - 65
New Jersey	66 - 67
New Mexico	68 - 69
New York	70 - 73
North Carolina	74 - 77
North Dakota	78 - 79
Ohio	80 - 83
Oklahoma	84 - 85
Oregon	86 - 87
Pennsylvania	88 - 91
Rhode Island	24 - 27
South Carolina	74 - 77
South Dakota	92 - 93
Tennessee	45 - 47
Texas	94 - 97
Utah	98 - 99
Vermont	64 - 65
Virginia	100 - 103
Washington	104 - 105
West Virginia	100 - 103
Wisconsin	106 - 107
Wyoming	108 - 109

Canada

Alberta	112 - 115
British Columbia	112 - 115
Manitoba	116 - 119
New Brunswick	126 - 127
Newfoundland and Labrador	126 - 127
Nova Scotia	126 - 127
Ontario	120 - 123
Prince Edward Island	126 - 127
Québec	124 - 125
Saskatchewan	116 - 119

City Maps

Albuquerque	129
Atlanta	128
Austin	130
Baltimore	129
Birmingham	129
Boston	130 - 131
Buffalo	132
Charlotte	130
Chicago	132 - 133
Cincinnati	134
Cleveland	137
Columbus	135
Dallas	134 & 136
Denver	135
Detroit	138 - 139
Fort Lauderdale	142 - 143
Fort Worth	134 & 136
Greensboro	138 - 139
Hartford	137
Houston	140
Indianapolis	139
Jacksonville	137
Kansas City	142 - 143
Las Vegas	143
Los Angeles	144 - 145
Louisville	139
Memphis	146
Mexico City	160
Miami	142 - 143
Milwaukee	146 - 147
Minneapolis	141
Nashville	144
New Orleans	146
New York	148 - 149
Newark	148 - 149
Norfolk	146 - 147
Orlando	153
Ottawa	111
Philadelphia	150 - 151
Phoenix	147
Pittsburgh	152 - 153
Portland	151
Raleigh	154
St. Louis	150 - 151
St. Paul	141
St. Petersburg	154 - 155
Sacramento	154 - 155
Salt Lake City	157
San Antonio	155
San Diego	154
San Francisco	156 - 157
Seattle	152 - 153
Tampa	154 - 155
Toronto	158
Vancouver	158
Washington D.C.	158 - 159
Winston-Salem	138 - 139

BEST OF THE ROAD® TRIPS

If you're like us, you love road trips. Here are some favorites from our Best of the Road collection. They follow scenic routes along stretches of coastline, both east and west; to forests and mountains; and through small towns and big cities.

Mt. Washington Cog Railway

Northern New England Summits & Shores

American heritage took root in New England four centuries ago, and Vermont, New Hampshire, and Maine have proudly preserved that legacy. En route to the coast, you'll travel through mountainous national forests and take in treasured heritage sites.

Bennington, VT

Bennington Center for the Arts Covered Bridge Museum. A gallery here is dedicated to Vermont's iconic covered bridges, 104 of which are still operational. An interactive map helps you plan a bridge tour; five of them are nearby. *44 Gypsy Ln., (802) 442-7158, www.thebennington.org.*

Manchester

Hildene. Robert Todd Lincoln built this Georgian Revival mansion in 1905. It's filled with original furniture and presidential and Lincoln family memorabilia. The 412-acre grounds encompass a farm, gardens, trails, and woods. *1005 Hildene Rd., (802) 362-1788, www.hildene.org.*

Rutland

Norman Rockwell Museum of Vermont. Displays include more than 2,500 *Saturday Evening Post* and other magazine covers, advertisements, and paintings by this iconic artist. *654 Rte. 4 E. (Rte.100), (877) 773-6095, www.normanrockwellvt.com.*

Waterbury

Ben & Jerry's Factory Tour. Guided half-hour tours let you lap up the history of a beloved brand. Free ice cream samples are part of the deal. *1281 Waterbury-Stowe Rd., (866) 258-6877, www.benjerry.com.*

Bretton Woods, NH

Mt. Washington Cog Railway. Channel the little engine that could on a 3-mile ride up the northeast's tallest peak on the world's second-steepest railway, built in 1869. *3168 Base Station Rd., 6 mi off Rte. 302, (603) 278-5404, www.thecog.com.*

Gorham

Mount Washington Auto Road. Get your "This Car Climbed Mount Washington" bumper sticker by driving up to almost 6,300 feet along this curvaceous 7-plus-mile toll road, open (weather permitting) since 1861. *Rte. 16, Pinkham Notch, (603) 466-3988, mtwashingtonautoroad.com.*

Wolfeboro

The Winnipesaukee Belle. The *Winni Belle*, a 2-story, 65-foot paddle-wheeler makes 90-minute round-trip tours of Lake Winnipesaukee. *90 N. Main St., (609) 569-3016, www.winnipesaukeebelle.com.*

Portsmouth

Strawbery Banke Museum. Colonial life gets real at this living history museum. Downtown Portsmouth also has lots of historic buildings—many housing boutiques, restaurants, and inns. *14 Hancock St., (603) 433-1100, www.strawberybanke.org.*

Kittery, ME

Kittery Trading Post. The town of Kittery (founded in 1647) has a proud history and a robust shopping scene—one that includes several outlet malls and this rustic-looking, multilevel emporium, which has been outfitting outdoors enthusiasts since 1938. *301 U.S. 1, (888) 587-6246, www.kitterytradingpost.com.*

Ogunquit

Ogunquit Beach. This broad, gradually sloping, white-sand beach is consistently ranked one of America's 10 best. It covers 1.5 miles of oceanfront and another 3.5 miles along the Ogunquit River, behind frontal dunes. *(207) 646-2939, ogunquit.org.*

Old Orchard Beach

Old Orchard Beach & Pier. In warm months, this 7-mile stretch of coastline buzzes. At the center of the sandy beach is the Pier, a shop- and restaurant-lined boardwalk. It's all anchored by the **Palace Playland** (207/934-2001, www.palaceplayland.com) amusement park. *(207) 934-2500, www.oldorchardbeachmaine.com.*

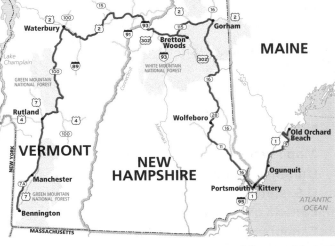

Atlas map I-1, p. 65
Distance: 425 miles point to point.

Blue Ridge Parkway near Asheville, NC

Inspirational Blue Ridge Parkway

Between Virginia's Shenandoah Valley and North Carolina's Great Smoky Mountains is one of this country's greatest treasures: the **Blue Ridge Parkway**. The scenery along the way is spectacular, and, just off the way, are charming communities with general stores, folk-art marketplaces, down-home restaurants, and cultural museums.

Atlas map F-9, p. 103
Distance: 450 miles point to point

Charlottesville, VA

Monticello. The author of the Declaration of Independence, third president of the U.S., and founder of the University of Virginia put his vast knowledge of the arts and sciences to good use throughout his 5,000-acre estate. *931 Thomas Jefferson Pkwy. (Rte. 53), (434) 984-9800, www. monticello.org.*

Grottoes

Grand Caverns. Tours of America's oldest show caves (discovered in 1804) take in popcorn, flowstone, drapery, shield, and soda-straw formations in chambers with evocative names like the Persian Palace, Dante's Inferno, and Cathedral Hall. *5 Grand Caverns Dr., (540) 249-5705, www.grandcaverns.com.*

Natural Bridge

Natural Bridge State Park. In the 19th and 20th centuries, this 215-foot-high, 90-foot-span arch appeared on Wonders of the World lists and became a popular tourist attraction. Today the majestic formation is part of a 1,500-acre state park. *6477 S. Lee Hwy., (540) 291-1324, www.dcr.virginia.gov/state-parks.*

Floyd

Mabry Mill Restaurant. The restaurant offers all kinds of down-home specialties.

Another plus? Breakfast is served all day. But this living history complex also offers a glimpse at life in the early 20th century, with a gristmill, sawmill, blacksmith shop, and the Matthews Cabin. *Blue Ridge Pkwy., MP 176.1, (276) 952-2947, www.mabrymillrestaurant.com.*

Mount Airy, NC

Wally's Service Station. In actor Andy Griffith's hometown—the basis for the fictional Mayberry—see *Andy Griffith Show*–related sites such as Floyd's City Barber Shop; the **Andy Griffith Museum** (218 Rockford St., 336/786-1604, www.andygriffithmuseum.com); and Wally's Service Station, where you can sign up for guided town tours in a reproduction Mayberry squad car. *625 S. Main St., (336) 789-6743, www.tourmayberry.com.*

Blowing Rock

Blowing Rock. Stand at the precipice 3,000 feet above the Johns River Gorge to experience powerful gusts sweep up and over the rim like invisible ocean waves. Hours are weather permitting; call ahead. *432 The Rock Rd., (828) 295-7111, www.theblowingrock.com.*

Tweetsie Railroad. Owing to its shrill whistle, locals gave the original East Tennessee and Western North Carolina Railroad this nickname. Today the steam locomotive is one of several rides and attractions. *300 Tweetsie Railroad Ln., (828) 264-9061, tweetsie.com.*

Valle Crucis

Original Mast General Store. This country store opened around 1883, and things haven't changed much since then. A pot-bellied stove sits in the store's center, and shelves are stocked with a lot of cool things you didn't know people made any more. *3565 Hwy. 194 S., (828) 963-6511, www.mastgeneralstore.com.*

Asheville

Biltmore Estate. Modeled after a 16th-century Loire Valley chateau, George W. Vanderbilt's 250-room mansion was completed in 1895. America's largest privately owned home has more than 4 acres of floor space, 65 fireplaces, 43 bathrooms, 34 bedrooms, and 3 kitchens. Allow a day to explore the estate; reserving tour tickets saves a few bucks. *1 Lodge Rd., (800) 411-3812, www.biltmore.com.*

4

Wisconsin shoreline

Along Lake Michigan in Wisconsin

The blue waters of Lake Michigan form the backdrop for this road trip that begins in the brewing (and Harley-Davidson) mecca of Milwaukee and ends in the Packer's capital of Green Bay. In between, the winding route hugs the lake's western shore, passing through regions rich in natural beauty and towns rich in Wisconsin history.

Milwaukee

Miller Brewery Tour. A guided tour traces Miller's brewing history since 1855, takes in the original storage caves, and highlights today's high-tech production lines. At the end, enjoy an ice-cold brew. *4251 W. State St., (414) 931-2337, www.millercoors.com/breweries.*

Harley-Davidson Museum. Displays showcase some 450 motorcycles, trace the history of an iconic company—which is still based in Milwaukee—and celebrate the brand's aficionados. *400 W. Canal St., (414) 287-2789, www.harley-davidson.com.*

RiverWalk District. Lined by trendy shops, cafes, restaurants, pubs, and sculptures, the lively RiverWalk follows the Milwaukee River for 2 miles through the city's heart. *milwaukeeriverwalkdistrict.com.*

Sturgeon Bay

Door County Maritime Museum. In addition to learning about shipbuilding and commercial fishing at this waterfront museum, you'll meet a colorful cast of characters. Its Baumgartner Gallery explores the history of the county's numerous lighthouses. *120 N. Madison Ave., (920) 743-5958, www.dcmm.org.*

Carlsville

Door Peninsula Winery. The oldest and largest winery in Door County has grown into a multilevel complex that houses a tasting room as well as a restaurant and a distillery. *5806 State Hwy. 42, (920) 743-7431, store.dcwine.com/winery.*

Egg Harbor

Wood Orchard Market. This is one the best of the county's famous produce stands. Watch for its giant apple along State Highway 42. While you shop, your kids can enjoy the property's go-cart track. *8112 State Hwy. 42, (920) 868-2334, www.woodorchard.com.*

Door County Trolley. These bright red trolleys are a familiar sight along this region's byways, and a narrated trip (several tours are offered) on one of them lets you concentrate on the scenery instead of the road. *8030 State Hwy. 42, (920) 868-1100, www.doorcountytrolley.com.*

Fish Creek

Peninsula State Park. This 3,776-acre expanse of woods, wetlands, meadows, and dolostone cliffs is bordered by 8 miles of Green Bay shoreline and is home to one of Door County's loveliest lighthouses, Eagle Bluff. *9462 Shore Rd., (920) 868-3258, dnr.wi.gov/topic/parks.*

Sister Bay

The Shoreline Charters. With 300 miles of coastline, some of Door County's best views are from the water, and this charter company offers a number of memorable boat excursions. *Sister Bay Marina, 10733 N. Bay Shore Dr., (920) 854-4707, www.shorelinecharters.net.*

Green Bay

Green Bay Packers Hall of Fame. Located at Lambeau Field, this hall of fame is packed with Packers artifacts and memorabilia. There's even a re-creation of legendary coach Vince Lombardi's office. You can also tour the stadium and shop for green-and-gold items in the pro shop. *1265 Lombardi Ave., (920) 569-7512, www.packers.com/lambeau-field.*

National Railroad Museum. With more than 70 locomotives and railroad cars, this is one of the nation's largest rail museums. Highlights include a 600-ton Union Pacific Big Boy and a Pullman Porters exhibit. *2285 S. Broadway, (920) 437-7623, www.nationalrrmuseum.org.*

Atlas map G-6, p. 107
Distance: 213 miles point to point.

Colorado River in Grand Canyon

Canyon Country

On this journey, the Grand Canyon is just one of many magnificent natural wonders. Denver is a great place to acclimate to higher elevations and brush up on frontier history. Near the Utah border, the majestic Rocky Mountains are replaced by glowing-red sandstone peaks and valleys in a trio of national parks. In Arizona, follow a stretch of historic Route 66 before reaching the Grand Canyon, a place that's older than time, with views that never get old.

Atlas map C-6, p. 23
Distance: 1,055 miles point to point.

Denver, CO

U.S. Mint–Denver. In 1859, a year after gold was discovered in Colorado, the U.S. Government established this bastion of both gold and silver bullion. Reservations are required for the free, guided, 45-minute tours of the current facility (circa 1906). *320 W. Colfax Ave., (303) 405-4761, www.usmint.gov.*

Grand Junction

Museums of Western Colorado. Exhibits at the **Museum of the West** (462 Ute Ave., 970/242-0971) highlight 1,000 years of history. At the **Cross Orchards Historic Site** (3073 F Rd., 970/434-9814), costumed docents demonstrate pioneer life. *www.museumofwesternco.com.*

Moab, UT

Arches National Park. Here, an azure sky contrasts with a crimson and gold panorama of graceful arches, spires, and fins. This park protects more than 2,000 arches, the world's largest concentration. A scenic drive winds more than 20 miles each way. *N. Hwy. 191, (435) 719-2299, www.nps.gov/arch.*

Bryce Canyon City

Bryce Canyon National Park. Paiute lore has it that Coyote became displeased with the Legend People who lived in Bryce Canyon, turned them to stone, and left them frozen in time. Geologists have it that the fantastic spires, bridges, and hoodoos are the work of ongoing erosion. Take in the ever-changing panorama along the 37-mile round-trip park road or one of several short trails. *Entrance a few miles south of intersection of Hwy. 12 & Hwy. 63, (435) 834-5322, www.nps.gov/brca.*

Springdale

Zion National Park. The rugged high-plateau terrain is a hiker's paradise, with everything from forests of piñon and juniper pine to red rock canyons. Note that April through October shuttles (mandatory) take you from the Springdale visitors center along the Zion Canyon Scenic Drive to the upper canyon. *State Rte. 9, (435) 772-3256, www.nps.gov/zion.*

Page, AZ

Glen Canyon National Recreation Area. Glen Canyon's reddish sandstone formations contrast with the sleek blue waters of 186-mile-long Lake Powell, formed when the 710-foot Glen Canyon Dam was completed in 1966. At the Carl Hayden Visitors Center find out about trails and arrange a dam tour. *691 Scenic View Dr., (928) 608-6200, www.nps.gov/glca.*

Flagstaff

Lowell Observatory. Founded in 1894, Lowell Observatory is where astronomer Clyde Tombaugh discovered Pluto in 1930. Its hands-on exhibit hall lets you peer through mighty telescopes. *1400 W. Mars Hill Rd., (928) 774-3358, lowell.edu.*

Grand Canyon

Grand Canyon National Park. The popular South Rim has the main Mather Point visitors center and Grand Canyon Village, with its many amenities—including the depot for the **Grand Canyon Railway** (233 N. Grand Canyon Blvd., 800/843-8724, www.thetrain.com) out of Williams. North Rim amenities are fewer, and access is seasonal, but the views are spectacular. To see the West Rim, nearer to Las Vegas, consider a walk on the famous Skywalk. Regardless of where you visit, make reservations (for everything!) as far ahead as possible. *(928) 638-7888, www.nps.gov/grca.*

Golden Gate Bridge, San Francisco

San Francisco and the Central Coast

California's glorious Highway 1 hugs the coast, showcasing windswept bluffs and ocean vistas at every turn. And those are just some of the intriguing sites on this trip from San Francisco south along the Central Coast.

San Francisco

Alcatraz. Over a million people tour "The Rock," America's most renowned prison, each year. Ferries depart from attraction-filled Fisherman's Wharf. *Fort Mason, B201, (415) 561-4900, www.nps.gov/alca.*

Ferry Building. The epicenter of the city's epic food scene serves up things like organic hot dogs, fresh Dungeness crab, rose-flavored gelato, and pumpkin milkshakes. *1 The Embarcadero, (415) 983-8030, www.ferrybuildingmarketplace.com.*

Golden Gate Park. The 1,017-acre park has trails, museums, gardens, windmills, lakes, and much, much more. *7th Ave., between Lincoln Way and Fulton St., (415) 831-5510, www.golden-gate-park.com.*

Moss Beach

Fitzgerald Marine Reserve. Don your water shoes, and hike down the cliff to tidal pools rife with marine life. Be on the lookout for seals. *200 Nevada Ave., (650) 728-3584, www.fitzgeraldreserve.org.*

Santa Cruz

Santa Cruz Beach Boardwalk. Among this seaside amusement park's more than 30 rides are a historic carousel and roller coaster. *400 Beach St., (831) 423-5590, www.beachboardwalk.com.*

Monterey

Monterey Bay Aquarium. Located in historic shop- and restaurant-filled Cannery

Atlas map F-2, p. 18
Distance: 394 miles point to point.

Row, the aquarium showcases sea otters, kelp forests, sharks, jellyfish, and sardines. *886 Cannery Row, (831) 648-4800, www.montereybayaquarium.org.*

Carmel

Carmel Walks. Take in the town's storybook buildings and beautiful beaches on a two-hour guided walk with this company. *Ocean Ave. and Lincoln St., (831) 373-2813 (info), (888) 284-8405 (tickets), carmelwalks.com.*

Big Sur

Julia Pfieffer Burns State Park. An 80-foot waterfall plunges into the ocean, and trails meander along bluffs, offering peeks of migrating gray whales (in winter), sea lions, and seals. The bird-watching is great, too. *Big Sur Station #1, (831) 667-2315, www.parks.ca.gov.*

Nepenthe Restaurant. Some say the buzz surpasses the food and the service. Still, it's a requisite Big Sur stop—if only for the views or the locally made art and body products, books, and more sold in the emblematic Phoenix Store. *48510 Hwy. 1, (831) 667-2345, www.nepenthebigsur.com.*

San Simeon

Hearst Castle. William Randolph Hearst's spectacular 165-room mansion—on 127 equally spectacular acres—contains thousands of priceless antiques and works of art. *750 Hearst Castle Rd., (805) 927-2010, hearstcastle.org.*

San Luis Obispo

Mission San Luis Obispo de Tolosa. Take a free, self-guided tour of one of the original nine California missions (circa 1772). *751 Palm St., (805) 781-8220, www.missionsanluisobispo.org.*

Solvang

Hans Christian Andersen Museum. The Danish writer is honored at this small museum. Downstairs, purchase copies of his fairy tales at the Book Loft and then stroll cobblestone streets through the Danish-style village of Solvang. *1680 Mission Dr., (805) 688-2052, www.bookloftsolvang.com.*

Santa Barbara

Municipal Winemakers. This shabby-chic downtown winery is one of several on Santa Barbara's Urban Wine Trail. *22 Anacapa St., (805) 931-6864, www.municipalwinemakers.com.*

Ventura

Channel Islands National Park & Marine Sanctuary. Five of eight Channel Islands make up the national park; the sea for 6 nautical miles surrounding them makes up the marine sanctuary. *(805) 658-5730, www.nps.gov/chis.*

Mileage Chart

This handy chart offers more than 2,400 mileages covering 77 North American cities. Want more mileages? Visit **randmcnally.com/MC** and type in any two cities or addresses.

	Albuquerque, NM	Atlanta, GA	Billings, MT	Boston, MA	Charlotte, NC	Chicago, IL	Cincinnati, OH	Dallas, TX	Denver, CO	Detroit, MI	Houston, TX	Indianapolis, IN	Kansas City, MO	Los Angeles, CA	Memphis, TN	Miami, FL	Milwaukee, WI	Minneapolis, MN	New Orleans, LA	New York, NY	Omaha, NE	Orlando, FL	Philadelphia, PA	Phoenix, AZ	Pittsburgh, PA	Portland, OR	St. Louis, MO	Salt Lake City, UT	San Francisco, CA	Seattle, WA	Washington, DC	Wichita, KS
Albuquerque, NM		1386	998	2219	1626	1333	1387	647	446	1570	884	1279	784	786	1008	1952	1354	1225	1165	2001	863	1730	1924	425	1641	1363	1037	599	1086	1438	1885	591
Amarillo, TX	288	1102	965	1935	1342	1049	1103	363	424	1286	589	995	570	1072	720	1668	1132	1009	881	1716	647	1446	1640	746	1357	1669	752	883	1370	1743	1600	418
Atlanta, GA	1386		1831	1095	244	715	461	780	1404	722	794	533	800	2174	379	661	809	1127	468	882	992	440	780	1844	684	2603	555	1878	2472	2649	637	955
Atlantic City, NJ	1985	831	2072	338	590	818	632	1518	1792	644	1598	703	1187	2774	1063	1248	910	1232	1273	126	1272	1038	60	2447	365	2922	948	2201	2934	2889	188	1379
Austin, TX	705	920	1495	1959	1164	1121	1128	196	950	1358	163	1067	702	1381	643	1341	1204	1136	503	1737	839	1124	1658	1010	1411	2068	825	1304	1760	2143	1524	542
Baltimore, MD	1887	683	1953	400	442	699	513	1368	1673	524	1448	584	1068	2670	914	1082	792	1112	1124	192	1153	889	97	2349	246	2804	829	2081	2816	2771	39	1260
Billings, MT	998	1831		2236	1990	1246	1546	1425	551	1535	1652	1435	1026	1240	1477	2497	1173	838	1868	2041	845	2275	2011	1210	1713	891	1278	552	1173	818	1951	1064
Birmingham, AL	1241	146	1780	1177	390	660	466	636	1329	724	668	478	749	2030	233	746	754	1072	343	960	939	534	880	1700	748	2551	502	1826	2327	2598	745	810
Boise, ID	938	2177	621	2660	2336	1693	1943	1702	830	1960	1930	1835	1372	842	1825	2844	1732	1461	2216	2465	1225	2622	2435	914	2137	431	1622	340	639	503	2375	1338
Boston, MA	2219	1095	2236		841	983	870	1764	1970	724	1844	937	1421	2983	1312	1482	1074	1396	1520	216	1436	1288	306	2681	570	3086	1182	2365	3098	3054	439	1613
Branson, MO	864	652	1241	1433	868	545	601	435	806	784	602	493	209	1651	274	1284	630	643	597	1201	402	1062	1138	1326	851	2013	249	1288	1950	2060	1081	292
Calgary, AB	1542	2357	541	2615	2400	1627	1925	1967	1096	1916	2209	1814	1567	1557	2028	3018	1555	1221	2419	2439	1387	2797	2391	1524	2093	787	1820	869	1500	678	2334	1606
Charleston, SC	1703	319	2133	970	209	908	620	1099	1706	826	1105	726	1103	2491	696	583	1002	1324	742	768	1294	380	668	2165	654	2904	857	2180	2789	2951	532	1272
Charlotte, NC	1626	244	1990	841		769	477	1023	1556	616	1038	583	961	2414	619	728	867	1180	712	641	1151	526	539	2088	446	2761	714	2037	2712	2808	398	1092
Chicago, IL	1333	715	1246	983	769		289	926	1002	282	1085	181	526	2015	531	1381	90	408	923	787	470	1153	757	1795	459	2118	295	1398	2130	2063	697	724
Cincinnati, OH	1387	461	1546	870	477	289		934	1137	259	1055	109	584	2172	482	1127	381	703	804	637	722	905	571	1849	288	2369	348	1647	2380	2363	512	779
Cleveland, OH	1598	714	1597	638	514	344	248	1194	1330	169	1315	315	799	2342	729	1240	434	756	1057	460	797	1043	428	2060	134	2446	560	1725	2458	2414	370	992
Columbus, OH	1457	567	1606	763	426	354	107	1039	1251	212	1174	189	657	2244	587	1164	445	766	910	533	792	954	468	1920	174	2439	421	1718	2451	2425	411	851
Corpus Christi, TX	855	1001	1622	2051	1244	1338	1262	410	1077	1542	207	1228	919	1494	782	1394	1421	1353	554	1844	1056	1172	1754	1122	1561	2218	1042	1454	1873	2292	1619	758
Dallas, TX	647	780	1425	1764	1023	926	934		830	1163	239	873	489	1437	453	1307	1010	928	519	1548	656	1086	1467	1066	1221	2128	630	1403	1734	2193	1332	361
Denver, CO	446	1404	551	1970	1566	1002	1187	880		1270	1035	1083	603	1015	1097	2069	1042	913	1398	1775	534	1851	1732	908	1447	1256	854	533	1268	1320	1671	519
Des Moines, IA	983	902	946	1299	1057	335	580	683	670	599	938	474	194	1682	617	1567	375	244	1008	1105	135	1339	1074	1445	777	1786	350	1065	1798	1764	1015	391
Detroit, MI	1570	722	1535	724	616	282	259	1163	1270		1319	277	764	2281	742	1354	374	696	1066	613	736	1144	583	2032	285	2385	533	1664	2397	2353	522	964
Duluth, MN	1375	1187	860	1370	1239	466	760	1092	1053	754	1331	651	586	2076	963	1852	394	152	1354	1264	530	1632	1230	1838	932	1749	679	1458	2033	1677	1171	785
Edmonton, AB	1724	2391	722	2549	2443	1670	1968	2149	1278	1958	2391	1857	1626	1755	2147	3058	1598	1264	2538	2482	1445	2836	2434	1721	2136	966	1878	1069	1695	793	2377	1787
El Paso, TX	266	1418	1257	2373	1662	1455	1569	635	707	1702	744	1398	929	796	1089	1934	1497	1377	1095	2202	1004	1712	2102	424	1774	1630	1157	866	1175	1705	1967	730
Fargo, ND	1318	1361	607	1629	1414	641	937	1079	873	930	1321	825	600	1848	1054	2025	569	234	1445	1438	420	1807	1405	1780	1107	1497	841	1160	1781	1424	1348	685
Gatlinburg, TN	1439	196	1803	922	202	578	290	884	1376	552	964	396	773	2226	431	865	672	994	640	707	964	640	625	1901	493	2574	527	1850	2525	2621	490	905
Guadalajara, JA	1194	1739	2194	2789	1982	1954	1962	1028	1639	2191	948	1901	1535	1501	1482	2131	2037	1969	1292	2592	1672	1910	2492	1212	2261	2545	1658	1792	1963	2631	2356	1377
Gulfport, MS	1221	399	1912	1482	643	896	767	562	1336	1025	403	780	883	1949	365	792	988	1196	78	1266	1073	572	1180	1577	1052	2633	647	1909	2307	2730	1036	867
Houston, TX	884	794	1652	1844	1038	1085	1055	239	1035	1319		1021	732	1550	575	1186	1163	1171	348	1632	898	965	1547	1178	1354	2356	784	1634	1929	2431	1411	595
Indianapolis, IN	1279	533	1435	937	583	181	109	873	1033	277	1021		482	2068	464	1198	272	591	818	707	613	968	643	1742	359	2260	243	1541	2273	2253	582	674
Jacksonville, FL	1636	346	2183	1146	379	1068	796	992	1756	1002	871	874	1152	2421	677	349	1163	1474	547	939	1344	141	844	2050	825	2954	907	2230	2723	3001	706	1272
Kansas City, MO	784	800	1026	1421	961	526	584	489	603	764	732	482		1616	451	1466	565	436	844	1196	184	1246	1127	1246	840	1797	248	1073	1808	1844	1066	198
Key West, FL	2099	809	2646	1659	886	1534	1275	1455	2222	1515	1334	1348	1617	2884	1159	160	1632	1944	1010	1446	1807	387	1357	2514	1332	3417	1370	2693	3186	3464	1213	1735
Las Vegas, NV	572	1959	973	2714	2199	1746	1932	1220	747	2013	1457	1828	1349	270	1581	2525	1786	1656	1739	2518	1278	2303	2480	285	2190	1023	1600	419	569	1128	2428	1164
Lexington, KY	1371	369	1610	917	400	370	83	876	1136	344	996	184	581	2158	423	1030	464	782	745	701	771	817	638	1833	370	2381	334	1657	2392	2428	533	773
Little Rock, AR	877	515	1407	1447	754	650	617	319	955	885	439	583	381	1666	136	1147	724	815	425	1230	574	925	1150	1340	905	2211	345	1488	1963	2275	1015	446
Los Angeles, CA	786	2174	1240	2983	2414	2015	2172	1437	1015	2281	1550	2068	1616		1794	2735	2055	1925	1894	2787	1546	2515	2713	370	2428	963	1821	688	380	1134	2670	1377
Memphis, TN	1008	379	1477	1312	619	531	482	453	1037	742	575	464	451	1794		1012	622	831	394	1094	641	778	1014	1471	768	2245	283	1524	2095	2299	879	577
Mexico City, DF	1404	1718	2301	2768	1962	2017	1979	1090	1756	2254	924	1963	1598	1839	1500	2111	2100	2032	1272	2571	1735	1889	2471	1469	2279	2768	1721	2003	2218	2842	2336	1440
Miami, FL	1952	661	2497	1482	728	1381	1127	1307	2059	1354	1186	1198	1466	2735	1012		1475	1791	861	1288	1658	235	1180	2362	1173	3260	1221	2544	3038	3315	1044	1587
Milwaukee, WI	1354	809	1173	1074	867	90	381	1010	1042	374	1163	272	565	2055	622	1475		337	1015	879	509	1258	849	1817	551	2062	379	1437	2170	1990	788	763
Minneapolis, MN	1225	1127	838	1396	1180	408	703	928	913	696	1171	591	436	1925	831	1791	337		1223	1204	372	1573	1171	1687	874	1727	563	1308	2040	1655	1110	634
Mobile, AL	1234	328	1874	1427	571	917	721	589	1414	978	468	733	850	2014	382	719	1011	1224	144	1202	1038	497	1101	1643	1000	2661	645	1936	2320	2727	965	894
Montréal, QC	2129	1218	2099	310	980	847	824	1722	1832	560	1884	847	1330	2845	1314	1647	938	1262	1640	382	1302	1437	454	2591	603	2948	1092	2228	2960	2916	587	1529
Nashville, TN	1219	248	1586	1099	408	469	273	664	1158	534	786	287	555	2006	209	913	564	881	532	884	747	692	802	1682	560	2357	307	1633	2306	2404	667	688
New Orleans, LA	1165	468	1868	1520	712	923	804	519	1398	1066	348	818	844	1894	394	861	1015	1223		1304	1032	641	1222	1523	1090	2642	675	1920	2252	2716	1087	880
New York, NY	2001	882	2041	216	641	787	637	1548	1775	613	1632	707	1196	2787	1094	1288	879	1204	1304		1245	1089	95	2463	369	2891	954	2170	2902	2858	228	1391
Norfolk, VA	1910	558	2132	569	328	878	605	1350	1758	704	1362	720	1155	2707	898	950	969	1295	1026	370	1335	755	271	2373	425	2962	911	2238	2973	2949	193	1349
Oklahoma City, OK	542	844	1203	1678	1084	792	846	206	631	1029	437	739	348	1326	466	1476	876	788	722	1460	452	1254	1384	1005	1101	1922	496	1200	1627	1948	1344	160
Omaha, NE	863	992	845	1436	1151	470	722	656	534	736	898	613	184	1546	641	1658	509	372	1032	1245		1436	1212	1325	914	1650	439	930	1662	1663	1151	298
Orlando, FL	1730	440	2275	1288	526	1153	905	1086	1851	1144	965	968	1246	2515	778	235	1258	1573	641	1089	1436		986	2145	975	3048	999	2323	2816	3093	849	1365
Ottawa, ON	2039	1158	1768	428	920	760	732	1632	1748	471	1804	757	1240	2763	1230	1618	859	1032	1582	440	1213	1408	447	2501	546	2660	1002	2142	2877	2586	566	1439
Philadelphia, PA	1924	780	2011	306	539	757	571	1467	1732	583	1547	643	1127	2713	1014	1180	849	1171	1222	95	1212	986		2387	305	2861	888	2140	2873	2828	137	1319
Phoenix, AZ	425	1844	1210	2681	2088	1795	1849	1066	908	2032	1178	1742	1246	373	1471	2362	1817	1687	1523	2463	1325	2145	2387		2104	1332	1499	653	749	1414	2348	1053
Pittsburgh, PA	1641	684	1713	570	446	459	288	1221	1447	285	1354	359	840	2428	768	1173	551	874	1090	369	914	975	305	2104		2563	604	1842	2574	2530	243	1035
Portland, ME	2315	1192	2333	107	938	1079	967	1861	2067	825	1940	1034	1518	3082	1408	1585	1176	1492	1616	304	1533	1385	402	2778	666	3186	1279	2461	3196	3151	535	1710
Portland, OR	1363	2603	891	3086	2761	2118	2369	2128	1256	2385	2356	2260	1797	963	2245	3260	2062	1727	2642	2891	1650	3048	2861	1332	2563		2050	765	635	174	2800	1764
Rapid City, SD	843	1508	323	1900	1670	912	1208	1061	397	1200	1291	1100	704	1312	1160	2173	840	575	1551	1708	525	1956	1675	1305	1378	1215	959	649	1384	1142	1618	699
Reno, NV	1019	2396	958	2881	2555	1913	2163	1668	1051	2180	1904	2056	1591	470	2029	3063	1953	1818	2186	2685	1445	2841	2656	733	2357	578	1844	518	218	720	2595	1558
Richmond, VA	1832	532	2051	547	293	797	512	1278	1671	622	1329	627	1069	2620	824	944	888	1210	1002	334	1259	742	245	2294	344	2869	822	2145	2880	2868	108	1261
St. Louis, MO	1037	555	1278	1182	714	295	348	630	854	533	784	243	248	1821	284	1221	379	563	675	954	439	999	888	1499	604	2050		1326	2061	2096	827	442
Salt Lake City, UT	599	1878	552	2365	2037	1398	1647	1403	533	1664	1634	1541	1073	688	1524	2544	1437	1308	1920	2170	930	2323	2140	653	1842	765	1326		735	839	2079	1042
San Antonio, TX	712	986	1480	2039	1230	1202	1210	276	935	1439	195	1149	766	1357	727	1379	1285	1205	541	1822	920	1160	1742	985	1495	2076	906	1311	1736	2150	1607	625
San Diego, CA	810	2138	1302	3046	2381	2080	2196	1359	1077	2346	1472	2089	1597	120	1819	2656	2118	1986	1816	2809	1613	2436	2738	355	2452	1083	1845	750	501	1256	2693	1401
San Francisco, CA	1086	2472	1173	3098	2712	2130	2380	1734	1268	2397	1929	2273	1808	382	2095	3038	2170	2040	2252	2902	1662	2816	2873	749	2574	635	2061	735		807	2812	1775
Santa Fe, NM	58	1379	943	2212	1618	1313	1379	640	391	1562	877	1272	766	846	998	1944	1336	1207	1158	1994	891	1723	1917	520	1634	1388	1029	625	1144	1463	1879	572
Sault Ste. Marie, ON	1777	1040	1273	923	947	483	577	1370	1428	348	1527	540	951	2465	972	1685	400	545	1355	921	850	1475	911	2240	614	2166	740	1848	2581	2090	854	1150
Seattle, WA	1438	2649	818	3054	2808	2063	2363	2193	1320	2353	2431	2253	1844	1134	2299	3315	1990	1655	2716	2858	1663	3093	2828	1414	2530	174	2096	839	807		2768	1828
Spokane, WA	1320	2369	541	2774	2528	1785	2084	1964	1091	2075	2192	1973	1564	1216	2018	3035	1712	1377	2409	2580	1383	2814	2550	1381	2252	352	1817	720	874	279	2490	1600
Tampa, FL	1746	451	2293	1342	578	1166	916	1102	1860	1178	980	984	1252	2525	779	280	1260	1578	651	1138	1445	85	1040	2153	1023	3064	1008	2340	2832	3111	904	1381
Toronto, ON	1800	963	1771	548	756	519	493	1393	1504	231	1551	518	1001	2517	983	1483	609	933	1306	489	974	1284	497	2262	316	2620	763	1899	2632	2588	486	1188
Tulsa, OK	645	782	1234	1576	1022	687	738	258	692	927	487	635	263	1433	402	1414	773	704	671	1350	380	1192	1282	1107	994	1938	392	1215	1731	2012	1234	175
Vancouver, BC	1575	2785	953	3188	2944	2198	2499	2338	1465	2487	2565	2389	1980	1275	2437	3451	2125	1790	2851	2993	1799	3229	2963	1550	2665	313	2232	973	947	141	2903	1973
Washington, DC	1885	637	1951	439	398	697	512	1332	1671	522	1411	582	1066	2670	879	1044	788	1110	1087	228	1151	849	137	2348	244	2800	827	2079	2812	2768		1258
Wichita, KS	591	955	1064	1613	1092	724	779	361	519	964	595	674	198	1377	577	1587	763	634	880	1391	298	1365	1319	1053	1035	1764	442	1042	1775	1828	1258	

Mileages in this chart are based upon the routes usually followed by motorists. Highway systems include interstate, U.S., and state highways.

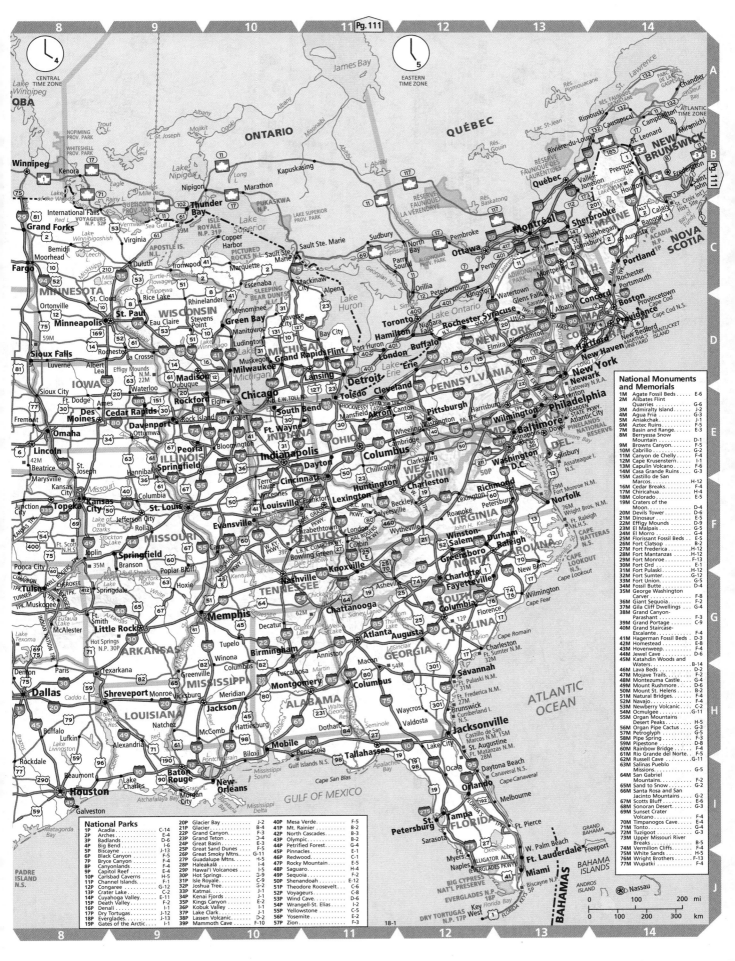

Pg. 111

National Monuments and Memorials

1M	Agate Fossil Beds	E-6
2M	Alibates Flint Quarries	G-6
3M	Admiralty Island	J-2
4M	Agua Fria	F-4
5M	Aniakchak	J-1
6M	Aztec Ruins	F-5
7M	Basin and Range	E-3
8M	Berryessa Snow Mountain	D-1
9M	Browns Canyon	F-5
10M	Cabrillo	G-2
11M	Canyon de Chelly	F-4
12M	Cape Krusenstern	I-1
13M	Capulin Volcano	F-6
14M	Casa Grande Ruins	G-3
15M	Castillo de San Marcos	H-12
16M	Cedar Breaks	F-4
17M	Chiricahua	H-4
18M	Colorado	E-5
19M	Craters of the Moon	D-4
20M	Devils Tower	D-6
21M	Dinosaur	E-5
22M	Effigy Mounds	D-9
23M	El Malpais	F-5
24M	El Morro	F-5
25M	Florissant Fossil Beds	F-5
26M	Fort Clatsop	B-2
27M	Fort Frederica	H-12
28M	Fort Matanzas	H-12
29M	Fort Monroe	F-13
30M	Fort Ord	E-1
31M	Fort Pulaski	H-12
32M	Fort Sumter	G-12
33M	Fort Union	G-5
34M	Fossil Butte	D-4
35M	George Washington Carver	F-8
36M	Giant Sequoia	F-2
37M	Gila Cliff Dwellings	G-4
38M	Grand Canyon-Parashant	F-3
39M	Grand Portage	C-9
40M	Grand Staircase-Escalante	F-4
41M	Hagerman Fossil Beds	D-3
42M	Homestead	E-8
43M	Hovenweep	F-4
44M	Jewel Cave	D-6
45M	Katahdin Woods and Waters	B-14
46M	Lava Beds	D-2
47M	Mojave Trails	F-2
48M	Montezuma Castle	F-4
49M	Mount Rushmore	D-6
50M	Mount St. Helens	B-2
51M	Natural Bridges	F-4
52M	Navajo	F-4
53M	Newberry Volcanic	C-2
54M	Ocmulgee	G-11
55M	Organ Mountains Desert Peaks	H-5
56M	Organ Pipe Cactus	G-3
57M	Petroglyph	F-5
58M	Pipe Spring	F-3
59M	Pipestone	D-8
60M	Rainbow Bridge	F-4
61M	Rio Grande del Norte	F-5
62M	Russell Cave	G-11
63M	Salinas Pueblo Missions	G-5
64M	San Gabriel Mountains	F-2
65M	Sand to Snow	G-2
66M	Santa Rosa and San Jacinto Mountains	G-2
67M	Scotts Bluff	E-6
68M	Sonoran Desert	G-3
69M	Sunset Crater Volcano	F-4
70M	Timpanogos Cave	F-4
71M	Tonto	G-4
72M	Tuzigoot	F-4
73M	Upper Missouri River Breaks	B-5
74M	Vermilion Cliffs	F-3
75M	White Sands	H-5
76M	Wright Brothers	F-13
77M	Wupatki	F-4

National Parks

1P	Acadia	C-14
2P	Arches	E-4
3P	Badlands	D-6
4P	Big Bend	I-6
5P	Biscayne	J-13
6P	Black Canyon	F-5
7P	Bryce Canyon	F-4
8P	Canyonlands	F-4
9P	Capitol Reef	F-4
10P	Carlsbad Caverns	H-5
11P	Channel Islands	F-1
12P	Congaree	G-12
13P	Crater Lake	C-2
14P	Cuyahoga Valley	E-11
15P	Death Valley	F-2
16P	Denali	I-1
17P	Dry Tortugas	J-12
18P	Everglades	J-13
19P	Gates of the Arctic	I-1
20P	Glacier Bay	J-2
21P	Glacier	B-4
22P	Grand Canyon	F-3
23P	Grand Teton	J-4
24P	Great Basin	E-3
25P	Great Sand Dunes	F-5
26P	Great Smoky Mtns.	G-11
27P	Guadalupe Mtns.	H-5
28P	Haleakalā	I-4
29P	Hawai'i Volcanoes	I-5
30P	Hot Springs	G-8
31P	Isle Royale	C-9
32P	Joshua Tree	G-2
33P	Katmai	J-1
34P	Kenai Fjords	J-1
35P	Kings Canyon	E-2
36P	Kobuk Valley	I-1
37P	Lake Clark	J-1
38P	Lassen Volcanic	D-2
39P	Mammoth Cave	F-10
40P	Mesa Verde	F-5
41P	Mt. Rainier	B-2
42P	North Cascades	B-3
43P	Olympic	B-2
44P	Petrified Forest	G-4
45P	Pinnacles	E-1
46P	Redwood	C-1
47P	Rocky Mountain	E-5
48P	Saguaro	G-4
49P	Sequoia	E-2
50P	Shenandoah	E-12
51P	Theodore Roosevelt	C-6
52P	Voyageurs	C-8
53P	Wind Cave	D-6
54P	Wrangell-St. Elias	C-5
55P	Yellowstone	C-4
56P	Yosemite	E-2
57P	Zion	F-3

18-1

Alabama state facts

Nickname: The Heart of Dixie
Capital: Montgomery, F-4

Population: 4,779,736 (rank: 23rd)
Largest city: Birmingham, 212,237, D-3

Land area: 50,645 sq. mi. (rank: 28th)
Highest point: Cheaha Mountain, 2,407 ft., D-5

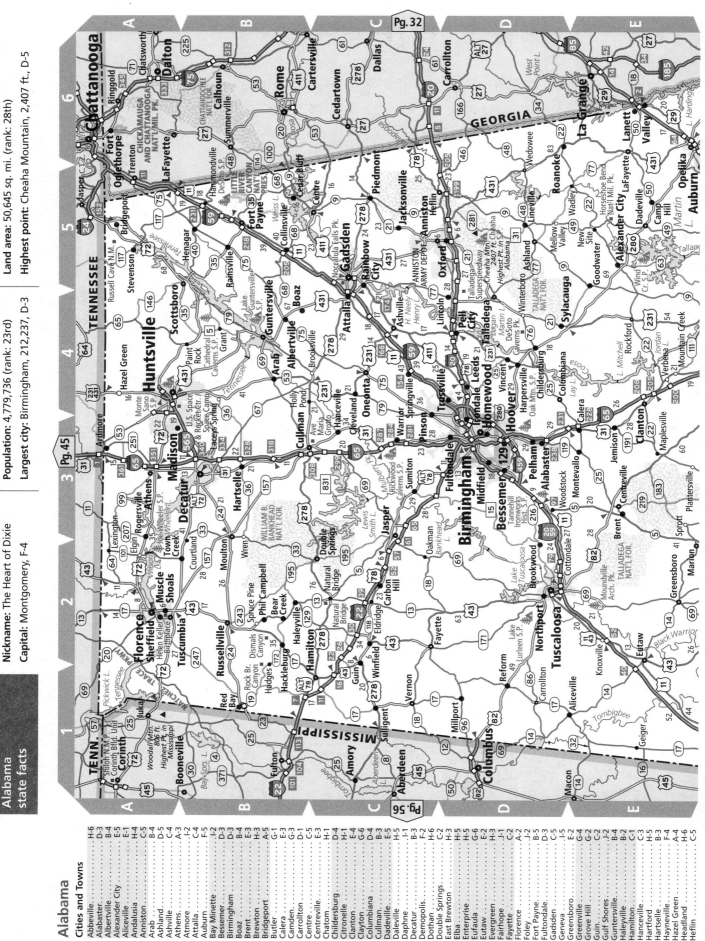

Alabama

Cities and Towns

Abbeville	H-6
Alabaster	D-3
Albertville	B-4
Alexander City	E-5
Aliceville	E-1
Andalusia	H-4
Anniston	C-5
Arab	B-4
Ashland	D-5
Ashville	C-4
Athens	A-3
Atmore	J-2
Attalla	C-4
Auburn	F-5
Bay Minette	J-2
Bessemer	D-3
Birmingham	D-3
Boaz	B-4
Brent	E-3
Brewton	H-3
Bridgeport	A-5
Butler	G-1
Calera	E-3
Camden	G-3
Carrollton	D-1
Centre	B-5
Centreville	E-3
Chatom	H-1
Childersburg	D-4
Citronelle	H-1
Clanton	E-4
Clayton	G-6
Columbiana	D-4
Cullman	B-3
Dadeville	E-5
Daleville	H-5
Daphne	J-1
Decatur	B-3
Demopolis	F-2
Dothan	H-6
Double Springs	B-2
East Brewton	H-3
Elba	H-5
Enterprise	H-5
Eufaula	G-6
Eutaw	E-2
Evergreen	H-4
Fairhope	J-1
Fayette	C-2
Florence	A-2
Foley	J-2
Fort Payne	B-5
Fultondale	D-3
Gadsden	C-4
Geneva	J-5
Greensboro	E-2
Greenville	G-4
Grove Hill	G-2
Guin	C-2
Gulf Shores	J-2
Guntersville	B-4
Haleyville	B-2
Hamilton	C-2
Hanceville	C-3
Hartford	J-5
Hartselle	B-3
Hayneville	F-4
Headland	H-6
Heflin	C-5

TENNESSEE

GEORGIA

MISSISSIPPI

Pg. 32
Pg. 45
Pg. 56

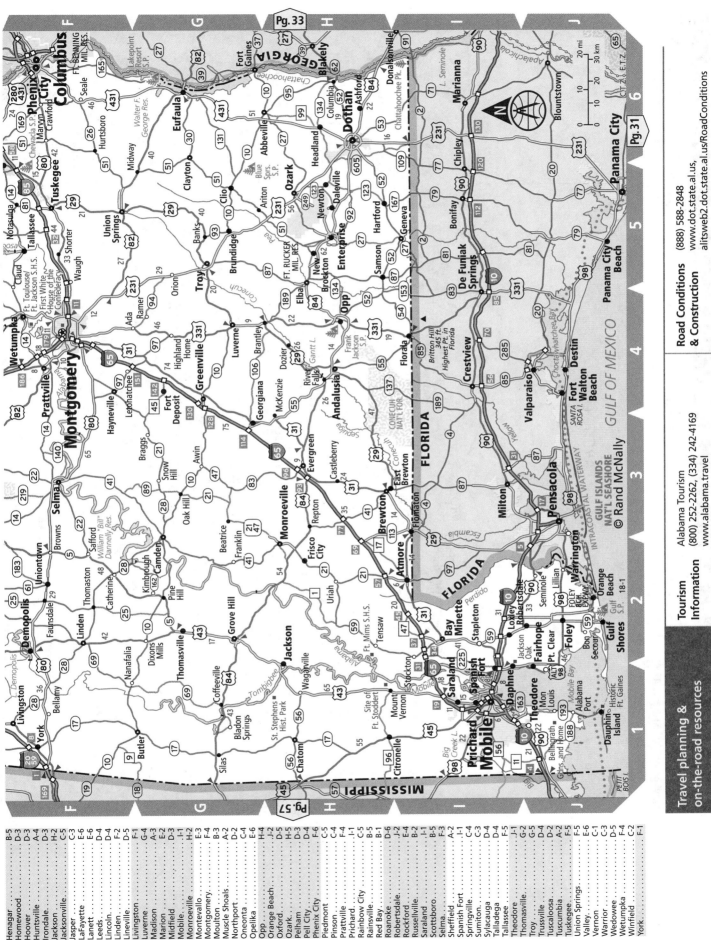

© Rand McNally

GULF OF MEXICO

Tourism Information	Alabama Tourism (800) 252-2262, (334) 242-4169 www.alabama.travel
Road Conditions & Construction	(888) 588-2848 www.dot.state.al.us, alitsweb2.dot.state.al.us/RoadConditions

Travel planning & on-the-road resources

Henagar B-5
Homewood D-3
Hoover D-3
Huntsville A-4
Irondale D-3
Jackson H-2
Jacksonville C-5
Jasper C-3
LaFayette E-6
Lanett E-6
Leeds D-4
Lincoln D-4
Linden F-2
Lineville D-5
Livingston F-1
Luverne G-4
Madison A-3
Marion E-2
Midfield D-3
Mobile J-1
Monroeville H-2
Montevallo E-3
Montgomery F-4
Moulton B-3
Muscle Shoals A-2
Northport D-2
Oneonta C-4
Opelika E-6
Opp H-4
Orange Beach J-2
Oxford D-5
Ozark H-5
Pelham D-3
Pell City D-4
Phenix City F-6
Piedmont C-5
Pinson C-4
Prattville F-4
Prichard J-1
Rainbow City C-5
Rainsville B-5
Red Bay B-1
Roanoke D-6
Robertsdale J-2
Rockford E-4
Russellville B-2
Saraland J-1
Selma F-3
Sheffield A-2
Spanish Fort J-1
Springville C-4
Sumiton C-3
Sylacauga D-4
Talladega D-5
Tallassee F-5
Theodore J-1
Thomasville G-2
Troy G-5
Trussville D-4
Tuscaloosa D-2
Tuscumbia A-2
Tuskegee F-5
Union Springs F-5
Valley E-6
Vernon C-1
Warrior C-3
Wedowee D-5
Wetumpka F-4
Winfield C-2
York F-1

Alaska state facts

Nickname: The Last Frontier
Capital: Juneau, E-6
Population: 710,231 (rank: 47th)

Largest city: Anchorage, 291,826, D-4
Land area: 570,641 sq. mi. (rank: 1st)
Highest point: Denali, 20,320 ft., D-3

Travel planning & on-the-road resources

Tourism Information
Alaska Tourism
www.travelalaska.com

Road Conditions & Construction
511, (907) 465-8952
511.alaska.gov,
www.dot.state.ak.us

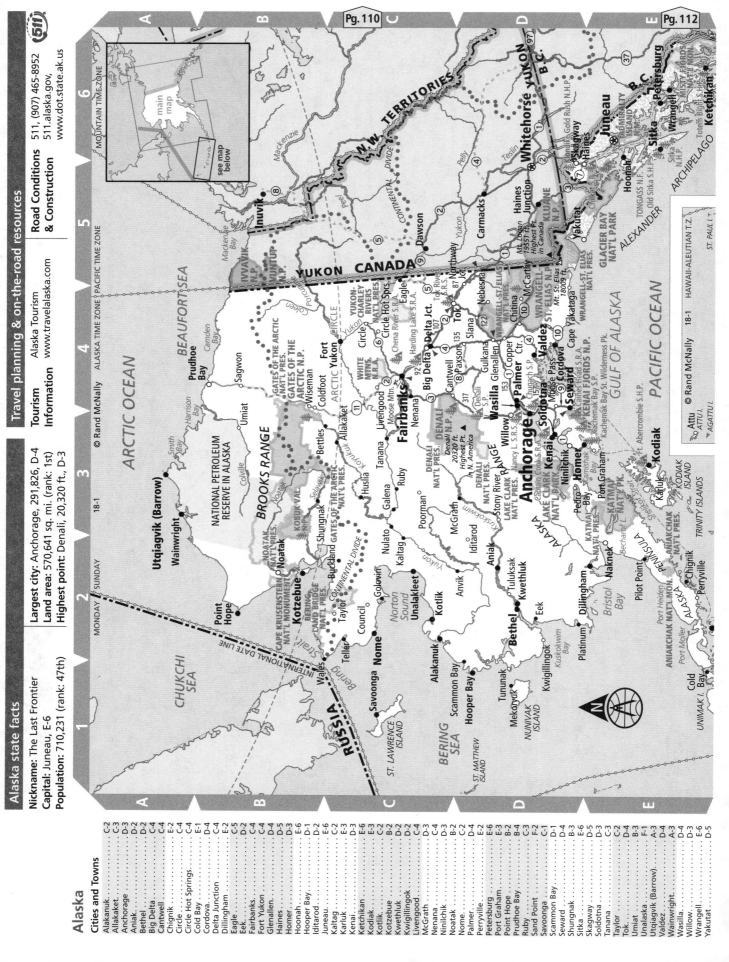

Pg. 110
Pg. 112

© Rand McNally

Alaska

Cities and Towns

Alakanuk C-2
Allakaket C-3
Anchorage D-3
Aniak D-2
Bethel D-2
Big Delta C-4
Cantwell C-4
Chignik E-2
Circle C-4
Circle Hot Springs C-4
Cold Bay E-1
Cordova D-4
Delta Junction E-2
Dillingham C-5
Eagle C-5
Eek D-2
Fairbanks C-4
Fort Yukon C-4
Glenallen D-4
Haines D-5
Homer D-4
Hoonah E-6
Hooper Bay D-1
Iditarod D-2
Juneau E-6
Kaltag C-2
Kenai D-3
Ketchikan E-6
Kodiak E-3
Kotlik C-2
Kotzebue B-2
Kwethluk D-2
Kwigillingok D-2
Livengood C-4
McGrath D-3
Nenana C-4
Ninilchik D-3
Noatak B-2
Nome C-2
Palmer D-4
Perryville E-2
Petersburg E-6
Port Graham E-3
Point Hope B-2
Prudhoe Bay B-4
Ruby C-3
Sand Point F-2
Savoonga C-1
Scammon Bay D-1
Seward D-4
Shungnak B-3
Sitka E-6
Skagway D-5
Soldotna D-3
Tanana C-3
Taylor C-2
Tok D-4
Umiat B-3
Unalaska F-1
Utqiagvik (Barrow) A-3
Valdez D-4
Wainwright A-3
Wasilla D-4
Willow D-3
Wrangell E-6
Yakutat D-5

NOTE: Maps are not always in alphabetical order.
See Page 1 for map location in this atlas.

Alaska • Hawaii   13

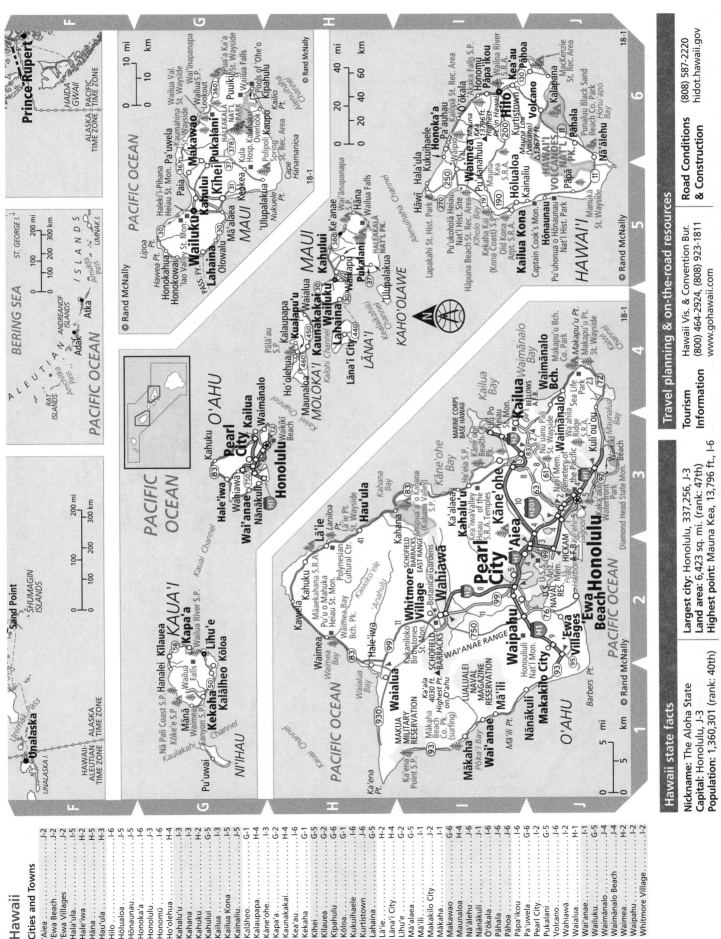

© Rand McNally

Hawaii

Cities and Towns

'Aiea J-2
'Ewa Beach J-2
'Ewa Villages J-2
Hala'ula H-5
Hale'iwa H-2
Hāna H-5
Hau'ula I-6
Hilo I-6
Hōlualoa J-5
Honaunau J-6
Honoka'a I-6
Honolulu J-3
Honomū H-4
Ho'olehua H-4
Kahalu'u I-3
Kahana H-2
Kahului G-5
Kailua I-3
Kailua Kona J-5
Kainaliu J-5
Kaunakakai G-1
Kekaha G-2
Kea'au I-6
Kīhei G-5
Kīlauea G-2
Kipahulu G-6
Koloa G-6
Kukuihaele I-6
Kurtistown I-6
Lahaina H-2
Lā'ie H-2
Lāna'i City H-4
Līhu'e G-2
Mā'alaea J-2
Mā'ili I-1
Makaha H-1
Makakilo City J-2
Makawao H-4
Maunaloa H-1
Nā'ālehu J-6
Nānākuli I-6
O'ōkala I-6
Pāhala J-6
Pāhoa I-6
Pāpa'ikou I-6
Pearl City J-2
Pukalani G-5
Volcano J-6
Wahiawā H-1
Waialua H-1
Wai'anae I-1
Wailuku G-5
Waimānalo I-4
Waimānalo Beach I-4
Waimea H-2
Waipahu J-2
Whitmore Village I-2

Hawaii state facts

Nickname: The Aloha State
Capital: Honolulu, J-3
Population: 1,360,301 (rank: 40th)
Largest city: Honolulu, 337,256, J-3
Land area: 6,423 sq. mi. (rank: 47th)
Highest point: Mauna Kea, 13,796 ft., I-6

Travel planning & on-the-road resources

| Tourism Information | Hawaii Vis. & Convention Bur. (800) 464-2924, (808) 923-1811 www.gohawaii.com |
| Road Conditions & Construction | (808) 587-2220 hidot.hawaii.gov |

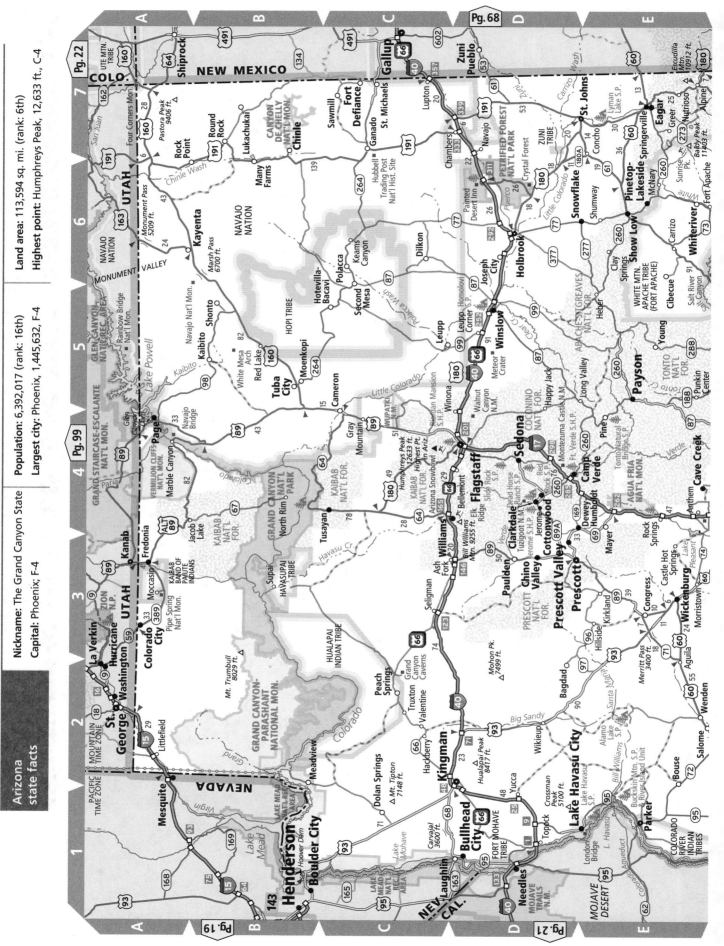

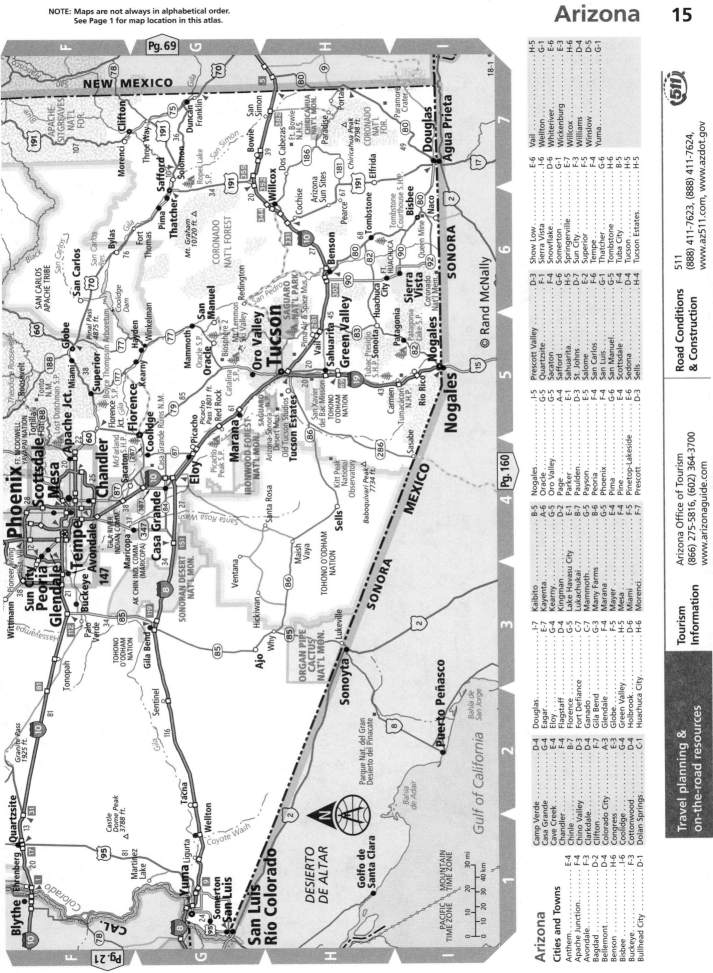

Arkansas
Cities and Towns

Arkadelphia E-3
Arkansas City F-6
Ash Flat A-6
Ashdown F-2
Augusta C-6
Batesville B-6
Bella Vista A-1
Benton D-4
Bentonville A-2
Berryville A-3
Blytheville B-8
Booneville C-2
Cabot D-5
Camden F-4
Charleston C-2
Clarendon D-6
Clarksville C-3
Clinton B-4
Conway C-4
Corning A-7
Crossett G-5
Danville C-3
Dardanelle C-3
De Queen E-1
De Valls Bluff D-6
De Witt E-6
Des Arc D-6
Dumas F-6
El Dorado G-4
Eureka Springs A-2
Fayetteville A-2
Fordyce F-4
Forrest City D-7
Fort Smith C-1
Greenwood C-1
Hamburg G-5
Hampton F-4
Harrisburg B-7
Harrison A-3
Heber Springs C-5
Helena-W. Helena D-7
Hope F-2
Hot Springs E-3
Hot Springs Village D-3
Huntsville A-2
Jacksonville D-5
Jasper B-3
Jonesboro B-7
Lake City B-7
Lake Village G-6
Lewisville G-2
Little Rock D-4
Lonoke D-5
Magnolia G-3
Malvern E-4
Marianna D-7
Marion C-8
Marshall B-4
McGehee F-6
Melbourne B-5
Mena D-1
Monticello F-5
Morrilton C-4
Mount Ida D-2
Mountain Home A-4
Mountain View B-5
Murfreesboro E-2
Nashville F-2
Newport B-6
North Little Rock D-5
Osceola B-8
Ozark C-2
Paragould B-7
Paris C-2
Perryville D-4
Piggott A-8
Pine Bluff E-5
Pocahontas A-7
Prescott F-3
Rison F-5
Rogers A-2
Russellville C-3
Salem A-5
Searcy C-5
Sheridan E-4
Siloam Springs A-1
Springdale A-2
Star City F-5
Stuttgart E-6
Texarkana G-2
Trumann B-7
Van Buren C-1
Waldron D-2
Walnut Ridge A-7
Warren F-5
West Memphis C-8
Wynne C-7
Yellville A-4

Land area: 52,035 sq. mi. (rank: 27th)

Highest point: Magazine Mtn., 2753 ft, C-2

Population: 2,915,918 (rank: 32nd)

Largest city: Little Rock, 193,524, D-4

Nickname: The Natural State

Capital: Little Rock, D-4

Arkansas state facts

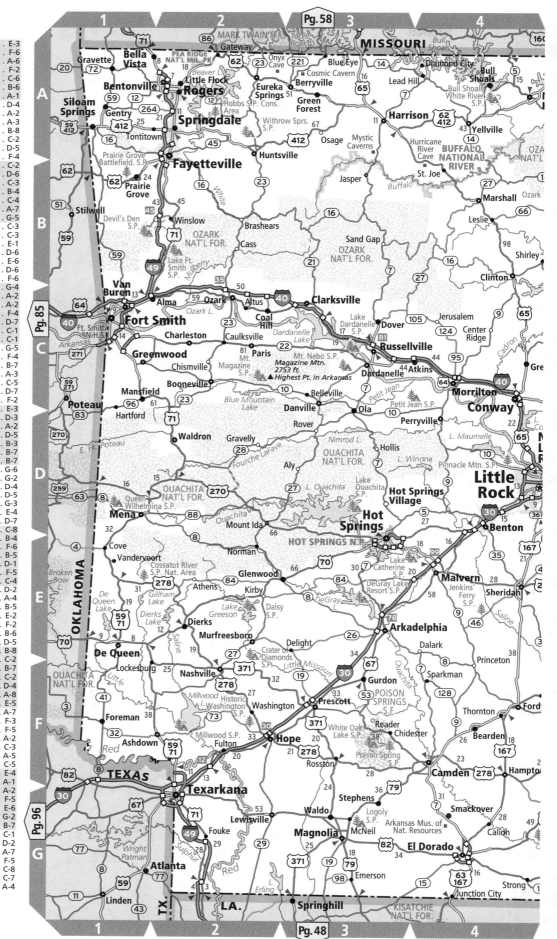

NOTE: Maps are not always in alphabetical order.
See Page 1 for map location in this atlas.

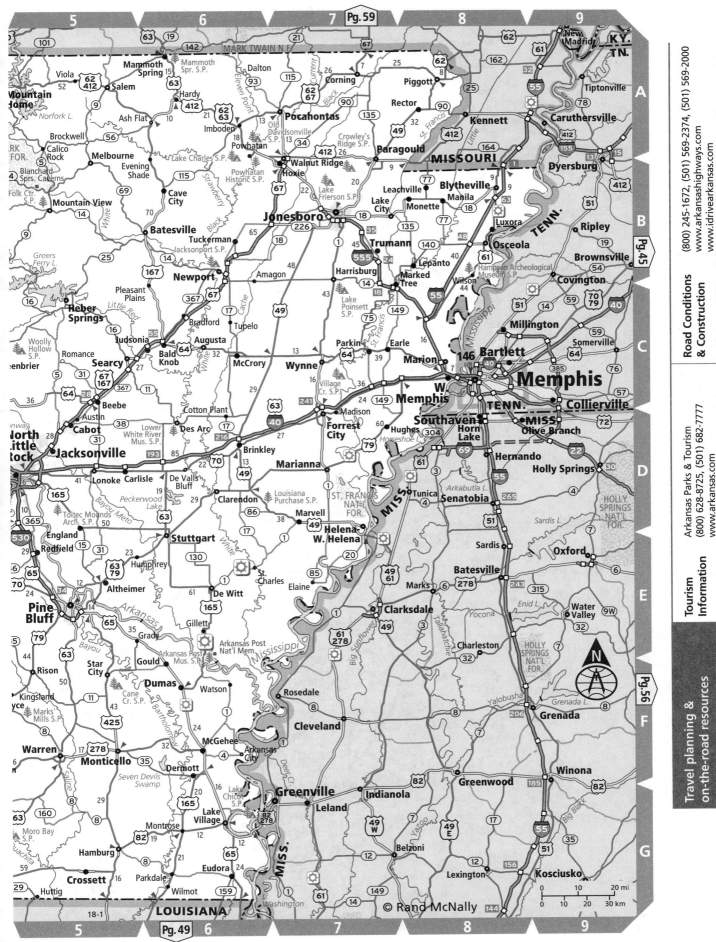

Road Conditions & Construction

(800) 245-1672, (501) 569-2374, (501) 569-2000
www.arkansashighways.com
www.idrivearkansas.com

Tourism Information

Arkansas Parks & Tourism
(800) 628-8725, (501) 682-7777
www.arkansas.com

Travel planning & on-the-road resources

© Rand McNally

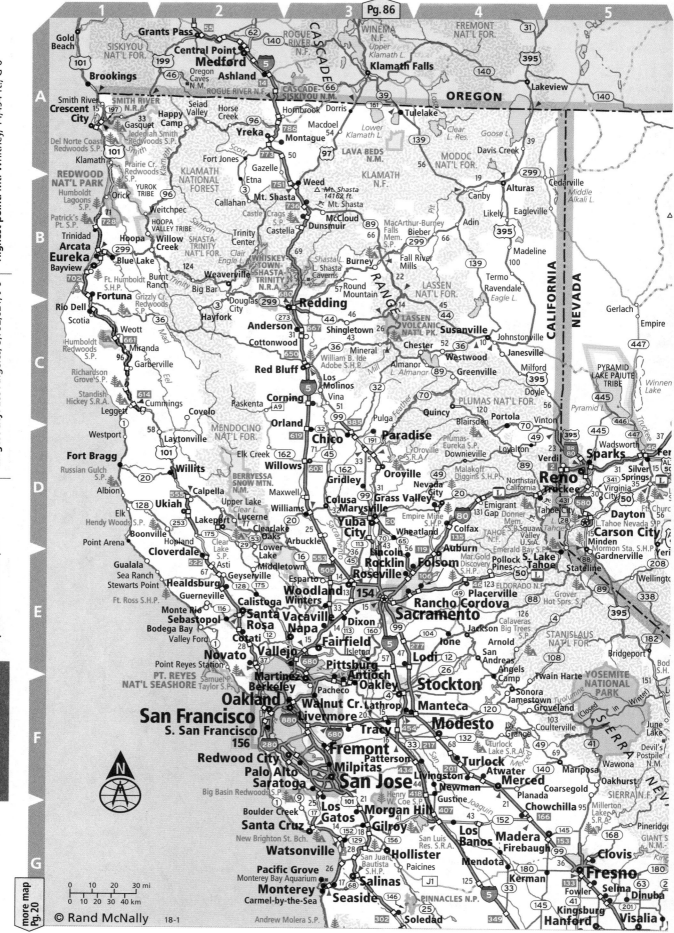

California state facts

Nickname: The Golden State
Capital: Sacramento, E-3

Population: 37,253,956 (rank: 1st)
Largest city: Los Angeles, 3,792,621, J-6

Land area: 155,799 sq. mi. (rank: 3rd)
Highest point: Mt. Whitney, 14,494 ft., G-6

© Rand McNally   18-1

more map Pg.20

NOTE: Maps are not always in alphabetical order.
See Page 1 for map location in this atlas.

California • Nevada/Northern

19

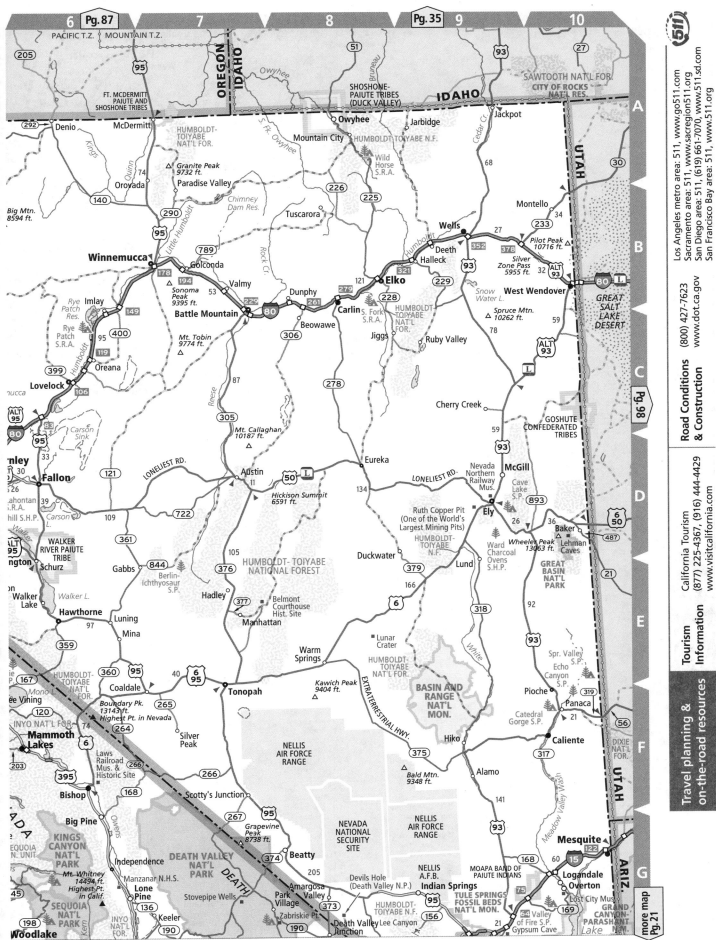

Los Angeles metro area: 511, www.go511.com
Sacramento area: 511, www.sacregion511.org
San Diego area: 511, (619) 661-7070, www.511sd.org
San Francisco Bay area: 511, www.511.org

Road Conditions & Construction
(800) 427-7623
www.dot.ca.gov

Tourism Information
California Tourism
(877) 225-4367, (916) 444-4429
www.visitcalifornia.com

Travel planning & on-the-road resources

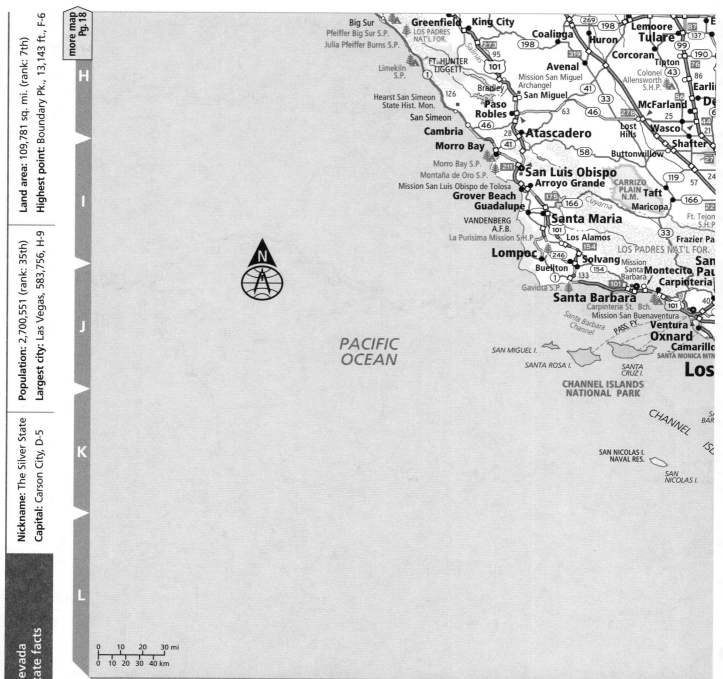

more map Pg. 18

Land area: 109,781 sq. mi. (rank: 7th) • **Highest point:** Boundary Pk., 13,143 ft., F-6

Population: 2,700,551 (rank: 35th) • **Largest city:** Las Vegas, 583,756, H-9

Nickname: The Silver State • **Capital:** Carson City, D-5

Nevada state facts

PACIFIC OCEAN

0 10 20 30 mi
0 10 20 30 40 km

California

Cities and Towns

Adelanto	J-7	Bishop	F-6
Alpine	L-8	Blythe	J-10
Alturas	B-4	Borrego Springs	K-8
Anaheim	J-7	Brawley	K-9
Anderson	C-3	Brentwood	F-3
Angels Camp	E-4	Bridgeport	E-5
Antioch	F-3	Buellton	I-4
Apple Valley	J-7	Calexico	L-9
Arcata	B-1	California City	I-7
Arroyo Grande	I-4	Calipatria	K-9
Arvin	I-6	Calistoga	E-2
Atascadero	H-4	Camarillo	J-6
Atwater	F-4	Cambria	H-4
Auburn	E-4	Carlsbad	K-7
Avalon	K-6	Carmel-by-the-Sea	G-3
Avenal	H-4	Carpinteria	J-5
Bakersfield	I-6	Chico	D-3
Barstow	I-7	Chowchilla	G-4
Bayview	B-1	Chula Vista	L-7
Beaumont	J-8	Clearlake Oaks	D-2
Berkeley	F-3	Cloverdale	E-2
		Clovis	G-5
		Coalinga	H-4
		Colusa	D-3

Corcoran	H-5	Frazier Park	I-6
Corning	C-3	Fremont	F-3
Corona	J-7	Fresno	G-5
Cotati	E-2	Gilroy	G-3
Cottonwood	C-3	Glendale	J-6
Crescent City	A-1	Grass Valley	D-4
Delano	H-5	Greenfield	H-3
Desert Hot Springs	J-8	Gridley	D-3
Dinuba	G-5	Grover Beach	I-4
Dixon	E-3	Guadalupe	I-4
Downieville	D-4	Guerneville	E-2
Earlimart	H-5	Gustine	F-4
El Cajon	L-8	Hanford	G-5
El Centro	K-9	Healdsburg	E-2
Encinitas	K-7	Hemet	J-8
Escondido	K-7	Hesperia	J-7
Eureka	B-1	Hollister	G-3
Exeter	H-5	Holtville	K-9
Fairfield	E-3	Huron	H-5
Firebaugh	G-4	Imperial	K-9
Folsom	E-4	Independence	G-6
Fort Bragg	D-1	Indio	J-8
Fortuna	B-1	Ione	E-4
Fowler	G-5	Irvine	K-7

Jackson	E-4	Manteca	F-4
Jamestown	F-4	Mariposa	F-5
JKerman	G-5	Martinez	F-3
King City	H-4	Marysville	D-3
Kingsburg	G-5	McFarland	H-5
Lake Elsinore	K-7	Mendota	G-4
Lakeport	D-2	Merced	F-4
Lancaster	I-6	Milpitas	F-3
Lathrop	F-3	Modesto	F-3
Lemoore	H-5	Montecito	J-5
Lincoln	E-3	Monterey	G-3
Lindsay	H-5	Moorpark	J-6
Livermore	F-3	Morgan Hill	F-3
Livingston	F-4	Morro Bay	I-4
Lodi	E-3	Mount Shasta	B-3
Loma Linda	J-7	Napa	E-3
Lompoc	I-4	National City	L-7
Long Beach	J-6	Needles	I-10
Los Angeles	J-6	Nevada City	D-4
Los Banos	G-4	Newman	F-4
Los Gatos	F-3	Newport Beach	K-7
Lucerne	D-2	Novato	E-2
Madera	G-5	Oakhurst	F-5
Mammoth Lakes	F-6	Oakland	F-3

NOTE: Maps are not always in alphabetical order.
See Page 1 for map location in this atlas.

California • Nevada/Southern   21

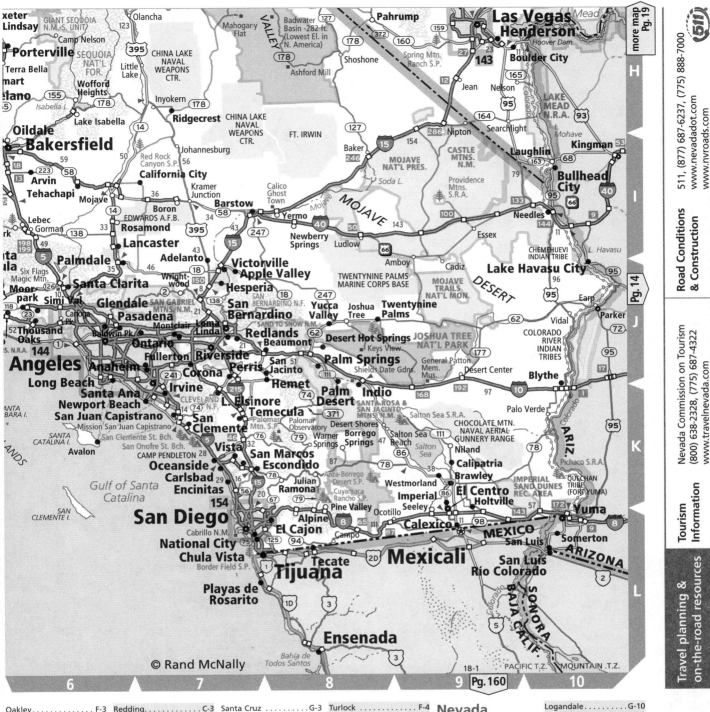

more map Pg. 19

Pg. 14

Road Conditions & Construction
511, (877) 687-6237, (775) 888-7000
www.nevadadot.com
www.nvroads.com

Tourism Information
Nevada Commission on Tourism
(800) 638-2328, (775) 687-4322
www.travelnevada.com

Travel planning & on-the-road resources

Pg. 160

Oakley F-3
Oceanside K-7
Oildale I-6
Ontario J-7
Orland D-3
Oroville D-3
Oxnard J-5
Pacific Grove G-3
Palm Desert J-8
Palm Springs J-8
Palmdale J-6
Palo Alto F-3
Paradise D-3
Pasadena J-6
Paso Robles H-4
Patterson F-4
Perris J-7
Pittsburg F-3
Placerville E-4
Porterville H-6
Quincy C-4
Ramona K-8
Rancho Cordova E-3
Red Bluff C-3

Redding C-3
Redlands J-7
Redwood City F-3
Ridgecrest H-7
Rio Dell C-1
Riverside J-7
Rocklin E-4
Rosamond I-6
Roseville E-3
Sacramento E-3
Salinas G-3
San Andreas E-4
San Bernardino J-7
San Clemente K-7
San Diego L-7
San Francisco F-2
San Jacinto J-8
San Jose F-3
San Juan Capistrano . K-7
San Luis Obispo I-4
San Marcos K-7
Santa Ana J-7
Santa Barbara J-5
Santa Clarita J-6

Santa Cruz G-3
Santa Maria I-4
Santa Paula J-5
Santa Rosa E-2
Saratoga F-3
Seaside G-3
Sebastopol E-2
Selma G-5
Shafter H-5
Simi Valley J-6
Soledad G-3
Solvang I-4
Sonora E-4
South Lake Tahoe . . . E-5
South San Francisco . . F-2
Stockton F-3
Susanville C-4
Taft I-5
Tehachapi I-6
Temecula K-7
Thousand Oaks J-6
Tracy F-3
Truckee D-4
Tulare H-5

Turlock F-4
Twain Harte F-4
Twentynine Palms . . . J-8
Ukiah D-2
Vacaville E-3
Vallejo E-3
Ventura J-5
Victorville J-7
Visalia G-5
Vista K-7
Wasco H-5
Watsonville G-3
Weaverville B-2
Williams D-3
Willits D-2
Willows D-3
Winters E-3
Woodlake G-5
Woodland E-3
Yreka A-2
Yuba City D-3
Yucca Valley J-8

Nevada
Cities and Towns
Alamo F-9
Amargosa Valley G-8
Battle Mountain B-7
Beatty G-8
Boulder City H-9
Caliente F-10
Carlin B-8
Carson City D-5
Dayton D-5
Elko B-8
Ely D-9
Eureka D-8
Fallon D-6
Fernley D-5
Gardnerville E-5
Hawthorne E-6
Henderson H-9
Indian Springs G-9
Jackpot A-9
Las Vegas H-9
Laughlin I-10

Logandale G-10
Lovelock C-6
McGill D-9
Mesquite G-10
Minden D-5
Overton G-10
Owyhee A-8
Pahrump H-8
Panaca F-10
Pioche F-10
Reno D-5
Schurz D-6
Searchlight H-9
Silver Springs D-5
Sparks D-5
Stateline D-5
Tonopah E-7
Verdi D-5
Virginia City D-5
Wadsworth D-5
Walker Lake E-6
Wells B-9
West Wendover B-10
Winnemucca B-7
Yerington D-5

© Rand McNally

Colorado

Cities and Towns

Akron	B-8
Alamosa	F-5
Arvada	C-6
Aspen	D-3
Aurora	C-6
Basalt	D-3
Bennett	C-6
Boulder	C-5
Breckenridge	C-4
Brighton	C-6
Brush	B-7
Buena Vista	D-4
Burlington	D-9
Cañon City	E-5
Carbondale	D-3
Castle Rock	D-6
Center	F-4
Central City	C-5
Cheyenne Wells	D-9
Clifton	D-2
Colorado City	F-6
Colorado Springs	D-6
Conejos	G-4
Cortez	G-1
Craig	B-3
Creede	F-3
Cripple Creek	E-5
Del Norte	F-4
Delta	D-2
Denver	C-6
Dove Creek	F-1
Durango	G-2
Eads	E-8
Eagle	C-4
Eaton	B-6
Englewood	C-6
Estes Park	B-5
Evans	B-6
Fairplay	D-4
Florence	E-6
Fort Collins	B-6
Fort Lupton	C-6
Fort Morgan	B-7
Fountain	E-6
Frederick	B-6
Fruita	D-1
Fruitvale	D-2
Georgetown	C-5
Glenwood Springs	C-3
Golden	C-5
Grand Junction	D-1
Greeley	B-6
Gunnison	E-3
Gypsum	C-3
Holyoke	B-9
Hot Sulphur Springs	C-4
Hugo	D-7
Julesburg	A-9
Kiowa	D-6
Lake City	F-3
Lakewood	C-6
Lamar	E-8
Las Animas	F-8
Leadville	D-4
Limon	D-7
Lincoln Park	E-5
Littleton	C-6
Longmont	B-6
Loveland	B-6
Manitou Springs	D-6
Meeker	C-2
Monte Vista	F-4
Montrose	E-2
Ordway	E-7
Ouray	F-2
Pagosa Springs	G-3
Palisade	D-2
Parker	C-6
Penrose	E-6
Platteville	B-6
Pueblo	E-6
Rangely	B-1
Rifle	C-2
Rocky Ford	F-7
Saguache	F-4
Salida	E-4
San Luis	G-5
Silverton	F-2
Springfield	G-9
Steamboat Springs	B-4
Sterling	B-8
Telluride	F-2
Thornton	C-6
Trinidad	G-6
Vail	C-4
Walden	B-4
Walsenburg	F-6
Wellington	B-6
Westcliffe	E-5
Windsor	B-6
Woodland Park	D-6
Wray	B-9
Yuma	B-8

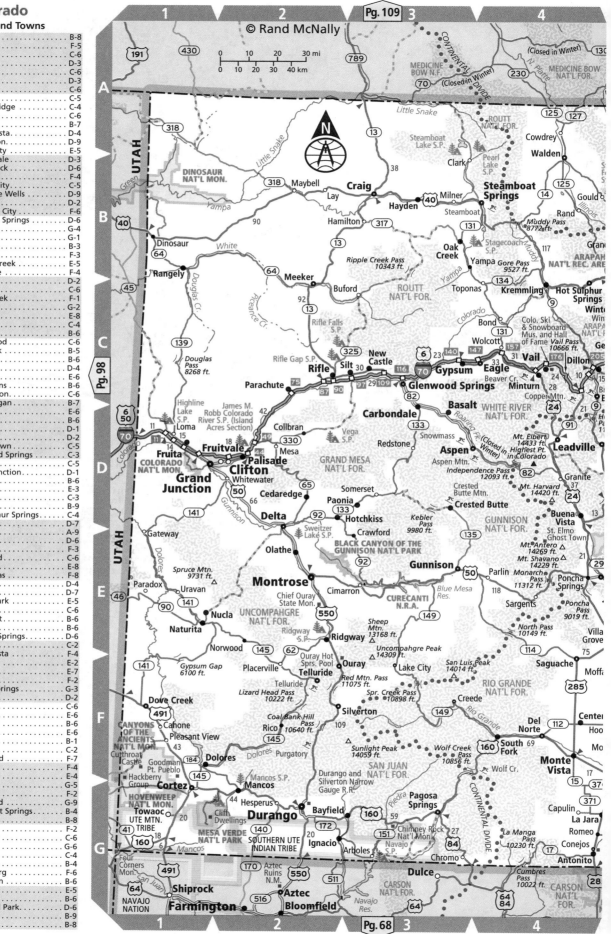

Pg. 109

Pg. 98

Pg. 68

© Rand McNally

NOTE: Maps are not always in alphabetical order.
See Page 1 for map location in this atlas.

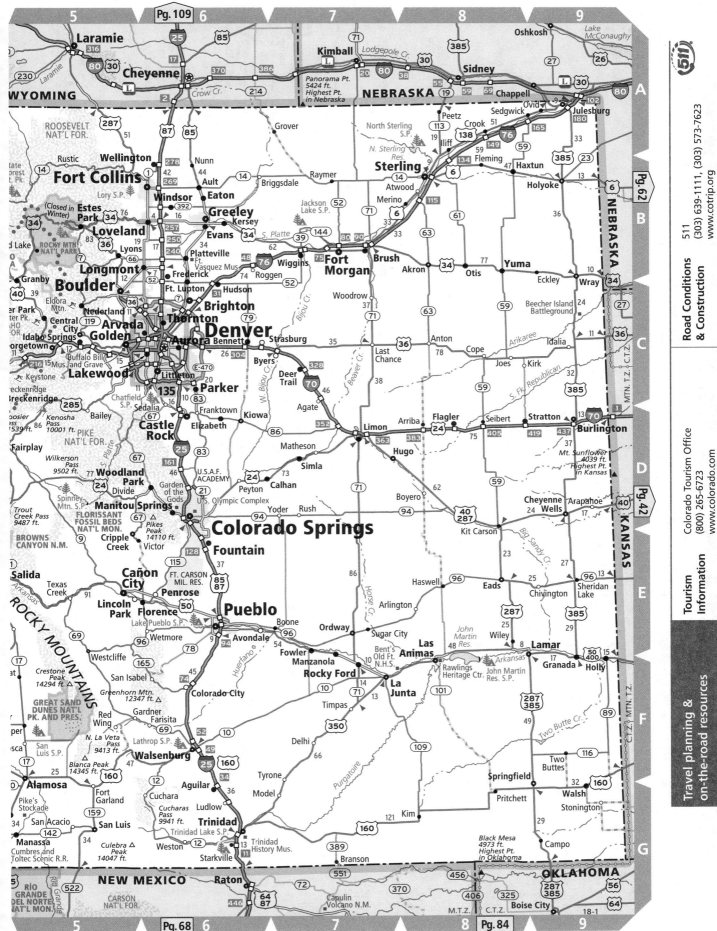

Road Conditions & Construction

511
(303) 639-1111, (303) 573-7623
www.cotrip.org

Tourism Information

Colorado Tourism Office
(800) 265-6723
www.colorado.com

Travel planning & on-the-road resources

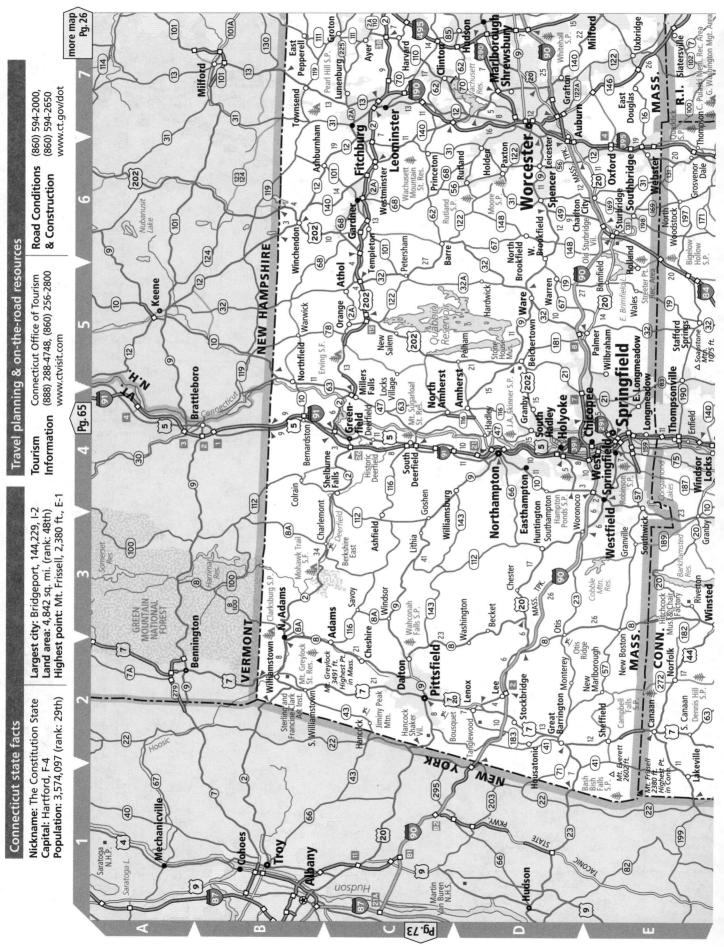

more map Pg. 26

Travel planning & on-the-road resources

Tourism Information	Connecticut Office of Tourism (888) 288-4748, (860) 256-2800 www.ctvisit.com
Road Conditions & Construction	(860) 594-2000, (860) 594-2650 www.ct.gov/dot

Connecticut state facts

Nickname: The Constitution State
Capital: Hartford, F-4
Population: 3,574,097 (rank: 29th)

Largest city: Bridgeport, 144,229, I-2
Land area: 4,842 sq. mi. (rank: 48th)
Highest point: Mt. Frissell, 2,380 ft., E-1

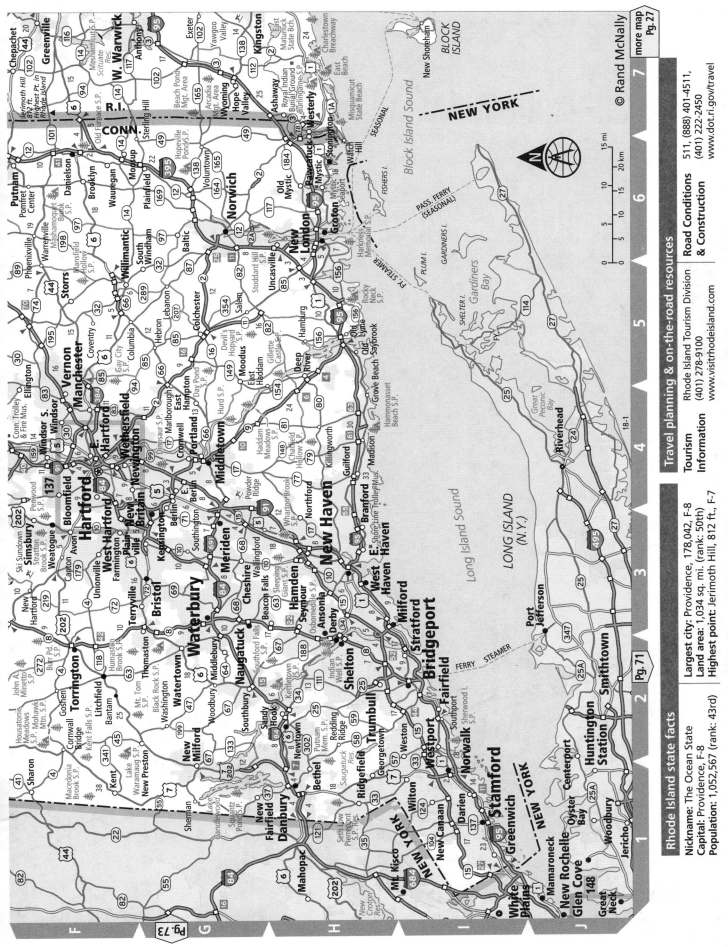

more map Pg.27

© Rand McNally

NEW YORK

Travel planning & on-the-road resources

Tourism Information	Road Conditions & Construction
Rhode Island Tourism Division (401) 278-9100 www.visitrhodeisland.com	511, (888) 401-4511, (401) 222-2450 www.dot.ri.gov/travel

Rhode Island state facts

Nickname: The Ocean State
Capital: Providence, F-8
Population: 1,052,567 (rank: 43rd)

Largest city: Providence, 178,042, F-8
Land area: 1,034 sq. mi. (rank: 50th)
Highest point: Jerimoth Hill, 812 ft., F-7

Connecticut

Cities and Towns

Ansonia	H-3
Avon	H-2
Baltic	G-6
Beacon Falls	H-3
Bethel	H-1
Bloomfield	F-4
Branford	H-3
Bridgeport	I-2
Bristol	G-3
Brooklyn	F-6
Canaan	E-2
Cheshire	G-3
Colchester	G-5
Columbia	F-5
Cromwell	G-4
Danbury	H-1
Danielson	F-6
Darien	I-1
Deep River	H-5
Derby	H-2
East Hampton	G-4
East Hartford	F-4
East Haven	H-3
Ellington	F-4
Fairfield	I-2
Farmington	F-3
Georgetown	H-1
Greenwich	I-1
Groton	H-6
Guilford	H-4
Hamden	H-3
Hartford	F-4
Kensington	G-4
Lakeville	E-1
Litchfield	F-2
Manchester	F-4
Meriden	G-3
Middlebury	G-2
Middletown	G-4
Milford	I-2
Moosup	F-6
Mystic	H-6
Naugatuck	H-3
New Britain	G-3
New Canaan	I-1
New Fairfield	H-1
New Haven	H-3
New London	H-6
New Milford	G-1
Newington	F-4
Newtown	H-2
Norfolk	E-2
Northford	H-3
Norwalk	I-1
Norwich	G-6
Old Mystic	H-6
Pawcatuck	H-6
Plainfield	G-6
Plainville	G-3
Portland	G-4
Putnam	F-6
Ridgefield	H-1
Seymour	H-2
Shelton	H-2
Simsbury	F-3
South Windham	G-5
South Windsor	F-4
Southbury	G-2
Stafford Springs	E-5
Stamford	I-1

Gloucester	C-10
Great Barrington	D-2
Greenfield	C-4
Harwich	F-12
Harwich Port.	G-12
Haverhill	B-9
Hingham	D-9
Holden	D-6
Holliston	D-8
Holyoke	D-4
Hudson	D-7
Hyannis	G-11
Ipswich	B-10
Kingston	E-10
Lawrence	B-9
Lee	D-2
Leicester	D-6
Leominster	C-7
Lexington	C-8
Lincoln	C-8
Longmeadow	E-4
Lowell	B-8
Lunenburg	C-7
Lynn	C-9
Lynnfield	C-9
Mansfield	E-8
Marblehead	C-10
Marlborough	D-7
Marshfield	E-10
Maynard	C-8
Medfield	D-8
Methuen	B-9
Middleborough	F-9
Middleton	B-9
Millis	D-8
Nantucket	H-12
Natick	D-8
New Bedford	G-9
Newton	C-8
North Adams	B-3
North Amherst	C-4
North Andover	B-9
North Attleboro	E-8
North Billerica	C-8
North Brookfield	D-5
Northampton	D-4
Norton	E-9
Norwood	D-8
Oak Bluffs	G-11
Orange	C-5
Orleans	F-12
Oxford	E-6
Palmer	D-5
Peabody	C-9
Pittsfield	C-2
Plymouth	E-10
Pocasset	F-10
Provincetown	E-12
Quincy	D-9
Randolph	D-9
Revere	C-9
Rockland	E-9
Rockport	B-10
Rutland	D-6
Salem	C-9
Salisbury	B-10
Sandwich	F-11
Saugus	C-9
Scituate	D-10
Sharon	E-8
Shelburne Falls	C-4
Shrewsbury	D-7

more map Pg. 24
Pg. 65

Storrs	F-5
Stratford	J-2
Terryville	G-3
Thomaston	G-3
Thompsonville	E-4
Torrington	F-2
Trumbull	H-2
Uncasville	H-6
Unionville	F-3
Vernon	F-4
Waterbury	G-3
Watertown	G-2
Weatogue	F-3
West Hartford	F-4
West Haven	H-3
Weston	I-2
Westport	I-2
Wethersfield	F-4
Willimantic	F-5
Wilton	I-1
Windsor	F-4
Windsor Locks	E-4
Winsted	E-3

Smith Mills	G-9
Somerset	F-9
South Deerfield	C-4
South Hadley	D-4
South Yarmouth	G-12
Southampton	D-4
Southbridge	E-6
Spencer	D-6
Springfield	E-4
Stoneham	C-9
Sturbridge	D-6
Sudbury Center	C-9
Swampscott	C-9
Taunton	F-9
Topsfield	B-9
Uxbridge	E-7
Vineyard Haven	G-10
Wakefield	C-9
Walpole	D-8
Waltham	C-9
Ware	D-5
Wareham Center	F-10
Wayland	C-9
Webster	E-6
Wellesley	C-9
West Bridgewater	E-9
West Springfield	E-4
West Yarmouth	G-12
Westfield	E-4
Whitman	D-9
Wilbraham	E-5
Williamstown	B-2
Wilmington	B-9
Winchendon	B-6
Woburn	C-9
Worcester	D-7
Wrentham	E-8

Massachusetts

Cities and Towns

Adams	C-2
Amesbury	B-9
Amherst	D-4
Andover	B-9
Athol	C-5
Attleboro	E-8
Auburn	D-7
Ayer	C-7
Barnstable	F-11
Bedford	C-8
Belchertown	D-5
Bellingham	E-8
Beverly	C-9
Billerica	C-8
Boston	D-9
Braintree	D-9
Brewster	F-12
Bridgewater	E-9
Brockton	E-9
Brookline	D-9
Buzzards Bay	F-10
Cambridge	D-9
Chicopee	E-4
Clinton	C-7
Cohasset	D-10
Concord	C-8
Dalton	C-2
Danvers	C-9
Dartmouth	G-9
Dedham	D-9
Dennis	F-12
East Douglas	E-7
East Falmouth	G-11
East Longmeadow	E-4
East Pepperell	B-7
Easthampton	D-4
Edgartown	H-11
Everett	C-9
Fairhaven	G-9
Fall River	F-9
Falmouth	G-10
Fitchburg	C-7
Foxborough	E-8
Framingham	D-8
Gardner	C-6
Georgetown	B-9

Rhode Island

Cities and Towns

Anthony	F-7
Bristol	G-8
Central Falls	F-8
Cranston	F-8
East Greenwich	G-8
East Providence	G-7
Greenville	F-7
Jamestown	G-8
Kingston	F-7
Middletown	G-8
Narragansett Pier	H-8
Newport	G-8
North Kingstown	F-8
Pawtucket	F-8
Portsmouth	G-8
Providence	F-8
Tiverton	G-9
Warwick	F-8
West Warwick	F-8
Westerly	H-7
Woonsocket	E-8

Tourism Information
Mass. Office of Travel & Tourism (800) 227-6277, (617) 973-8500 www.massvacation.com

Road Conditions & Construction
511, Metro Boston: (617) 986-5511, Central: (508) 499-5511, Western: (413) 754-5511 www.mass511.com, www.mhd.state.ma.us

Travel planning & on-the-road resources 511

© Rand McNally

more map Pg. 25

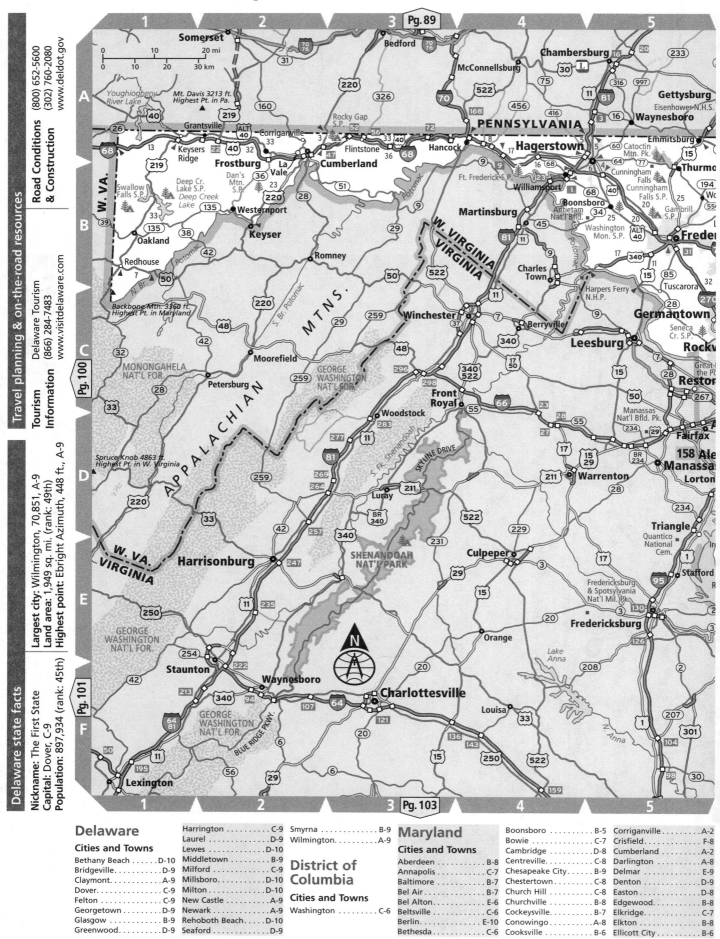

Pg. 89

Pg. 100

Pg. 101

Pg. 103

Travel planning & on-the-road resources

Road Conditions & Construction
(800) 652-5600
(302) 760-2080
www.deldot.gov

Tourism Information
Delaware Tourism
(866) 284-7483
www.visitdelaware.com

Delaware state facts

Nickname: The First State
Capital: Dover, C-9
Population: 897,934 (rank: 45th)

Largest city: Wilmington, 70,851, A-9
Land area: 1,949 sq. mi. (rank: 49th)
Highest point: Ebright Azimuth, 448 ft., A-9

Delaware

Cities and Towns

Bethany Beach D-10
Bridgeville D-9
Claymont A-9
Dover C-9
Felton C-9
Georgetown D-9
Glasgow B-9
Greenwood D-9
Harrington C-9
Laurel D-9
Lewes D-10
Middletown B-9
Milford C-9
Millsboro D-10
Milton D-10
New Castle A-9
Newark A-9
Rehoboth Beach D-10
Seaford D-9
Smyrna B-9
Wilmington A-9

District of Columbia

Cities and Towns

Washington C-6

Maryland

Cities and Towns

Aberdeen B-8
Annapolis C-7
Baltimore B-7
Bel Air B-7
Bel Alton E-6
Beltsville C-6
Berlin E-10
Bethesda C-6
Boonsboro B-5
Bowie C-7
Cambridge D-8
Centreville C-8
Chesapeake City B-9
Chestertown C-8
Church Hill C-8
Churchville B-8
Cockeysville B-7
Conowingo A-8
Cooksville B-6
Corriganville A-2
Crisfield F-8
Cumberland A-2
Darlington A-8
Delmar E-9
Denton D-8
Easton D-8
Edgewood B-8
Elkridge C-7
Elkton A-8
Ellicott City B-6

NOTE: Maps are not always in alphabetical order.
See Page 1 for map location in this atlas.

Delaware • Maryland 29

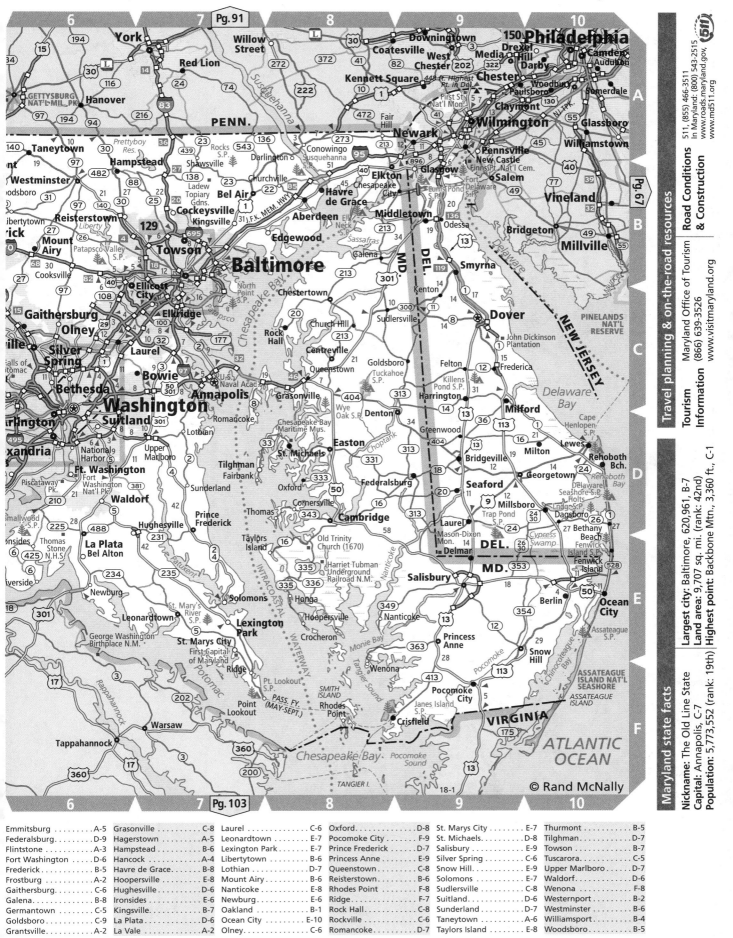

Travel planning & on-the-road resources

Road Conditions & Construction
511, (855) 466-3511
In Maryland: (800) 543-2515
www.roads.maryland.gov,
www.md511.org

Travel planning & Information

Tourism Maryland Office of Tourism (866) 639-3526 www.visitmaryland.org

Information

Maryland state facts

Nickname: The Old Line State
Capital: Annapolis, C-7
Population: 5,773,552 (rank: 19th)

Largest city: Baltimore, 620,961, B-7
Land area: 9,707 sq. mi. (rank: 42nd)
Highest point: Backbone Mtn., 3,360 ft., C-1

© Rand McNally

Emmitsburg A-5	Grasonville C-8	Laurel C-6	Oxford D-8	St. Marys City E-7	Thurmont B-5
Federalsburg D-9	Hagerstown A-5	Leonardtown E-7	Pocomoke City F-9	St. Michaels. D-8	Tilghman D-7
Flintstone A-3	Hampstead B-6	Lexington Park E-7	Prince Frederick . . . D-7	Salisbury E-9	Towson B-7
Fort Washington D-6	Hancock A-4	Libertytown B-6	Princess Anne E-9	Silver Spring C-6	Tuscarora C-5
Frederick. B-5	Havre de Grace B-8	Lothian D-7	Queenstown C-8	Snow Hill E-9	Upper Marlboro . . . D-7
Frostburg A-2	Hoopersville E-8	Mount Airy B-6	Reisterstown B-6	Solomons E-7	Waldorf D-6
Gaithersburg C-6	Hughesville D-6	Nanticoke E-8	Rhodes Point F-8	Sudlersville C-8	Wenona F-8
Galena. B-8	Ironsides E-6	Newburg E-6	Ridge F-7	Suitland D-6	Westernport B-2
Germantown C-5	Kingsville B-7	Oakland B-1	Rock Hall C-8	Sunderland D-7	Westminster B-6
Goldsboro C-9	La Plata D-6	Ocean City E-10	Rockville C-6	Taneytown A-6	Williamsport B-4
Grantsville A-2	La Vale A-2	Olney C-6	Romancoke D-7	Taylors Island E-8	Woodsboro B-5

Florida

Florida
state facts

Nickname: The Sunshine State

Capital: Tallahassee, B-1

Population: 18,801,310 (rank: 4th)

Largest city: Jacksonville, 821,784, B-4

Land area: 53,625 sq. mi. (rank: 26th)

Highest point: Britton Hill, 345 ft., I-2

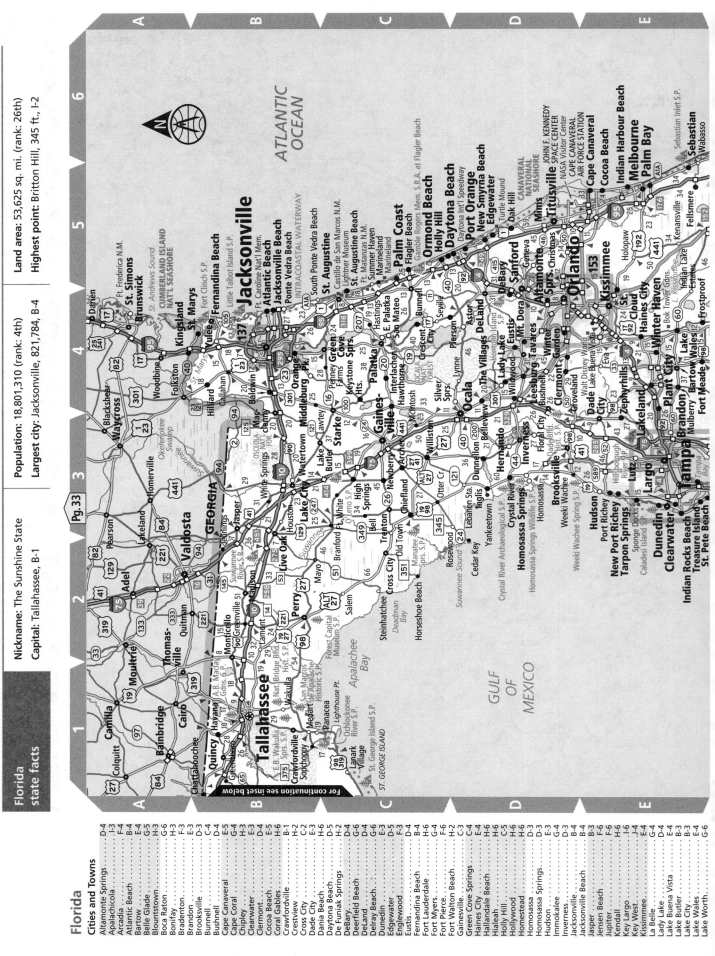

Cities and Towns

Altamonte Springs D-4
Apalachicola I-3
Arcadia F-4
Atlantic Beach B-4
Bartow E-4
Belle Glade G-5
Blountstown H-3
Boca Raton G-6
Bonifay H-3
Bradenton F-3
Brandon E-3
Brooksville D-3
Bunnell C-4
Cape Canaveral E-5
Cape Coral G-4
Chipley H-3
Clermont E-3
Clearwater E-3
Cocoa Beach E-5
Coral Gables H-6
Crawfordville B-1
Crestview H-2
Cross City C-2
Dade City E-3
Dania Beach H-6
Daytona Beach D-5
De Funiak Springs H-2
DeBary D-4
DeLand D-4
Delray Beach G-6
Dunedin E-3
Edgewater D-5
Englewood F-3
Eustis D-4
Fernandina Beach B-4
Fort Lauderdale H-6
Fort Myers G-4
Fort Pierce F-6
Fort Walton Beach H-2
Gainesville C-3
Green Cove Springs C-4
Haines City E-4
Hallandale Beach H-6
Hialeah H-6
Hollywood H-6
Hollly Hill C-5
Homestead H-6
Homosassa D-3
Homosassa Springs D-3
Hudson E-3
Immokalee G-4
Inverness D-3
Jacksonville B-4
Jacksonville Beach B-3
Jasper B-3
Jensen Beach F-6
Jupiter F-6
Kendall H-6
Key Largo I-6
Key West J-4
Kissimmee E-4
La Belle G-4
Lady Lake D-4
Lake Buena Vista E-4
Lake Butler B-3
Lake City B-3
Lake Wales E-4
Lake Worth G-6

NOTE: Maps are not always in alphabetical order.
See Page 1 for map location in this atlas.

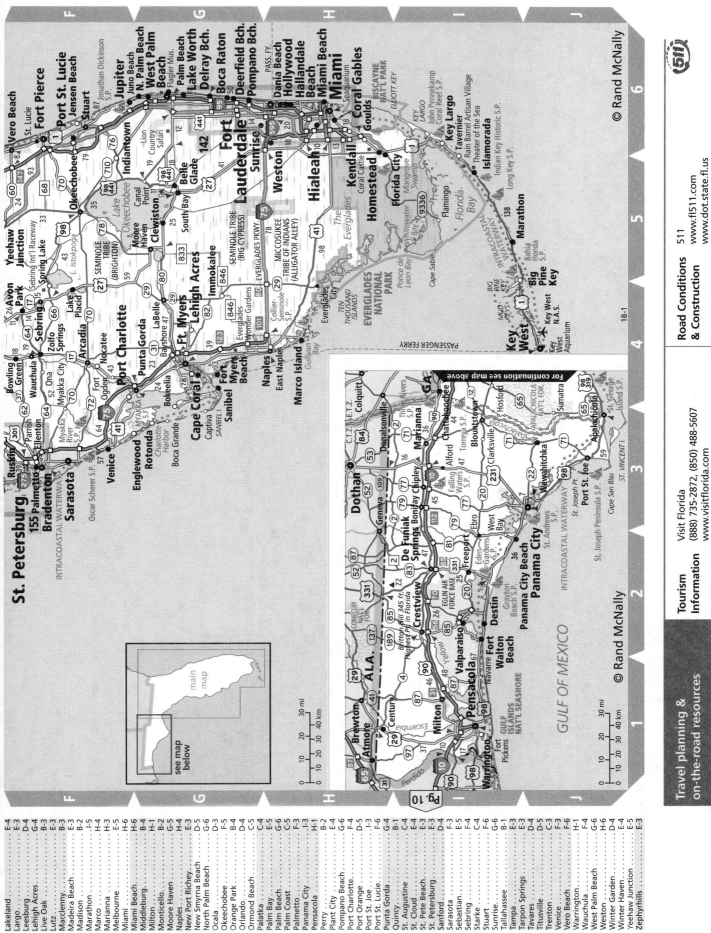

© Rand McNally

Lakeland E-4
Largo E-3
Leesburg D-4
Lehigh Acres G-4
Live Oak B-3
Lutz E-3
Macclenny B-3
Madeira Beach B-2
Madison B-2
Marathon J-5
Marco H-4
Marianna H-3
Melbourne E-5
Miami H-6
Miami Beach H-6
Middleburg B-4
Milton H-1
Monticello B-2
Moore Haven G-5
Naples H-4
New Port Richey E-3
New Smyrna Beach D-5
North Palm Beach G-6
Ocala D-3
Okeechobee F-5
Orange Park B-4
Orlando D-4
Ormond Beach C-5
Palatka C-4
Palm Bay E-5
Palm Beach G-6
Palm Coast C-5
Palmetto F-3
Panama City H-3
Pensacola H-1
Perry B-2
Plant City E-3
Pompano Beach G-6
Port Charlotte F-4
Port Orange D-5
Port St. Joe I-3
Port St. Lucie F-6
Punta Gorda G-4
Quincy B-1
St. Augustine C-4
St. Cloud E-4
St. Pete Beach E-3
St. Petersburg E-3
Sanford D-4
Sarasota F-3
Sebastian E-5
Sebring F-4
Starke C-4
Stuart F-6
Sunrise G-6
Tallahassee B-1
Tampa E-3
Tarpon Springs E-3
Tavares D-4
Titusville D-5
Trenton C-3
Venice F-3
Vero Beach F-6
Warrington H-1
Wauchula F-4
West Palm Beach G-6
Weston H-6
Winter Garden D-4
Winter Haven E-4
Yeehaw Junction E-5
Zephyrhills E-3

GULF OF MEXICO

For continuation see map above

Pg. 10

© Rand McNally

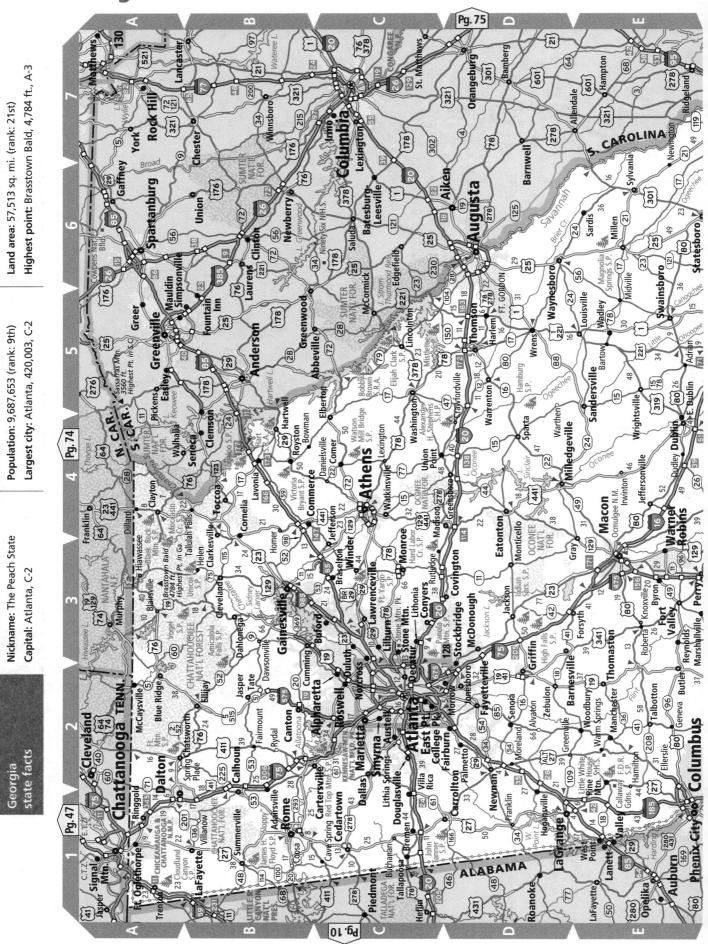

NOTE: Maps are not always in alphabetical order.
See Page 1 for map location in this atlas.

Georgia   33

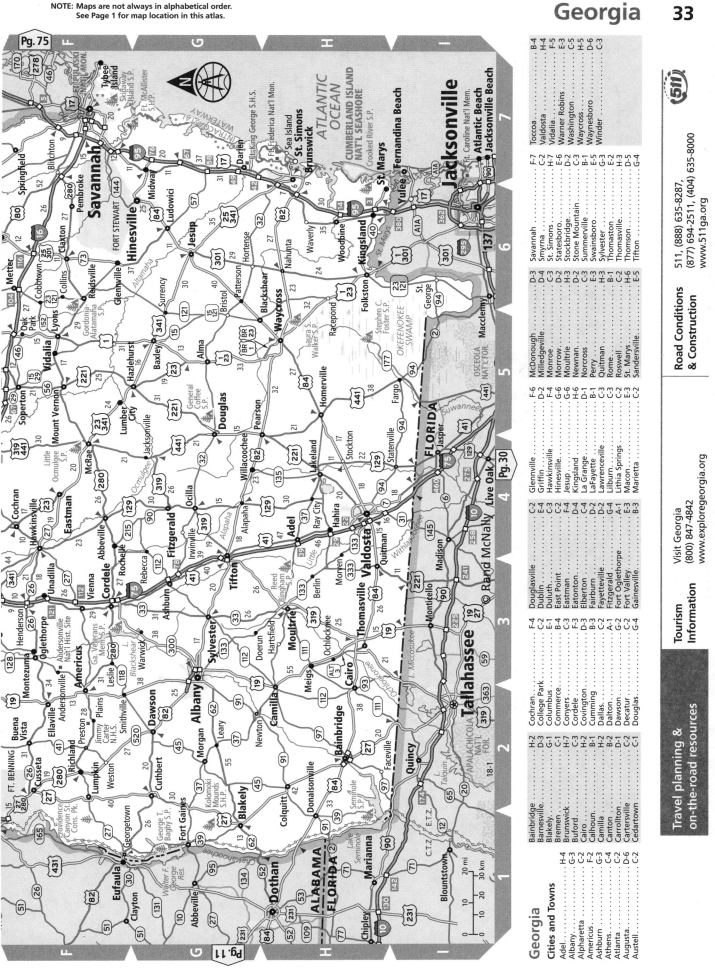

Georgia

Cities and Towns

Adel	H-4
Albany	G-3
Alpharetta	C-2
Americus	F-2
Ashburn	G-3
Athens	C-4
Atlanta	C-2
Augusta	D-6
Austell	C-2
Bainbridge	H-2
Barnesville	D-3
Blakely	G-1
Bremen	B-4
Brunswick	H-7
Buford	C-3
Cairo	H-2
Calhoun	B-1
Camilla	H-2
Canton	B-2
Carrollton	C-1
Cartersville	C-2
Cedartown	C-2
Cochran	H-2
College Park	D-3
Columbus	G-1
Commerce	B-4
Conyers	C-3
Cordele	F-3
Covington	D-3
Dallas	B-3
Dalton	A-1
Dawson	G-2
Decatur	C-2
Douglas	G-4
Douglasville	F-4
Dublin	C-2
Duluth	E-1
East Point	B-4
Eatonton	F-3
Elberton	D-3
Fairburn	B-3
Fayetteville	C-2
Fitzgerald	G-4
Fort Oglethorpe	G-2
Fort Valley	C-2
Gainesville	G-4
Glennville	C-2
Griffin	E-4
Hawkinsville	E-1
Hinesville	F-2
Jesup	F-4
Kingsland	D-4
La Grange	D-2
Lawrenceville	C-3
Lilburn	G-4
Lithia Springs	A-1
Macon	E-3
Marietta	B-3
McDonough	D-3
Milledgeville	D-4
Monroe	C-3
Morrow	D-2
Moultrie	H-3
Newnan	D-2
Norcross	C-3
Perry	E-3
Quitman	H-3
Rome	C-2
Roswell	C-3
St. Marys	H-6
Sandersville	E-5
Savannah	F-7
Smyrna	C-2
St. Simons	H-7
Statesboro	E-6
Stockbridge	D-2
Stone Mountain	C-3
Summerville	B-1
Swainsboro	E-5
Sylvester	G-3
Thomaston	E-2
Thomasville	H-3
Thomson	D-5
Tifton	G-4
Toccoa	B-4
Valdosta	H-4
Vidalia	F-5
Warner Robins	E-3
Washington	C-5
Waycross	H-5
Waynesboro	D-6
Winder	C-3

Travel planning & on-the-road resources

Tourism Information
Visit Georgia
(800) 847-4842
www.exploregeorgia.org

Road Conditions & Construction
511, (888) 635-8287,
(877) 694-2511, (404) 635-8000
www.511ga.org

Idaho
state facts

Nickname: The Gem State

Capital: Boise, H-2

Population: 1,567,582 (rank: 39th)

Largest city: Boise, 205,671, H-2

Land area: 82,643 sq. mi. (rank: 11th)

Highest point: Borah Peak, 12,662 ft., G-4

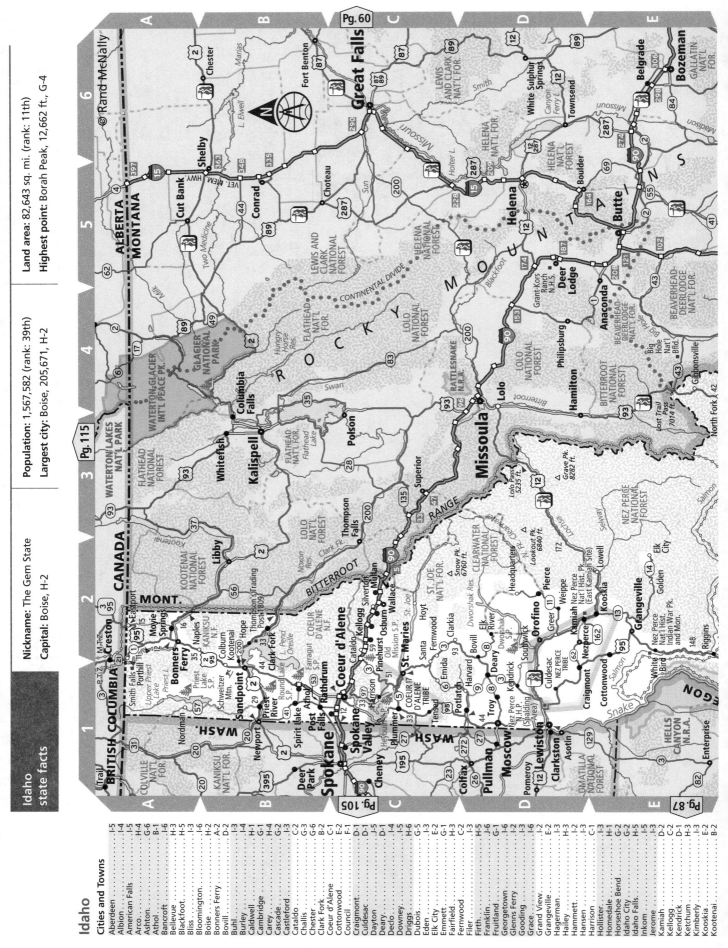

Idaho

Cities and Towns

Aberdeen	I-5
Albion	I-4
American Falls	I-5
Arco	H-4
Ashton	G-6
Athol	B-1
Bancroft	H-3
Bellevue	H-3
Blackfoot	H-5
Bloomington	I-6
Boise	H-2
Bonners Ferry	A-2
Bovill	D-2
Buhl	I-3
Burley	I-4
Caldwell	H-1
Cambridge	G-1
Carey	H-4
Cascade	G-2
Castleford	I-3
Cataldo	C-2
Challis	G-3
Chester	G-6
Clark Fork	B-2
Coeur d'Alene	C-1
Cottonwood	E-2
Council	F-1
Craigmont	D-1
Culdesac	D-1
Dayton	J-5
Deary	D-1
Declo	I-4
Downey	H-6
Driggs	G-5
Dubois	G-5
Eden	I-4
Elk City	E-2
Emmett	G-1
Fairfield	H-3
Fernwood	C-2
Filer	I-3
Firth	H-5
Franklin	J-6
Fruitland	G-1
Georgetown	I-6
Glenns Ferry	I-3
Gooding	I-3
Grace	H-6
Grand View	I-2
Grangeville	E-2
Hagerman	I-3
Hailey	H-3
Hammett	I-2
Hansen	I-3
Harrison	C-1
Hollister	I-3
Homedale	H-1
Horseshoe Bend	G-2
Idaho City	H-2
Idaho Falls	H-5
Inkom	H-5
Jerome	I-3
Kamiah	D-2
Kellogg	C-2
Kendrick	D-1
Ketchum	H-3
Kimberly	I-3
Kooskia	E-2
Kootenai	B-2

NOTE: Maps are not always in alphabetical order.
See Page 1 for map location in this atlas.

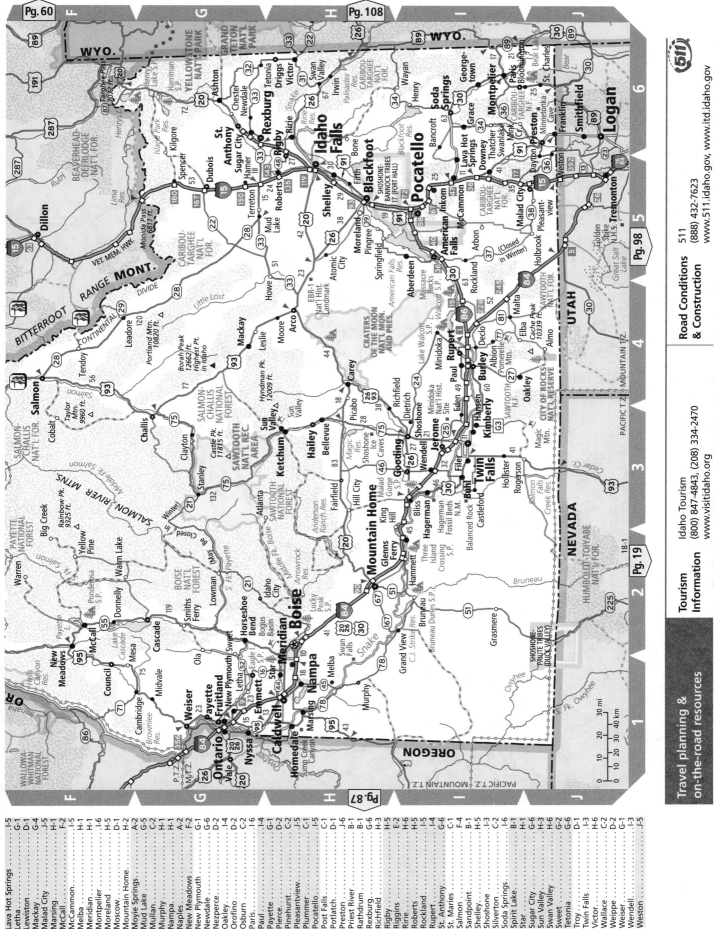

Pg. 60 Pg. 108 Pg. 98 Pg. 19 Pg. 87

Travel planning & on-the-road resources

Tourism Information	Road Conditions & Construction
Idaho Tourism (800) 847-4843, (208) 334-2470 www.visitidaho.org	511 (888) 432-7623 www.511.idaho.gov, www.itd.idaho.gov

Lava Hot Springs I-5
Letha G-1
Lewiston D-1
Mackay G-4
Malad City J-5
Marsing H-1
McCall F-2
McCammon I-5
Melba H-1
Meridian H-1
Montpelier I-6
Moreland H-5
Moscow A-2
Mountain Home G-5
Mud Lake G-5
Mullan C-2
Murphy H-1
Nampa H-1
Naples A-2
New Meadows F-1
New Plymouth G-1
Newdale G-6
Nezperce C-1
Oakley I-4
Orofino C-2
Osburn C-2
Paris I-6
Paul I-4
Payette G-1
Pierce D-2
Pinehurst C-2
Pleasantview J-5
Plummer B-1
Pocatello I-5
Post Falls C-1
Potlatch B-1
Preston J-6
Priest River B-1
Rathdrum C-1
Rexburg G-6
Richfield H-3
Rigby G-6
Riggins E-2
Ririe H-6
Roberts G-5
Rockland I-5
Rupert I-4
St. Anthony G-6
St. Maries C-1
Salmon F-4
Sandpoint B-1
Shelley H-5
Shoshone H-3
Silverton C-2
Soda Springs I-6
Spirit Lake B-1
Star H-1
Sugar City G-6
Sun Valley H-3
Swan Valley H-6
Sweet G-2
Tetonia G-6
Troy D-1
Twin Falls I-3
Victor H-6
Wallace C-2
Weippe D-2
Weiser G-1
Wendell I-3
Weston J-5

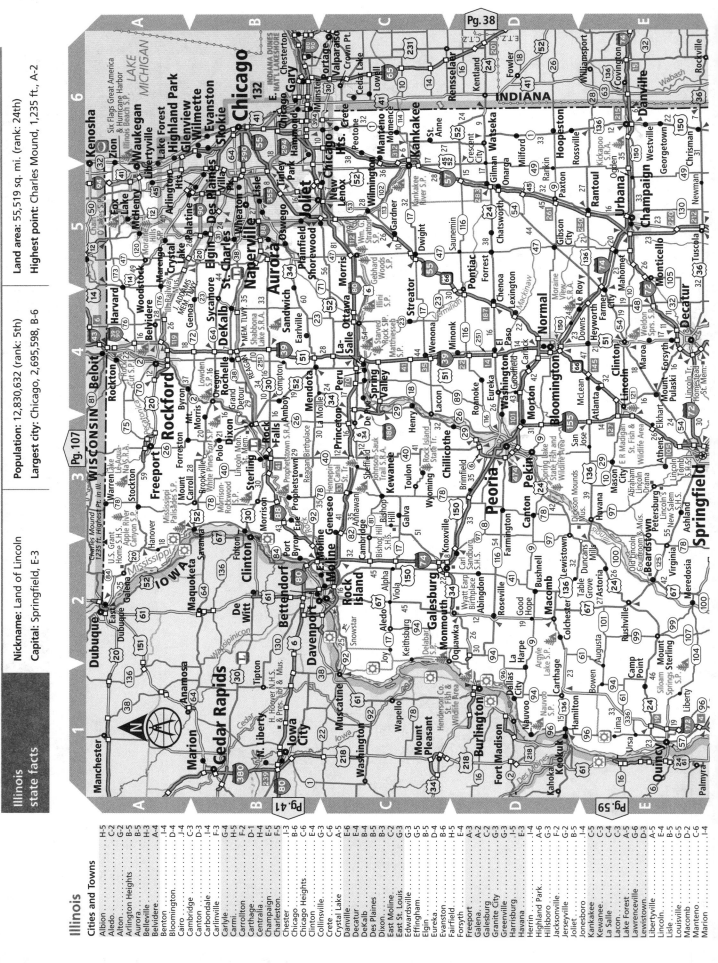

Illinois state facts

Nickname: Land of Lincoln

Capital: Springfield, E-3

Population: 12,830,632 (rank: 5th)

Largest city: Chicago, 2,695,598, B-6

Land area: 55,519 sq. mi. (rank: 24th)

Highest point: Charles Mound, 1,235 ft., A-2

Illinois

Cities and Towns

Albion	H-5
Aledo	C-2
Alton	G-2
Arlington Heights	B-5
Aurora	H-3
Belleville	A-4
Belvidere	J-4
Benton	J-4
Bloomington	D-4
Cairo	J-4
Cambridge	C-3
Canton	D-3
Carbondale	J-4
Carlinville	F-3
Carlyle	G-4
Carmi	H-5
Carrollton	F-2
Carthage	D-1
Centralia	H-4
Champaign	E-5
Charleston	G-6
Chester	J-3
Chicago	B-6
Chicago Heights	C-6
Clinton	E-4
Collinsville	G-3
Crete	C-6
Crystal Lake	A-5
Danville	E-6
Decatur	E-4
DeKalb	B-4
Des Plaines	B-5
Dixon	B-3
East Moline	C-2
East St. Louis	G-3
Edwardsville	G-3
Effingham	G-5
Elgin	B-5
Eureka	D-4
Fairfield	H-5
Forsyth	E-4
Freeport	A-3
Galena	A-2
Galesburg	C-3
Granite City	G-3
Greenville	G-3
Havana	D-3
Harrisburg	I-5
Herrin	J-4
Highland Park	A-6
Hillsboro	G-3
Jacksonville	F-2
Jerseyville	G-2
Joliet	B-5
Kankakee	C-5
Kewanee	C-3
La Salle	C-4
Lacon	D-4
Lawrenceville	G-6
Lewistown	D-3
Libertyville	A-5
Lincoln	E-4
Lisle	B-5
Louisville	G-5
Macomb	D-2
Manteco	C-6
Marion	J-4

NOTE: Maps are not always in alphabetical order.
See Page 1 for map location in this atlas.

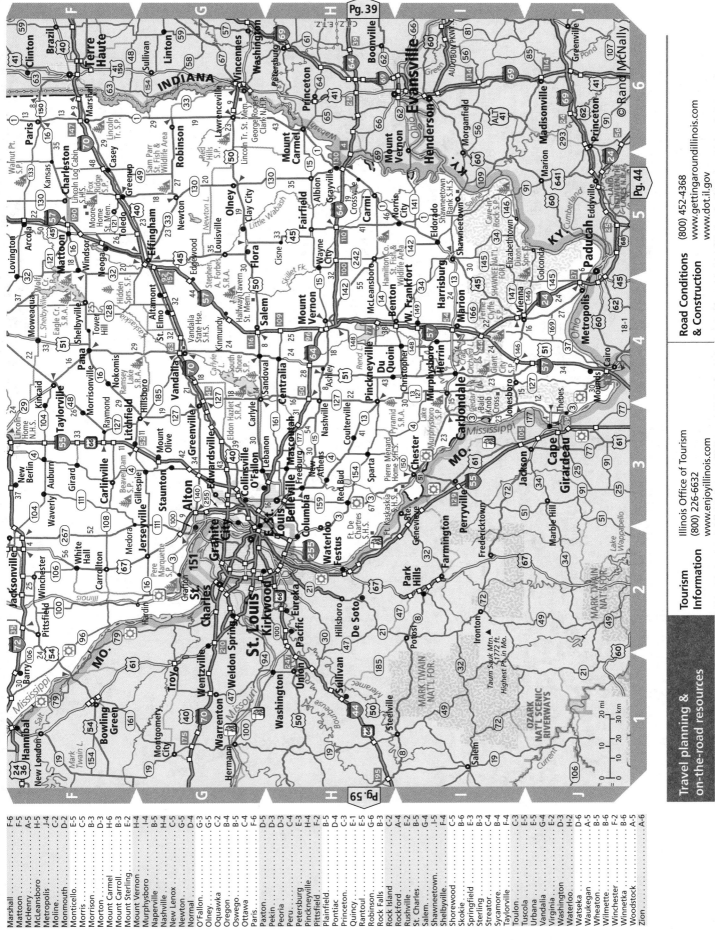

**Travel planning &
on-the-road resources**

Tourism Information	Illinois Office of Tourism (800) 226-6632 www.enjoyillinois.com	Road Conditions & Construction	(800) 452-4368 www.gettingaroundillinois.com www.dot.il.gov

Marshall F-6
Mattoon F-5
McHenry A-5
McLeansboro H-5
Metropolis J-4
Moline D-2
Monmouth D-2
Monticello C-5
Morris B-5
Morrison B-3
Morton C-5
Mount Carmel H-6
Mount Carroll B-3
Mount Sterling E-2
Mount Vernon H-4
Murphysboro I-4
Naperville B-5
Nashville H-4
New Lenox C-5
Newton G-5
Normal D-4
O'Fallon G-3
Olney G-5
Oquawka C-2
Oregon B-4
Oswego B-5
Ottawa B-5
Paris F-6
Paxton D-5
Pekin D-3
Peoria D-3
Peru C-4
Petersburg E-3
Pinckneyville H-4
Pittsfield F-2
Plainfield B-5
Pontiac D-4
Princeton C-3
Quincy E-1
Rantoul D-5
Robinson G-6
Rock Falls B-3
Rock Island C-2
Rockford A-4
Rushville D-2
St. Charles B-5
Salem H-4
Shawneetown I-5
Shelbyville E-4
Shorewood B-5
Skokie A-6
Springfield E-3
Sterling B-3
Streator C-4
Sycamore B-4
Taylorville F-4
Toulon C-3
Tuscola E-5
Urbana D-5
Vandalia G-4
Virginia E-2
Washington H-2
Waterloo H-3
Watseka D-6
Waukegan A-5
Wheaton B-5
Wilmette B-6
Winchester F-2
Winnetka B-6
Woodstock A-5
Zion A-6

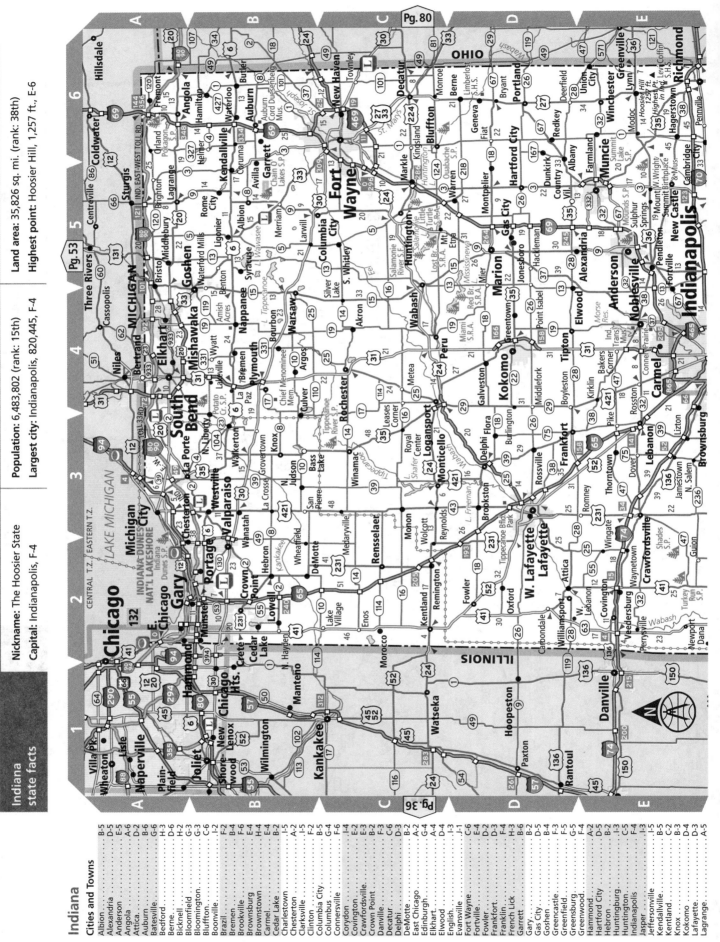

Indiana state facts

Nickname: The Hoosier State
Capital: Indianapolis, F-4

Population: 6,483,802 (rank: 15th)
Largest city: Indianapolis, 820,445, F-4

Land area: 35,826 sq. mi. (rank: 38th)
Highest point: Hoosier Hill, 1,257 ft., E-6

Indiana

Cities and Towns

Albion B-5
Alexandria D-5
Anderson E-5
Angola A-6
Attica D-2
Auburn B-6
Batesville G-6
Bedford H-3
Berne D-6
Bicknell H-2
Bloomfield G-3
Bloomington G-3
Bluffton C-6
Boonville I-2
Brazil F-2
Bremen B-4
Brookville F-6
Brownsburg E-4
Brownstown H-4
Carmel E-4
Cedar Lake B-2
Charlestown I-5
Chesterton A-2
Clarksville I-5
Clinton F-2
Columbia City B-5
Columbus G-4
Connersville F-6
Corydon I-4
Covington E-2
Crawfordsville E-3
Crown Point B-2
Danville F-3
Decatur C-6
Delphi D-3
DeMotte B-2
East Chicago A-2
Edinburgh G-4
Elkhart A-4
Elwood D-5
English I-3
Evansville J-1
Fort Wayne C-6
Fortville E-4
Fowler D-3
Frankfort E-3
Franklin F-4
French Lick H-3
Garrett B-6
Gary A-2
Gas City D-5
Goshen B-4
Greencastle F-3
Greenfield F-5
Greensburg G-5
Greenwood F-4
Hammond A-2
Hartford City D-5
Hebron B-2
Huntingburg I-3
Huntington C-5
Indianapolis F-4
Jasper I-3
Jeffersonville I-5
Kendallville B-5
Kentland C-2
Knox B-3
Kokomo D-4
Lafayette E-3
Lagrange A-5

NOTE: Maps are not always in alphabetical order.
See Page 1 for map location in this atlas.

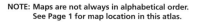

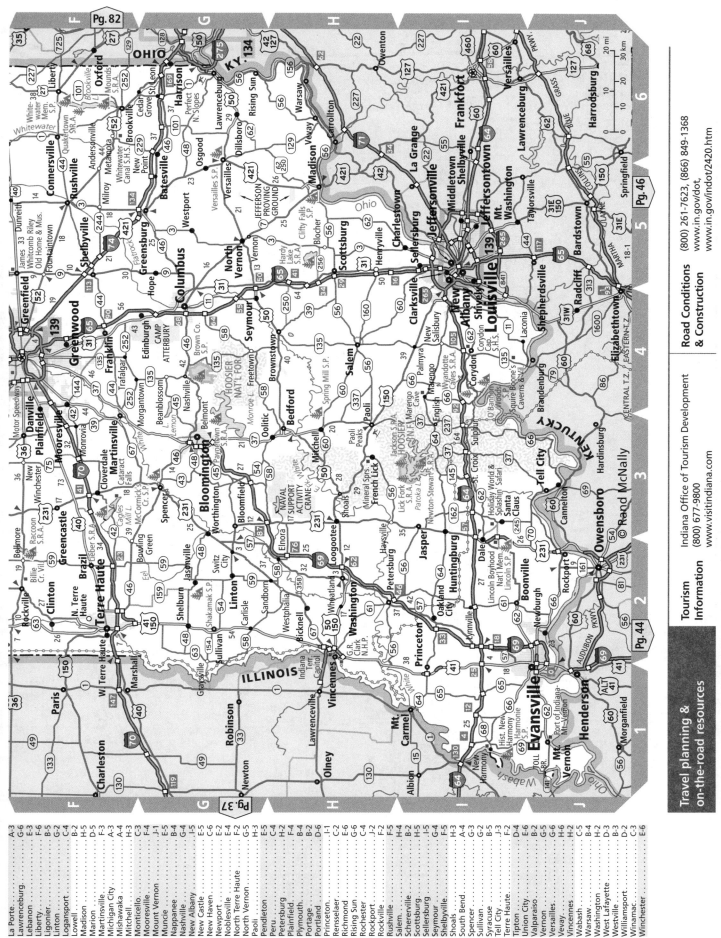

Travel planning & on-the-road resources

Tourism Information
Indiana Office of Tourism Development
(800) 677-9800
www.visitindiana.com

Road Conditions & Construction
(800) 261-7623, (866) 849-1368
www.in.gov/dot/
www.in.gov/indot/2420.htm

© Rand McNally

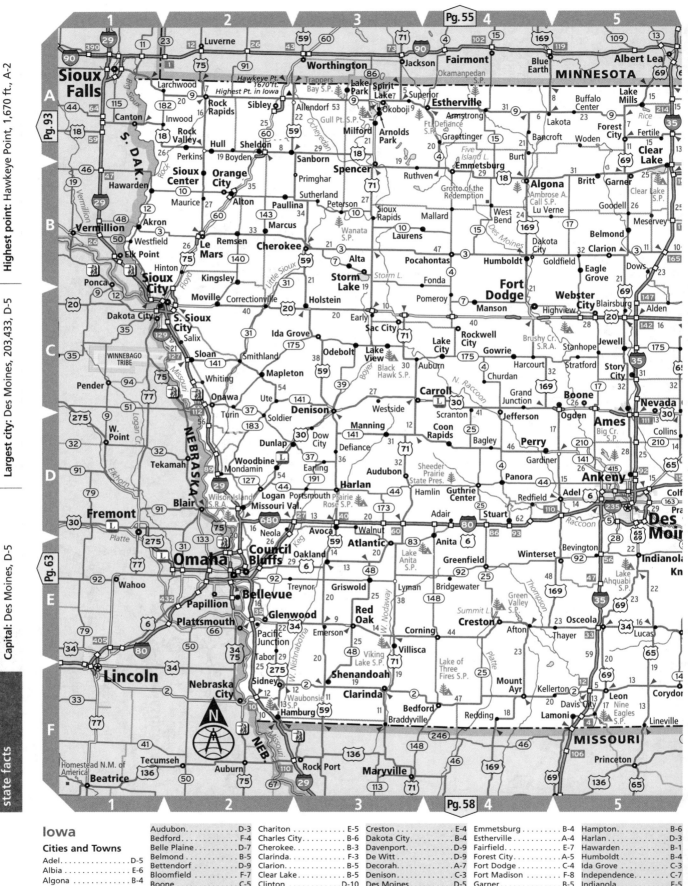

Iowa

Cities and Towns

Adel.............D-5	Audubon...........D-3	Chariton.............E-5
Albia.............E-6	Bedford...........F-4	Charles City........B-6
Algona...........B-4	Belle Plaine........D-7	Cherokee...........B-3
Allison...........B-6	Belmond...........B-5	Clarinda...........F-3
Ames.............C-5	Bettendorf..........D-9	Clarion.............B-5
Anamosa..........C-8	Bloomfield.........F-7	Clear Lake.........B-5
Ankeny...........D-5	Boone.............C-5	Clinton.............D-10
Atlantic...........E-3	Burlington..........F-8	Coralville..........D-8
	Carroll...........C-3	Corning.............E-4
	Cedar Falls........C-7	Corydon............F-5
	Cedar Rapids.......D-8	Council Bluffs......E-2
	Centerville.........F-6	Cresco.............A-7

Creston.............E-4	Emmetsburg........B-4	Hampton...........B-6
Dakota City........B-4	Estherville.........A-4	Harlan.............D-3
Davenport.........D-9	Fairfield............E-7	Hawarden.........B-1
De Witt...........D-9	Forest City........A-5	Humboldt.........B-4
Decorah..........A-7	Fort Dodge........C-4	Ida Grove.........C-3
Denison..........C-3	Fort Madison......F-8	Independence......C-7
Des Moines........D-5	Garner.............B-5	Indianola..........E-5
Dubuque..........C-9	Glenwood..........E-2	Iowa City..........D-8
Dyersville.........C-8	Greenfield.........E-4	Iowa Falls.........C-6
Eagle Grove.......B-5	Grinnell...........D-6	Jefferson..........D-4
Eldora............C-6	Grundy Center......C-6	Keokuk...........F-8
Elkader...........B-8	Guthrie Center......D-4	Keosauqua........F-7

NOTE: Maps are not always in alphabetical order.
See Page 1 for map location in this atlas.

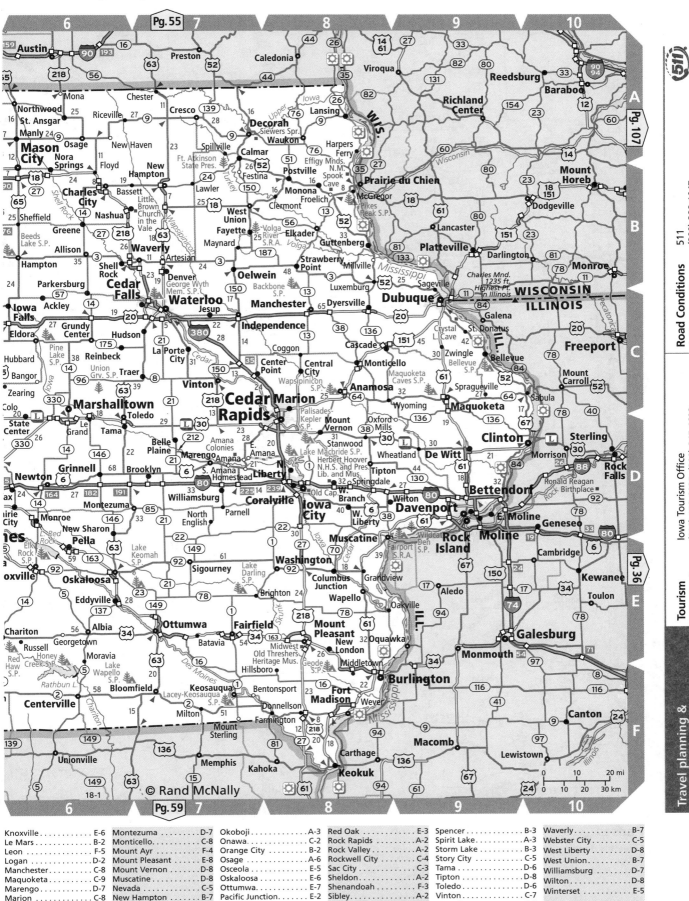

Pg. 55
Pg. 59
Pg. 107
Pg. 36

© Rand McNally

511
Road Conditions & Construction
511 (800) 288-1047 www.511ia.org, www.iowadot.gov

Tourism Information
Iowa Tourism Office (888) 472-6035, (800) 345-4692 www.traveliowa.com

Travel planning & on-the-road resources

Knoxville E-6
Le Mars B-2
Leon F-5
Logan D-2
Manchester C-8
Maquoketa C-9
Marengo D-7
Marion C-8
Marshalltown C-6
Mason City B-6
Milford A-3
Missouri Valley D-2

Montezuma D-7
Monticello C-8
Mount Ayr F-4
Mount Pleasant E-8
Mount Vernon D-8
Muscatine D-8
Nevada C-5
New Hampton B-7
Newton D-6
North Liberty D-8
Northwood A-6
Oelwein B-7

Okoboji A-3
Onawa C-2
Orange City B-2
Osage A-6
Osceola E-5
Oskaloosa E-6
Ottumwa E-7
Pacific Junction E-2
Pella E-6
Perry D-4
Pocahontas B-4
Primghar B-3

Red Oak E-3
Rock Rapids A-2
Rock Valley A-2
Rockwell City C-4
Sac City C-3
Sheldon B-2
Shenandoah F-3
Sibley A-2
Sidney F-2
Sigourney E-7
Sioux Center B-2
Sioux City C-2

Spencer B-3
Spirit Lake A-3
Storm Lake B-3
Story City C-5
Tama D-6
Tipton D-8
Toledo D-6
Vinton C-7
Wapello E-8
Washington E-8
Waterloo C-7
Waukon A-8

Waverly B-7
Webster City C-5
West Liberty D-8
West Union B-7
Williamsburg D-7
Wilton D-8
Winterset E-5

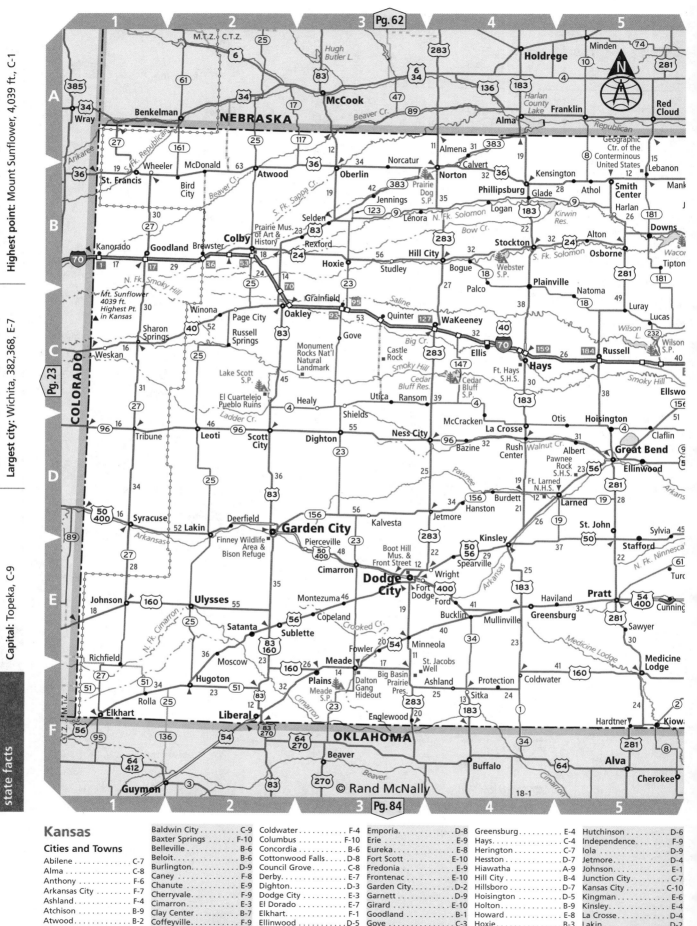

Kansas state facts

Land area: 81,759 sq. mi. (rank: 13th)
Highest point: Mount Sunflower, 4,039 ft., C-1
Population: 2,853,118 (rank: 33rd)
Largest city: Wichita, 382,368, E-7
Nickname: The Sunflower State
Capital: Topeka, C-9

Pg. 62
Pg. 84
Pg. 23

Kansas

Cities and Towns

Abilene	C-7	Baldwin City	C-9	Coldwater	F-4
Alma	C-8	Baxter Springs	F-10	Columbus	F-10
Anthony	F-6	Belleville	B-6	Concordia	B-6
Arkansas City	F-7	Beloit	B-6	Cottonwood Falls	D-8
Ashland	F-4	Burlington	D-9	Council Grove	C-8
Atchison	B-9	Caney	F-8	Derby	E-7
Atwood	B-2	Chanute	E-9	Dighton	D-3
Augusta	E-7	Cherryvale	F-9	Dodge City	E-3
		Cimarron	E-3	El Dorado	E-7
		Clay Center	B-7	Elkhart	F-1
		Coffeyville	F-9	Ellinwood	D-5
		Colby	B-2	Ellsworth	C-6

Emporia	D-8	Greensburg	E-4	Hutchinson	D-6
Erie	E-9	Hays	C-4	Independence	F-9
Eureka	E-8	Herington	C-7	Iola	D-9
Fort Scott	E-10	Hesston	D-7	Jetmore	D-4
Fredonia	E-9	Hiawatha	A-9	Johnson	E-1
Frontenac	E-10	Hill City	B-4	Junction City	C-7
Garden City	D-2	Hillsboro	D-7	Kansas City	C-10
Garnett	D-9	Hoisington	D-5	Kingman	E-6
Girard	E-10	Holton	B-9	Kinsley	E-4
Goodland	B-1	Howard	E-8	La Crosse	D-4
Gove	C-3	Hoxie	B-3	Lakin	D-2
Great Bend	D-5	Hugoton	F-2	Larned	D-5

NOTE: Maps are not always in alphabetical order.
See Page 1 for map location in this atlas.

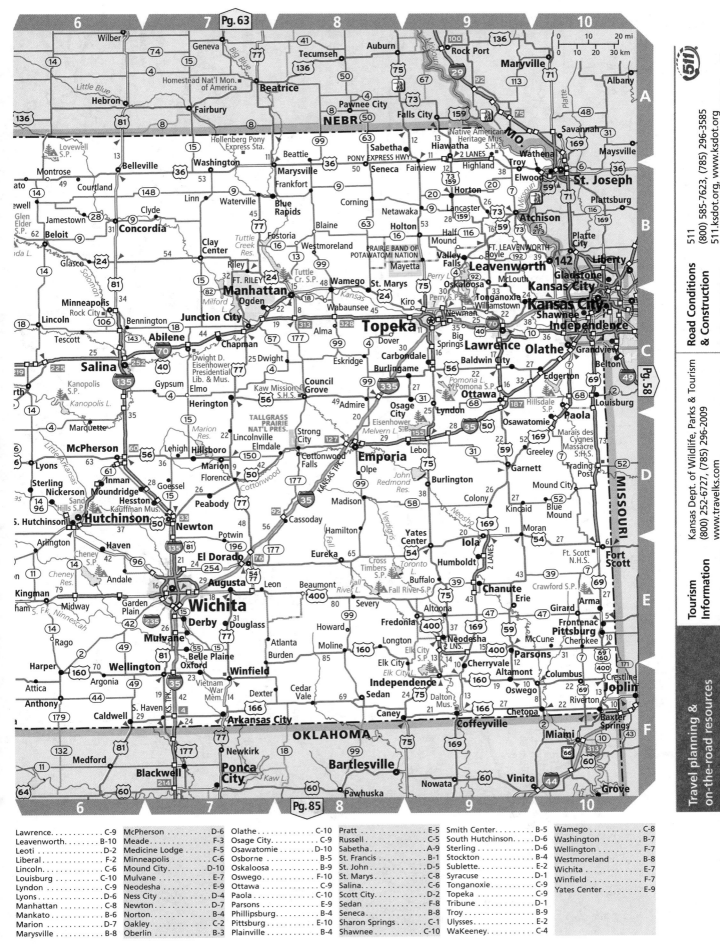

511

Road Conditions & Construction
511
(800) 585-7623, (785) 296-3585
511.ksdot.org, www.ksdot.org

Tourism Information
Kansas Dept. of Wildlife, Parks & Tourism
(800) 252-6727, (785) 296-2009
www.travelks.com

Travel planning & on-the-road resources

Lawrence	C-9	McPherson	D-6	Olathe	C-10	Pratt	E-5	Smith Center	B-5	Wamego	C-8
Leavenworth	B-10	Meade	F-3	Osage City	C-9	Russell	C-5	South Hutchinson	D-6	Washington	B-7
Leoti	D-2	Medicine Lodge	F-5	Osawatomie	D-10	Sabetha	A-9	Sterling	D-6	Wellington	F-7
Liberal	F-2	Minneapolis	C-6	Osborne	B-5	St. Francis	B-1	Stockton	B-4	Westmoreland	B-8
Lincoln	C-6	Mound City	D-10	Oskaloosa	B-9	St. John	D-5	Sublette	E-2	Wichita	E-7
Louisburg	C-10	Mulvane	E-7	Oswego	F-10	St. Marys	C-8	Syracuse	D-1	Winfield	F-7
Lyndon	C-9	Neodesha	E-9	Ottawa	C-9	Salina	C-6	Tonganoxie	C-9	Yates Center	E-9
Lyons	D-6	Ness City	D-4	Paola	C-10	Scott City	D-2	Topeka	C-8		
Manhattan	C-8	Newton	D-7	Parsons	E-9	Sedan	F-8	Tribune	D-1		
Mankato	B-6	Norton	B-4	Phillipsburg	B-4	Seneca	B-8	Troy	B-9		
Marion	D-7	Oakley	C-2	Pittsburg	E-10	Sharon Springs	C-1	Ulysses	E-2		
Marysville	B-8	Oberlin	B-3	Plainville	B-4	Shawnee	C-10	WaKeeney	C-4		

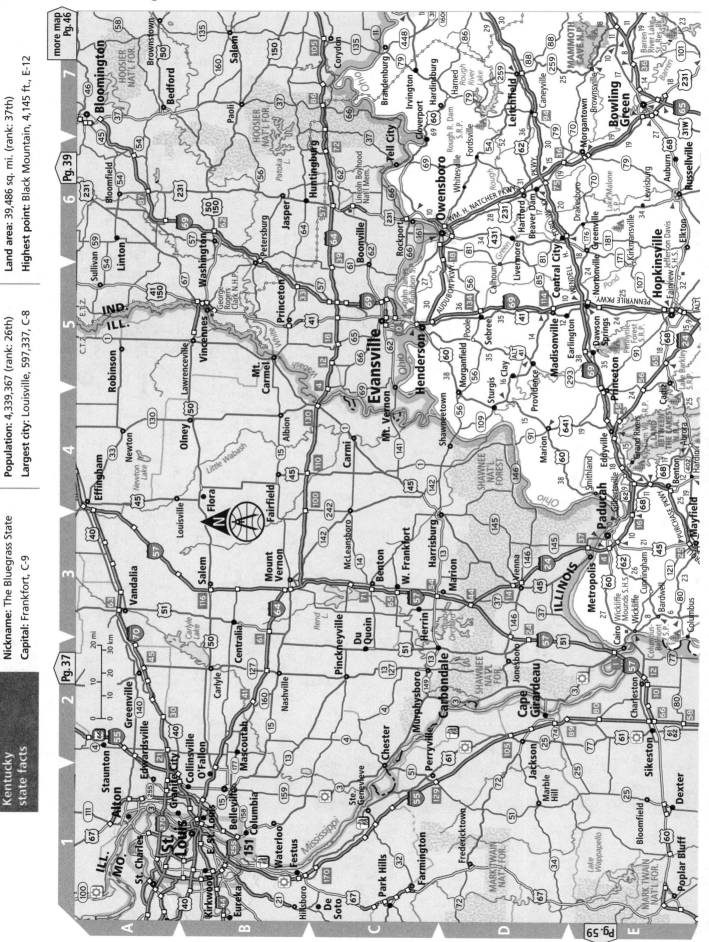

more map Pg.46

Pg.39

Pg.37

Pg.59

Kentucky state facts

Nickname: The Bluegrass State

Capital: Frankfort, C-9

Population: 4,339,367 (rank: 26th)

Largest city: Louisville, 597,337, C-8

Land area: 39,486 sq. mi. (rank: 37th)

Highest point: Black Mountain, 4,145 ft., E-12

NOTE: Maps are not always in alphabetical order.
See Page 1 for map location in this atlas.

Kentucky • Tennessee/Western

45

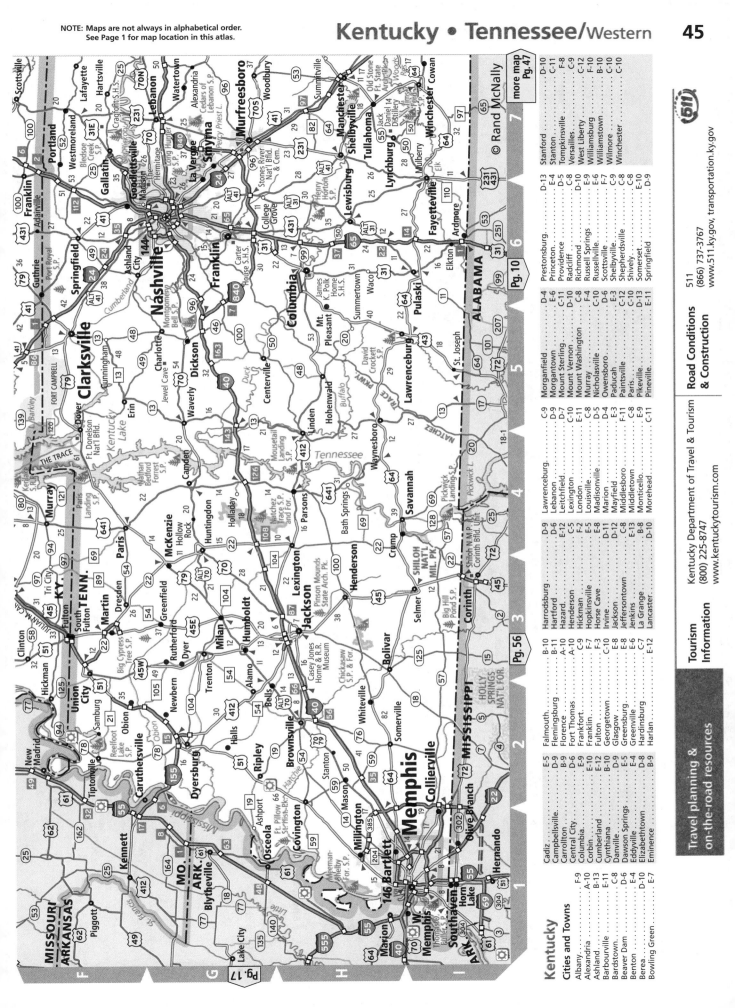

© Rand McNally

more map Pg.47

Stanford D-10
Stanton C-11
Tompkinsville F-8
Versailles C-9
West Liberty C-12
Williamsburg F-10
Williamstown B-10
Wilmore C-10
Winchester C-10

Road Conditions & Construction
511
(866) 737-3767
www.511.ky.gov, transportation.ky.gov

Kentucky Department of Travel & Tourism

Tourism Information
(800) 225-8747
www.kentuckytourism.com

Travel planning & on-the-road resources

Kentucky
Cities and Towns
Albany F-9
Alexandria A-10
Ashland B-13
Barbourville E-11
Bardstown C-8
Beaver Dam D-6
Benton E-4
Berea D-10
Bowling Green E-7

Cadiz E-5
Campbellsville D-9
Carrollton B-9
Central City D-6
Columbia E-9
Corbin E-10
Cumberland E-12
Cynthiana B-10
Danville C-9
Dawson Springs D-6
Eddyville E-4
Elizabethtown D-10
Eminence B-9

Falmouth B-10
Flemingsburg B-11
Florence A-10
Fort Thomas A-10
Frankfort C-9
Franklin E-8
Fulton E-3
Georgetown C-10
Glasgow E-8
Greensburg D-8
Greenville E-6
Hardinsburg C-7
Harlan E-12

Harrodsburg C-9
Hartford D-6
Hazard D-12
Henderson C-5
Hickman F-2
Hopkinsville E-5
Horse Cave E-8
Irvine C-11
Jackson D-12
Jeffersontown C-8
Jenkins D-13
La Grange B-9
Lancaster D-10

Lawrenceburg C-9
Lebanon D-9
Leitchfield D-7
Lexington C-10
London E-11
Louisville C-8
Madisonville D-5
Marion D-4
Mayfield E-3
Middlesboro F-11
Middletown C-8
Monticello E-9
Morehead C-11

Morganfield C-9
Morgantown D-9
Mount Sterling C-11
Mount Vernon D-10
Mount Washington . . C-8
Murray E-4
Nicholasville C-10
Owensboro D-6
Paducah E-3
Paintsville C-12
Paris B-10
Pikeville C-13
Pineville E-11

Prestonsburg D-4
Princeton E-6
Providence C-11
Radcliff D-10
Richmond C-8
Russell Springs F-4
Russellville C-10
Scottsville D-6
Shelbyville E-3
Shepherdsville C-8
Shively C-8
Somerset E-10
Springfield D-9

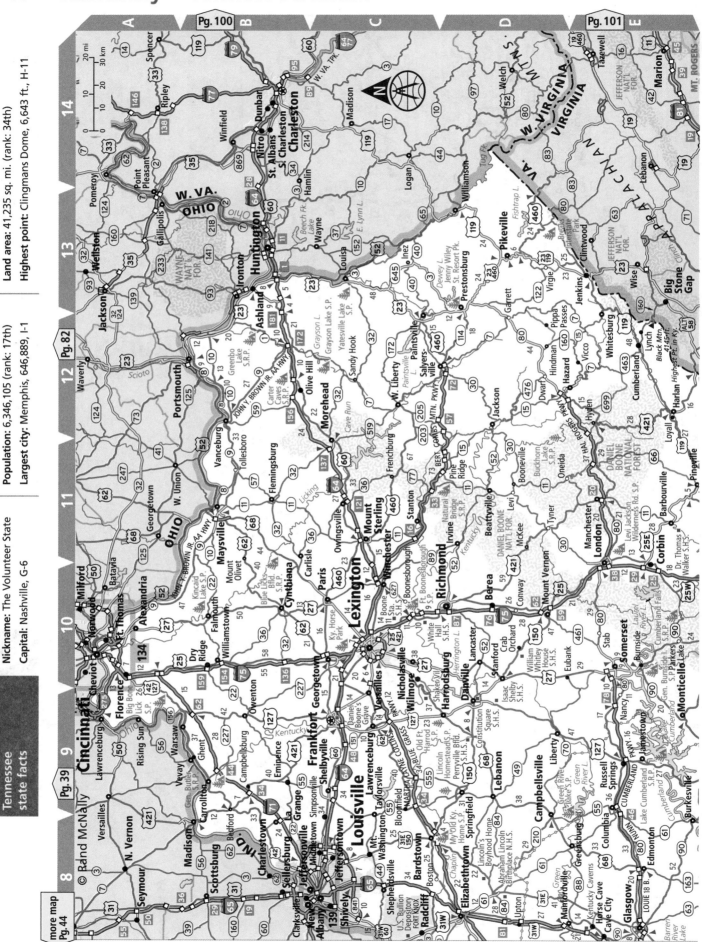

Tennessee state facts

Nickname: The Volunteer State
Capital: Nashville, G-6

Population: 6,346,105 (rank: 17th)
Largest city: Memphis, 646,889, I-1

Land area: 41,235 sq. mi. (rank: 34th)
Highest point: Clingmans Dome, 6,643 ft., H-11

NOTE: Maps are not always in alphabetical order.
See Page 1 for map location in this atlas.

Kentucky • Tennessee/Eastern **47**

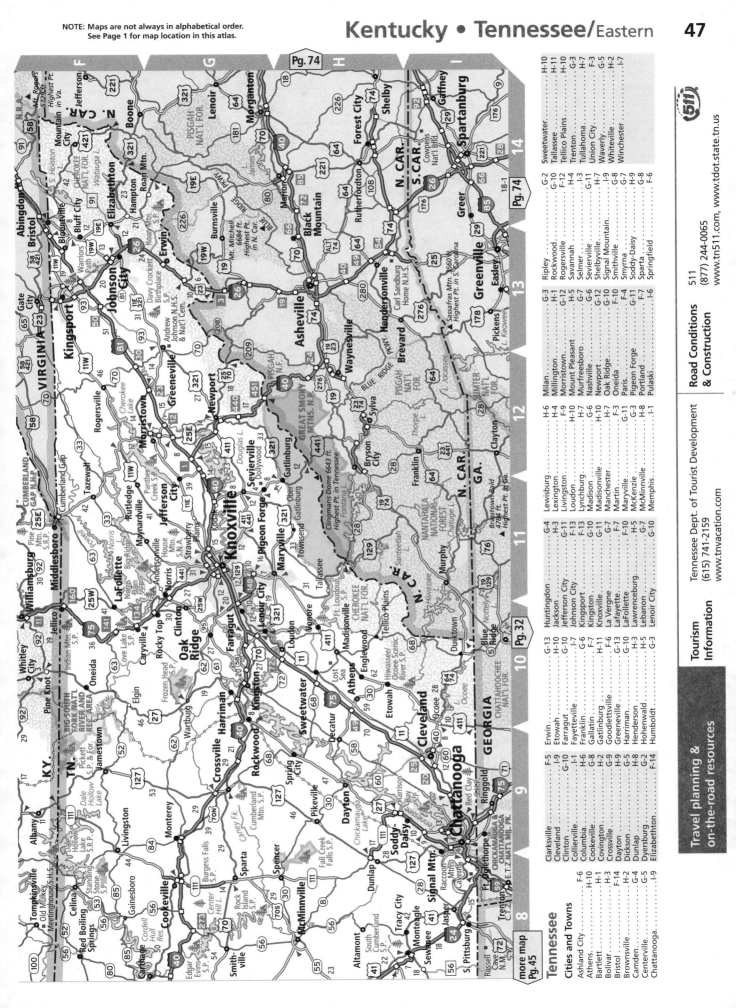

Tennessee

Cities and Towns

Ashland City	F-6
Athens	I-9
Bartlett	G-10
Bolivar	H-3
Bristol	F-14
Brownsville	H-2
Camden	G-4
Centerville	G-5
Chattanooga	I-9
Clarksville	G-3
Cleveland	H-1
Clinton	G-12
Collierville	G-7
Columbia	H-4
Cookeville	G-6
Covington	G-11
Crossville	H-7
Dayton	H-10
Dickson	F-3
Dunlap	G-5
Dyersburg	H-2
Elizabethton	I-7
Erwin	F-5
Etowah	I-9
Farragut	G-10
Fayetteville	I-1
Gallatin	G-8
Gatlinburg	H-2
Goodlettsville	G-9
Greeneville	H-9
Henderson	H-8
Hohenwald	H-2
Humboldt	F-14
Huntingdon	H-6
Jackson	H-4
Jefferson City	F-9
Johnson City	H-7
Kingsport	G-6
Kingston	H-7
Knoxville	H-11
La Vergne	G-11
Lafayette	F-10
LaFollette	G-10
Lawrenceburg	H-3
Lebanon	H-5
Lenoir City	G-10
Lewisburg	G-4
Lexington	H-3
Livingston	F-11
Loudon	F-13
Lynchburg	I-3
Madison	G-10
Madisonville	G-11
Manchester	G-7
Martin	F-3
Maryville	F-10
McKenzie	H-5
McMinnville	G-7
Memphis	I-6
Milan	H-6
Millington	H-4
Morristown	F-9
Mount Pleasant	H-7
Murfreesboro	H-7
Nashville	G-6
Newport	H-10
Oak Ridge	H-7
Oneida	F-3
Paris	G-11
Pigeon Forge	G-3
Portland	H-8
Pulaski	I-1
Ripley	G-2
Rockwood	H-1
Rogersville	F-12
Savannah	H-4
Selmer	I-3
Sevierville	G-11
Shelbyville	H-7
Signal Mountain	I-9
Smithville	G-8
Smyrna	G-7
Soddy-Daisy	H-9
Sparta	G-7
Springfield	F-6
Sweetwater	H-10
Tallassee	G-10
Tellico Plains	F-12
Trenton	H-4
Tullahoma	H-7
Union City	F-3
Waverly	G-5
Whiteville	H-2
Winchester	I-7

Tourism Information
Tennessee Dept. of Tourist Development
(615) 741-2159
www.tnvacation.com

Road Conditions & Construction
511
(877) 244-0065
www.tn511.com, www.tdot.state.tn.us

Travel planning & on-the-road resources

Louisiana

Cities and Towns

Abbeville	F-4
Alexandria	D-4
Amite	E-7
Arcadia	A-3
Baldwin	F-5
Bastrop	A-5
Baton Rouge	E-6
Benton	A-2
Bogalusa	D-8
Bossier City	A-2
Breaux Bridge	E-5
Broussard	F-4
Bunkie	D-4
Cameron	F-2
Chalmette	F-7
Clinton	D-6
Colfax	C-3
Columbia	B-4
Coushatta	B-2
Covington	E-7
Crowley	E-4
Delhi	B-5
Denham Springs	E-6
DeQuincy	E-2
DeRidder	D-2
Donaldsonville	F-6
Edgard	F-7
Eunice	E-4
Farmerville	A-4
Ferriday	C-5
Franklin	F-5
Franklinton	D-7
Gramercy	F-6
Greensburg	D-6
Greenwood	B-1
Gretna	F-7
Hahnville	F-7
Hammond	E-7
Harrisonburg	C-5
Haynesville	A-3
Homer	A-3
Houma	G-6
Iowa	E-3
Jackson	D-6
Jeanerette	F-5
Jena	C-4
Jennings	E-3
Jonesboro	B-3
Jonesville	C-5
Kaplan	F-4
Lafayette	E-4
Lake Arthur	F-3
Lake Charles	E-3
Lake Providence	A-6
Laplace	F-7
Leesville	D-3
Livingston	E-6
Mamou	E-4
Mandeville	E-7
Mansfield	B-2
Many	C-2
Marksville	D-4
Metairie	F-7
Minden	A-3
Monroe	A-4
Morgan City	F-6
Napoleonville	F-6
Natchitoches	C-3
New Iberia	F-5
New Orleans	F-7
New Roads	E-5
Oak Grove	A-5
Oakdale	D-3
Oberlin	E-3
Opelousas	E-4
Patterson	F-5
Plaquemine	E-6
Ponchatoula	E-7
Port Allen	E-6
Port Sulphur	G-8
Raceland	F-7
Rayne	E-4
Rayville	B-5
Ruston	A-3
St. Francisville	D-5
St. Joseph	C-6
St. Martinville	F-5
Scott	E-4
Shreveport	A-2
Simmesport	D-5
Slidell	E-8
Springhill	A-2
Sulphur	E-2
Tallulah	B-6
Thibodaux	F-6
Vidalia	C-5
Ville Platte	E-4
Vivian	A-2
Walker	E-6
Welsh	E-3
West Monroe	A-4
Winnfield	C-3
Winnsboro	B-5

Louisiana state facts

Land area: 43,204 sq. mi. (rank: 33rd)
Highest point: Driskill Mountain, 535 ft., B-3

Population: 4,533,372 (rank: 25th)
Largest city: New Orleans, 343,829, F-7

Nickname: The Pelican State
Capital: Baton Rouge, E-6

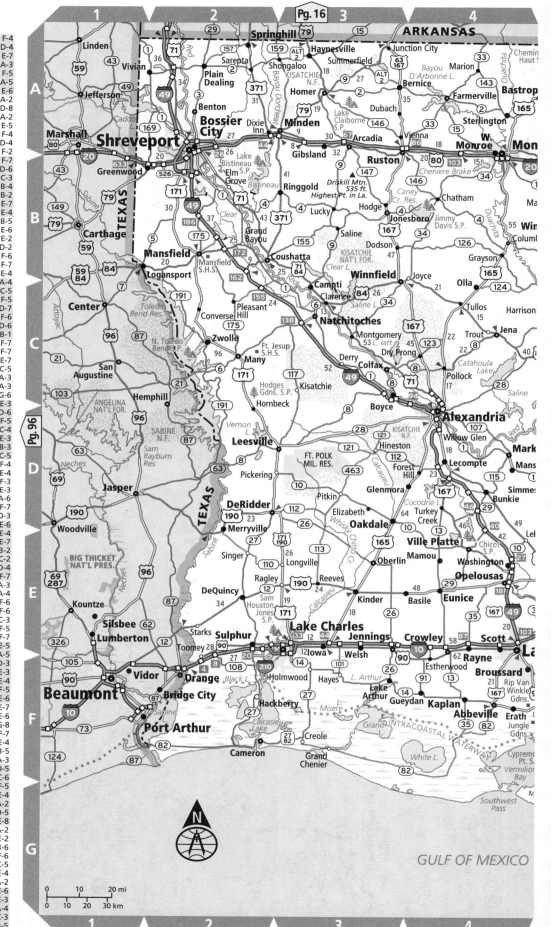

NOTE: Maps are not always in alphabetical order.
See Page 1 for map location in this atlas.

Louisiana 49

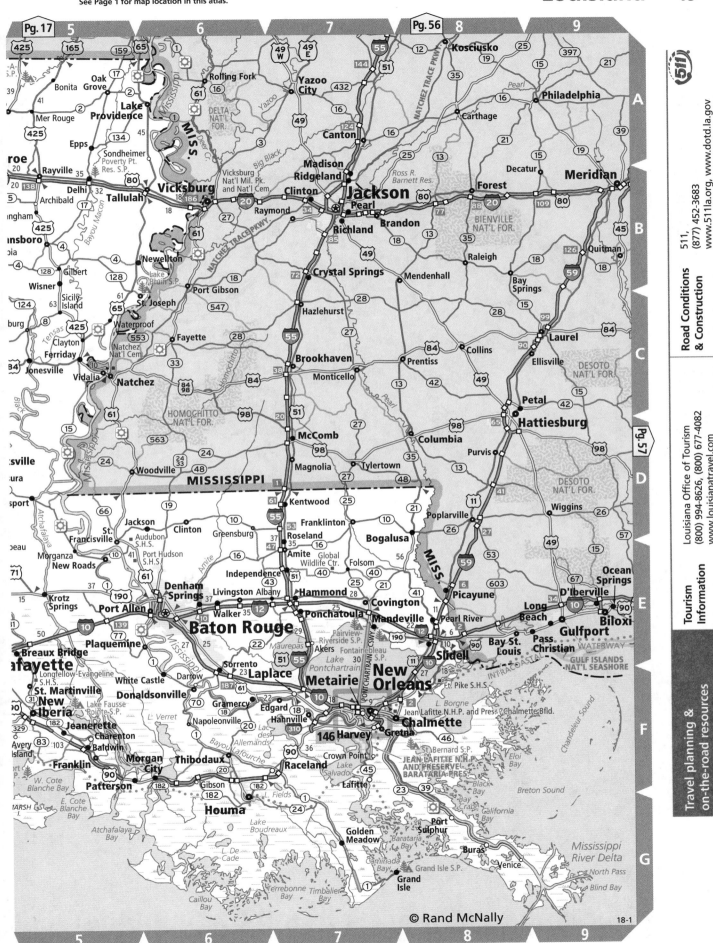

Pg. 17
Pg. 56
Pg. 57

511
Road Conditions & Construction
511, (877) 452-3683
www.511la.org, www.dotd.la.gov

Tourism Information
Louisiana Office of Tourism
(800) 994-8626, (800) 677-4082
www.louisianatravel.com

Travel planning & on-the-road resources

© Rand McNally

18-1

Pg. 126

Maine state facts

Nickname: The Pine Tree State
Capital: Augusta, G-2

Population: 1,328,361 (rank: 41st)
Largest city: Portland, 66,194, H-2

Land area: 30,843 sq. mi. (rank: 39th)
Highest point: Mount Katahdin, 5,268 ft., D-4

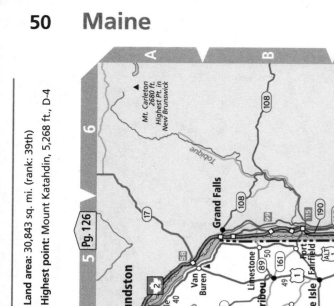

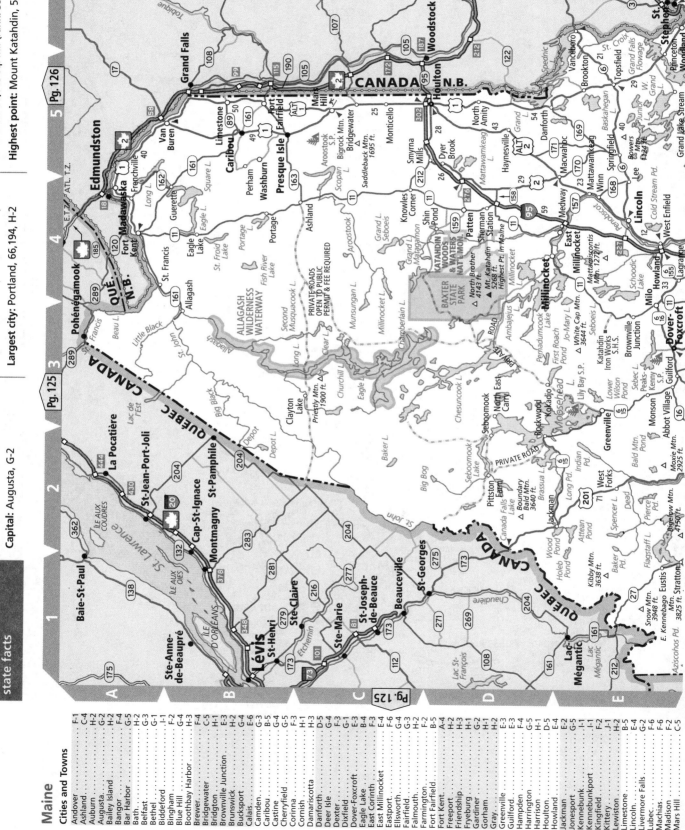

Maine

Cities and Towns

Andover	F-1
Ashland	C-4
Auburn	H-2
Augusta	G-2
Bailey Island	H-2
Bangor	F-4
Bar Harbor	G-5
Bath	H-2
Belfast	G-3
Bethel	G-1
Biddeford	I-1
Bingham	F-2
Blue Hill	G-4
Boothbay Harbor	H-3
Brewer	F-4
Bridgewater	C-5
Bridgton	H-1
Brownville Junction	E-3
Brunswick	H-2
Bucksport	G-4
Calais	E-6
Camden	G-3
Caribou	B-5
Castine	G-4
Cherryfield	G-5
Corinna	F-3
Cornish	H-1
Damariscotta	H-3
Danforth	D-5
Deer Isle	G-4
Dexter	F-3
Dixfield	G-1
Dover-Foxcroft	F-3
Eagle Lake	B-4
East Millinocket	E-4
Eastport	F-6
Ellsworth	G-4
Fairfield	G-3
Falmouth	H-2
Farmington	F-2
Fort Fairfield	B-5
Fort Kent	A-4
Freeport	H-2
Friendship	H-3
Fryeburg	H-1
Gardiner	G-2
Gorham	H-1
Gray	H-2
Greenville	E-3
Guilford	F-3
Hampden	F-4
Harrington	G-5
Harrison	H-1
Houlton	D-5
Howland	E-4
Jackman	E-2
Jonesport	G-5
Kennebunk	I-1
Kennebunkport	I-1
Kingfield	F-2
Kittery	J-1
Lewiston	H-2
Limestone	B-5
Lincoln	E-4
Livermore Falls	G-2
Lubec	F-6
Machias	F-6
Madison	F-2
Mars Hill	C-5

NOTE: Maps are not always in alphabetical order.
See Page 1 for map location in this atlas.

Maine   51

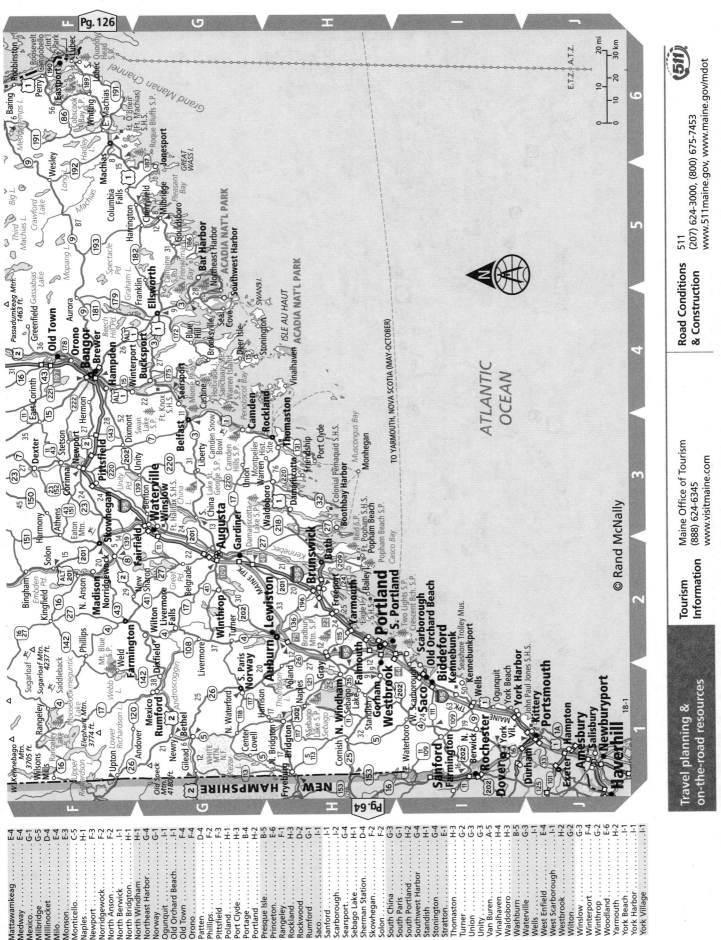

Tourism Information
Maine Office of Tourism
(888) 624-6345
www.visitmaine.com

Road Conditions & Construction
511
(207) 624-3000, (800) 675-7453
www.511maine.gov, www.maine.gov/mdot

Travel planning & on-the-road resources

© Rand McNally

Mattawamkeag E-4
Medway E-4
Mexico G-1
Milbridge G-5
Millinocket D-4
Milo E-4
Monson E-3
Monticello C-5
Naples H-1
Newport F-3
Norridgewock F-2
North Anson F-2
North Berwick H-1
North Bridgton H-1
North Windham H-1
Northeast Harbor G-4
Norway G-1
Ogunquit I-1
Old Orchard Beach I-1
Old Town F-4
Orono F-4
Patten D-4
Phillips F-2
Pittsfield F-3
Poland H-1
Port Clyde H-3
Portage B-4
Portland H-2
Presque Isle B-5
Princeton E-6
Rangeley F-1
Rockland G-3
Rockwood D-2
Rumford G-1
Saco I-1
Sanford I-1
Scarborough I-2
Searsport G-3
Sebago Lake H-1
Sherman Station D-4
Skowhegan F-2
Solon F-2
South China G-3
South Paris G-1
South Portland H-2
Southwest Harbor G-4
Standish H-1
Stonington G-4
Stratton E-1
Thomaston G-3
Turner G-2
Unity F-3
Van Buren A-5
Vinalhaven H-3
Waldoboro G-3
Washburn B-5
Waterville F-3
Wells I-1
West Enfield E-4
West Harbor I-1
Westbrook H-2
Wilton G-2
Winslow F-3
Winterport F-4
Winthrop G-2
Woodland E-6
Yarmouth H-2
York Beach I-1
York Harbor I-1
York Village I-1

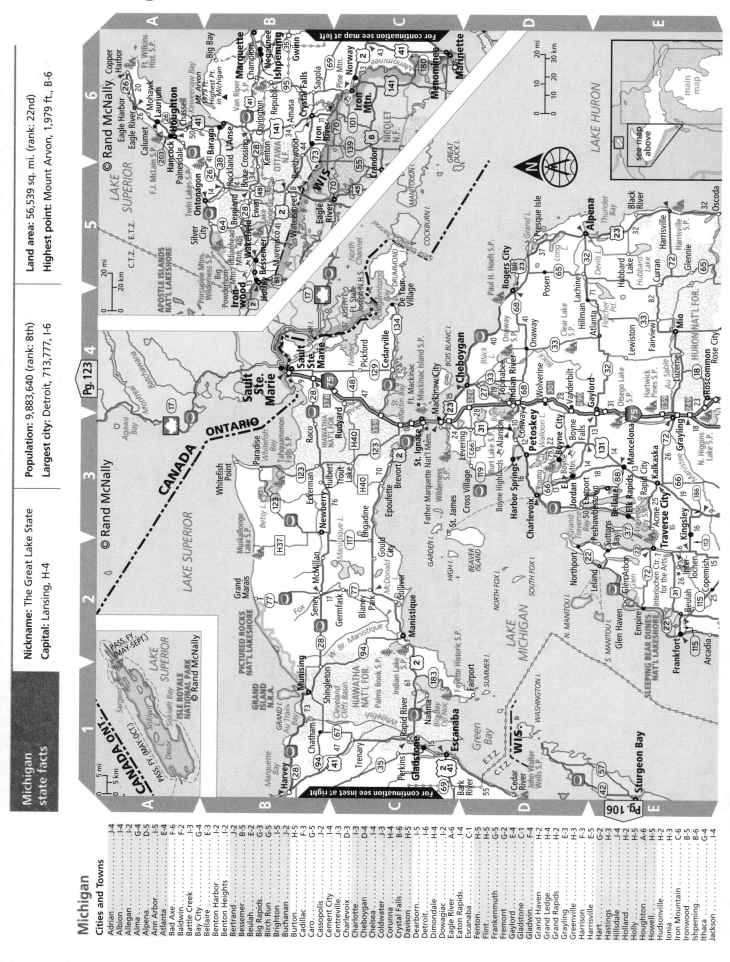

Michigan state facts

Nickname: The Great Lake State
Capital: Lansing, H-4

Population: 9,883,640 (rank: 8th)
Largest city: Detroit, 713,777, I-6

Land area: 56,539 sq. mi. (rank: 22nd)
Highest point: Mount Arvon, 1,979 ft., B-6

Michigan

Cities and Towns

Adrian J-4
Albion I-4
Allegan I-2
Alma G-4
Alpena D-5
Ann Arbor I-5
Atlanta E-4
Bad Axe F-6
Baldwin F-2
Battle Creek I-3
Bay City G-4
Bellaire E-3
Benton Harbor I-2
Bentron Heights I-2
Bertrand J-2
Bessemer B-5
Beulah E-2
Big Rapids G-3
Birch Run G-5
Brighton I-5
Buchanan J-2
Burton H-5
Cadillac F-3
Caro G-5
Cassopolis J-2
Cement City I-4
Centreville J-3
Charlevoix D-3
Charlotte I-4
Cheboygan D-4
Chelsea I-4
Coldwater J-3
Corunna H-4
Crystal Falls B-6
Davison H-5
Dearborn I-5
Detroit I-6
Dimondale H-4
Dowagiac I-2
Eagle River A-6
Eaton Rapids I-4
Escanaba C-1
Fenton H-5
Flint H-5
Frankenmuth G-5
Fremont G-2
Gaylord E-4
Gladstone C-1
Gladwin F-4
Grand Haven H-2
Grand Ledge H-4
Grand Rapids H-2
Grayling E-3
Greenville H-3
Harrison F-3
Harrisville E-5
Hart G-2
Hastings H-3
Hillsdale J-4
Holland H-2
Holly H-5
Houghton A-6
Howell H-5
Hudsonville H-2
Ionia H-3
Iron Mountain C-6
Ironwood B-5
Ishpeming B-6
Ithaca G-4
Jackson I-4

NOTE: Maps are not always in alphabetical order.
See Page 1 for map location in this atlas.

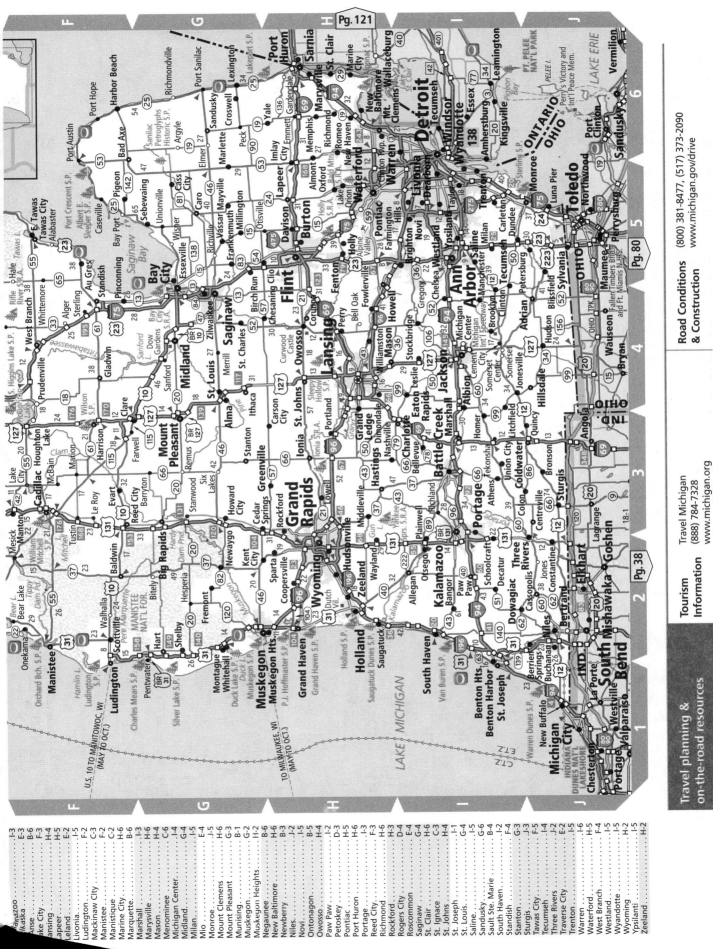

Pg. 121
Pg. 80
Pg. 38

Road Conditions & Construction

(800) 381-8477, (517) 373-2090
www.michigan.gov/drive

Tourism Information

Travel Michigan
(888) 784-7328
www.michigan.org

Travel planning & on-the-road resources

Pg. 106
Pg. 123
Pg. 123
Pg. 119
Pg. 79

Minnesota state facts

Nickname: The North Star State
Capital: St. Paul, H-5

Population: 5,303,925 (rank: 21st)
Largest city: Minneapolis, 382,578, H-4

Land area: 79,627 sq. mi. (rank: 14th)
Highest point: Eagle Mountain, 2,301 ft., A-5

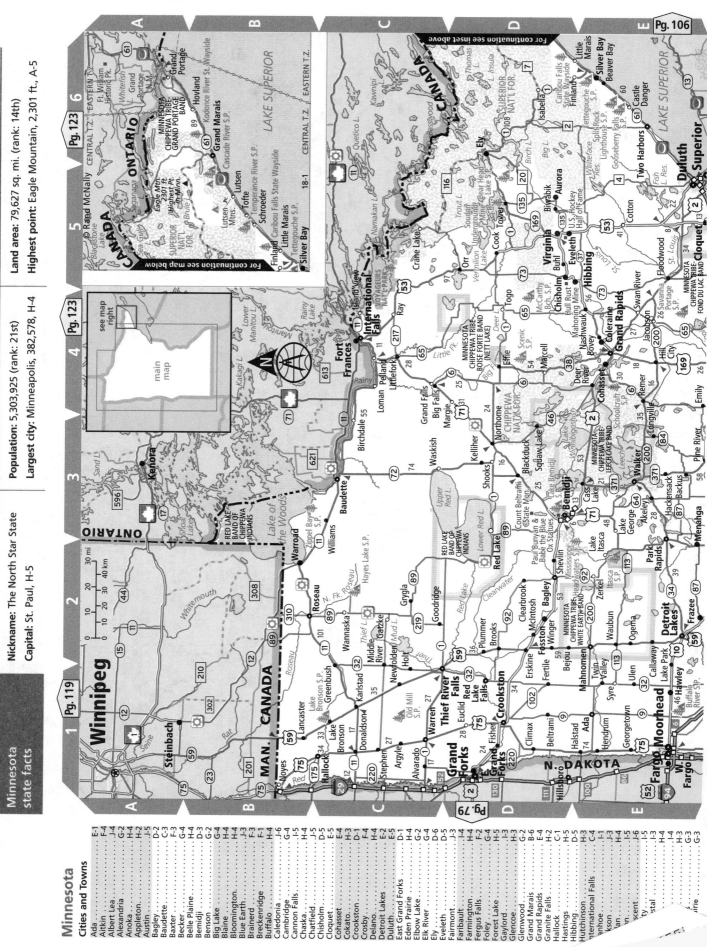

Minnesota
Cities and Towns

Ada	E-1
Aitkin	F-4
Albert Lea	J-4
Alexandria	G-2
Anoka	H-4
Appleton	H-2
Austin	J-5
Bagley	D-2
Baudette	C-3
Baxter	F-3
Becker	G-4
Belle Plaine	H-4
Bemidji	D-3
Benson	G-2
Big Lake	G-4
Blaine	H-4
Bloomington	H-4
Blue Earth	J-3
Brainerd	F-3
Breckenridge	F-1
Buffalo	H-4
Caledonia	J-6
Cambridge	G-4
Cannon Falls	H-4
Chaska	H-4
Chatfield	J-5
Chisholm	D-5
Cloquet	E-5
Cohasset	E-4
Cokato	H-3
Crookston	D-1
Crosby	F-4
Delano	H-4
Detroit Lakes	E-2
Duluth	E-5
East Grand Forks	D-1
Eden Prairie	H-4
Elbow Lake	G-2
Elk River	G-4
Ely	D-5
Eveleth	D-5
Fairmont	J-3
Faribault	H-4
Farmington	H-4
Fergus Falls	F-2
Foley	G-4
Forest Lake	H-5
Gaylord	H-3
Glencoe	H-3
Glenwood	G-2
Grand Marais	B-6
Grand Rapids	E-4
Granite Falls	H-2
Hallock	C-1
Hastings	H-5
Hibbing	D-5
Hutchinson	H-3
International Falls	C-4
...hoe	J-5
...kson	J-3
...scent	J-6
...ty	I-3
...stal	I-4

NOTE: Maps are not always in alphabetical order.
See Page 1 for map location in this atlas.

Minnesota 55

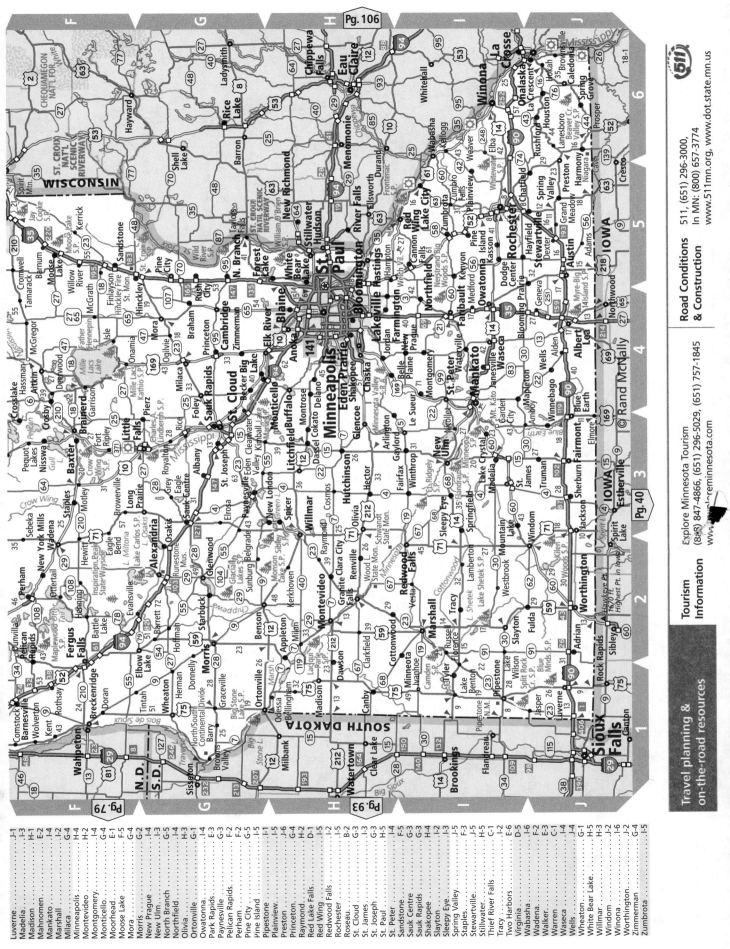

Luverne J-1
Madelia I-3
Madison H-1
Mahnomen E-2
Mankato I-4
Marshall I-2
Milaca G-4
Minneapolis H-4
Montevideo H-2
Montgomery I-4
Monticello H-4
Moorhead E-1
Moose Lake G-4
Mora G-4
Morris G-2
New Prague I-4
New Ulm I-3
North Branch H-4
Northfield I-4
Olivia H-3
Ortonville G-1
Owatonna I-4
Park Rapids E-3
Paynesville G-3
Pelican Rapids . . . F-2
Perham F-2
Pine City G-4
Pine Island I-5
Pipestone J-1
Plainview I-5
Preston J-6
Princeton G-4
Raymond H-2
Red Lake Falls . . . D-1
Red Wing I-5
Redwood Falls . . . I-2
Rochester I-5
Roseau B-2
St. Cloud G-3
St. James I-3
St. Joseph G-3
St. Paul H-5
St. Peter I-4
Sandstone G-4
Sauk Centre G-3
Sauk Rapids G-3
Shakopee H-4
Slayton I-2
Sleepy Eye I-3
Spring Valley J-5
Staples F-3
Stewartville J-5
Stillwater H-5
Thief River Falls . . C-1
Tracy I-2
Two Harbors E-6
Virginia D-5
Wabasha I-5
Wadena F-2
Walker E-3
Warren C-1
Waseca I-4
Wells I-4
Wheaton G-1
White Bear Lake . . H-5
Willmar H-3
Windom I-2
Winona I-6
Worthington J-2
Zimmerman G-4
Zumbrota I-5

Mississippi
state facts

Nickname: The Magnolia State

Capital: Jackson, F-3

Population: 2,967,297 (rank: 31st)

Largest city: Jackson, 173,514, F-3

Land area: 46,923 sq. mi. (rank: 31st)

Highest point: Woodall Mountain, 806 ft., B-6

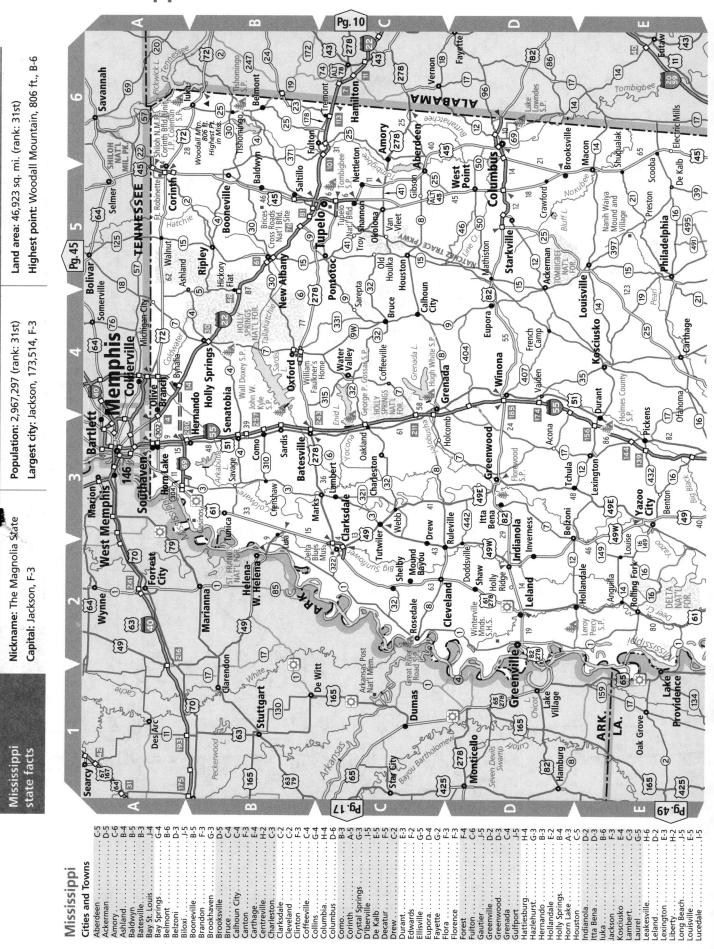

Mississippi
Cities and Towns

Aberdeen C-5
Ackerman D-5
Amory C-6
Ashland B-4
Baldwyn B-5
Batesville B-3
Bay St. Louis J-4
Bay Springs G-4
Belmont B-6
Belzoni D-3
Biloxi J-5
Booneville B-5
Brandon F-3
Brookhaven G-3
Brooksville D-5
Bruce C-4
Calhoun City C-4
Canton F-3
Carthage E-4
Centreville H-2
Charleston C-3
Clarksdale C-2
Cleveland C-2
Clinton F-3
Coffeeville C-4
Collins G-4
Columbia H-4
Columbus D-6
Como B-3
Corinth A-5
Crystal Springs G-3
D'Iberville J-5
De Kalb E-5
Decatur F-5
Drew C-2
Durant E-3
Edwards F-3
Ellisville G-5
Eupora D-4
Fayette G-2
Flora F-3
Florence F-3
Forest F-4
Fulton B-6
Gautier J-5
Greenville D-2
Greenwood D-3
Grenada C-4
Gulfport J-5
Hattiesburg H-4
Hazlehurst G-3
Hernando B-3
Hollandale E-2
Holly Springs B-4
Horn Lake A-3
Houston C-5
Indianola D-2
Itta Bena D-2
Iuka B-6
Jackson F-3
Kosciusko E-4
Lambert C-3
Laurel H-4
Leakesville H-6
Leland E-2
Lexington E-3
Liberty H-2
Long Beach J-5
Louisville E-5
Lucedale I-5

NOTE: Maps are not always in alphabetical order.
See Page 1 for map location in this atlas.

Mississippi 57

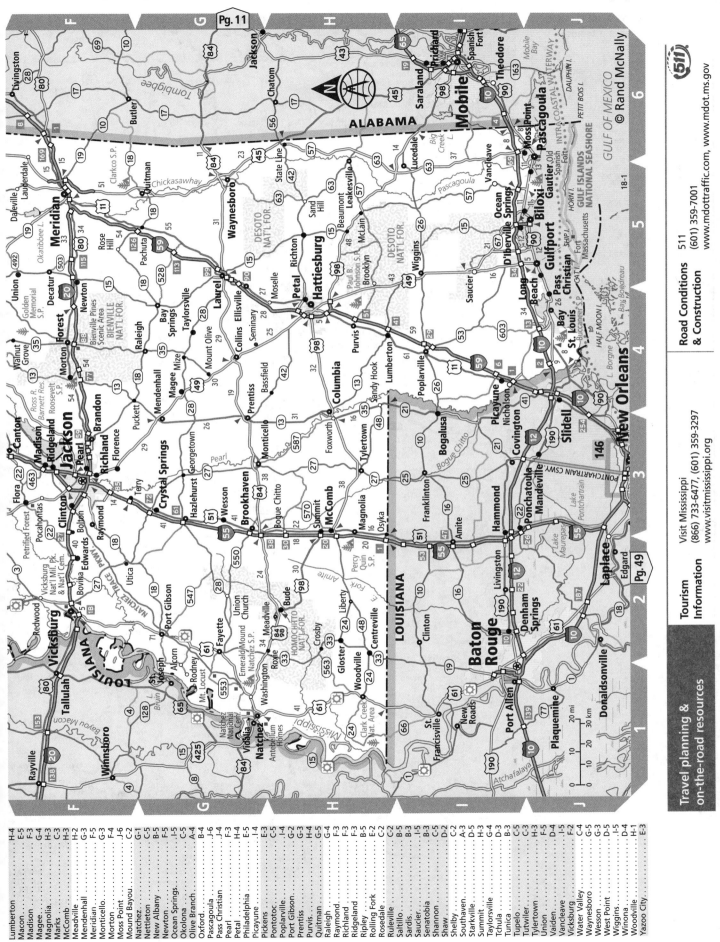

Pg. 11

Pg. 49

© Rand McNally

GULF OF MEXICO

GULF ISLANDS
NATIONAL SEASHORE

ALABAMA

LOUISIANA

Travel planning &
on-the-road resources

| Tourism Information | Visit Mississippi (866) 733-6477, (601) 359-3297 www.visitmississippi.org |
| Road Conditions & Construction | 511 (601) 359-7001 www.mdottraffic.com, www.mdot.ms.gov |

Lumberton H-4
Macon E-5
Madison F-3
Magee G-4
Magnolia H-3
Marks C-3
McComb H-3
Meadville H-2
Mendenhall G-3
Meridian F-5
Monticello G-3
Morton F-4
Moss Point J-6
Mound Bayou C-2
Natchez G-1
Nettleton C-5
New Albany B-5
Newton F-5
Ocean Springs J-5
Okolona C-5
Olive Branch A-4
Oxford B-4
Pascagoula J-6
Pass Christian J-4
Pearl F-3
Petal H-4
Philadelphia E-5
Picayune I-4
Pickens E-3
Pontotoc C-5
Poplarville I-4
Port Gibson G-2
Prentiss G-3
Purvis H-4
Quitman F-5
Raleigh G-4
Raymond F-3
Richland F-3
Ridgeland F-3
Ripley B-5
Rolling Fork E-2
Rosedale C-2
Ruleville C-3
Saltillo B-5
Sardis B-3
Saucier I-5
Senatobia B-3
Shannon C-5
Shaw C-2
Shelby C-2
Southaven A-3
Starkville D-5
Summit H-3
Taylorsville G-4
Tchula D-3
Tunica B-3
Tupelo C-5
Tutwiler C-3
Tylertown H-3
Union E-4
Vaiden D-4
Vancleave I-5
Vicksburg F-2
Water Valley C-4
Waynesboro G-5
Wesson G-3
West Point D-5
Wiggins I-5
Winona D-4
Woodville H-1
Yazoo City E-3

Missouri

Cities and Towns

Aurora	F-3
Belton	C-2
Blue Springs	C-3
Bolivar	E-4
Bonne Terre	E-7
Boonville	C-4
Bowling Green	B-6
Branson	F-4
Brookfield	B-4
Butler	D-2
California	D-4
Cameron	B-3
Cape Girardeau	E-8
Carrollton	C-3
Carthage	F-2
Caruthersville	G-8
Centralia	C-5
Charleston	F-8
Chillicothe	B-3
Clinton	D-3
Columbia	C-5
Crystal City	D-7
De Soto	D-7
Dexter	F-8
El Dorado Springs	E-3
Eldon	D-4
Eureka	D-7
Excelsior Springs	B-3
Farmington	E-7
Festus	D-7
Fredericktown	E-7
Fulton	C-5
Gladstone	C-2
Grandview	C-2
Hannibal	B-6
Harrisonville	C-2
Hollister	F-4
Independence	C-2
Jackson	E-8
Jefferson City	D-5
Joplin	F-2
Kansas City	C-2
Kearney	B-2
Kennett	G-7
Kirksville	A-4
Kirkwood	D-7
Lamar	E-3
Lebanon	E-4
Lexington	C-3
Liberty	C-2
Louisiana	B-6
Macon	B-5
Malden	F-8
Marshall	C-4
Marshfield	E-4
Maryville	A-2
Mexico	C-5
Moberly	B-5
Monett	F-3
Mount Vernon	F-3
Mountain Grove	F-5
Neosho	F-2
Nevada	E-2
New Madrid	F-8
Nixa	F-4
Odessa	C-3
Osage Beach	D-4
Ozark	F-4
Pacific	D-7
Park Hills	E-7
Perryville	E-8
Platte City	B-2
Pleasant Hill	C-3
Poplar Bluff	F-7
Republic	F-3
Richmond	C-3
Rolla	E-5
St. Charles	C-7
St. Clair	D-6
St. James	D-6
St. Joseph	B-2
St. Louis	C-7
Ste. Genevieve	D-7
Salem	E-6
Savannah	B-2
Scott City	F-8
Sedalia	C-4
Sikeston	F-8
Springfield	F-4
Sullivan	D-6
Trenton	A-3
Troy	C-6
Union	D-6
Vandalia	C-6
Villa Ridge	D-6
Warrensburg	C-3
Warrenton	C-6
Washington	D-6
Waynesville	E-5
Webb City	F-2
Weldon Spring	C-7
Wentzville	C-6
West Plains	F-5

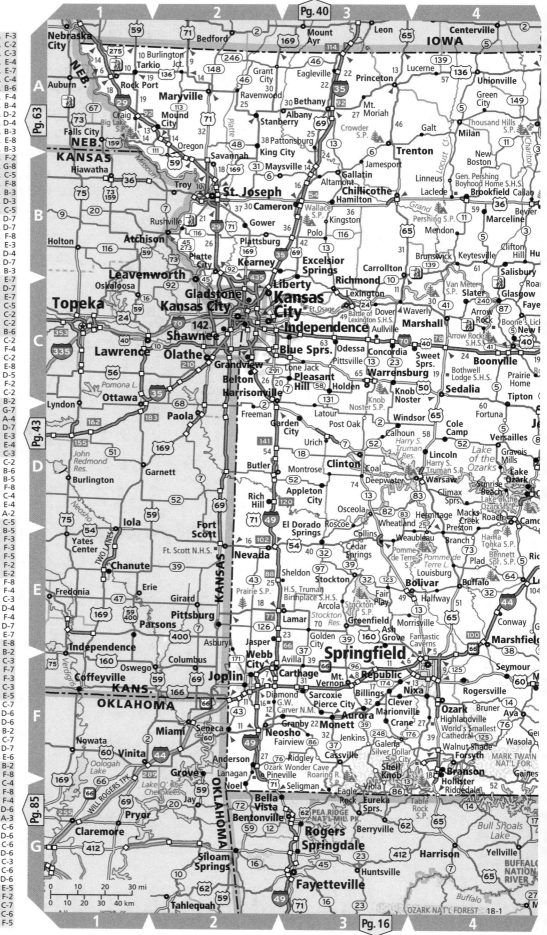

NOTE: Maps are not always in alphabetical order.
See Page 1 for map location in this atlas.

Missouri 59

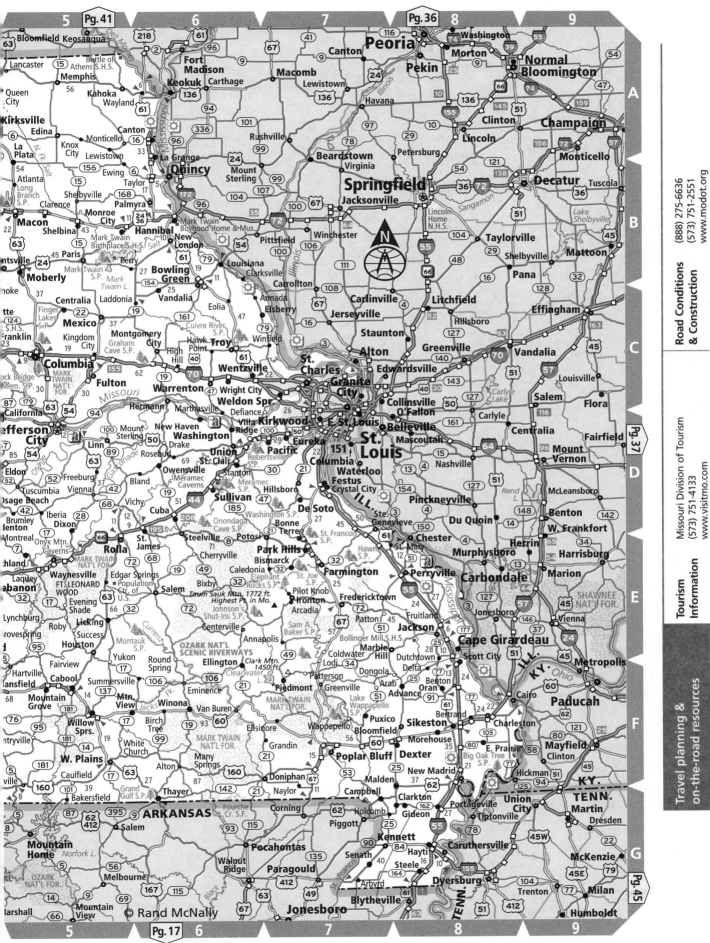

Road Conditions & Construction

(888) 275-6636
(573) 751-2551
www.modot.org

Tourism Information

Missouri Division of Tourism
(573) 751-4133
www.visitmo.com

Travel planning & on-the-road resources

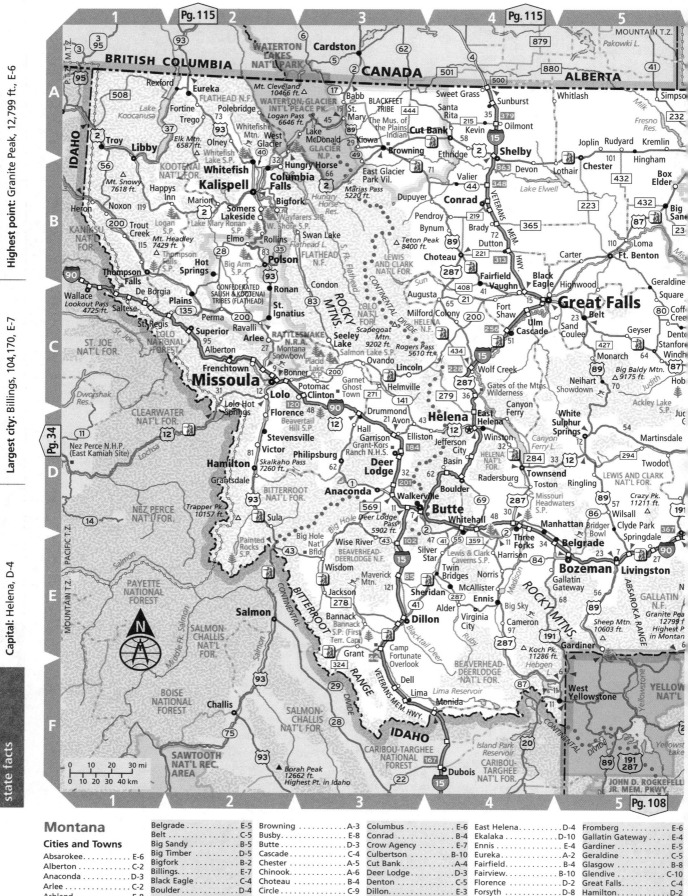

Montana state facts

Nickname: The Treasure State
Capital: Helena, D-4

Population: 989,415 (rank: 44th)
Largest city: Billings, 104,170, E-7

Land area: 145,546 sq. mi. (rank: 4th)
Highest point: Granite Peak, 12,799 ft., E-6

Montana

Cities and Towns

Absarokee	E-6	Belgrade	E-5	Browning	A-3	Columbus	E-6	East Helena	D-4	Fromberg	E-6
Alberton	C-2	Belt	C-5	Busby	E-8	Conrad	B-4	Ekalaka	D-10	Gallatin Gateway	E-4
Anaconda	D-3	Big Sandy	B-5	Butte	D-3	Crow Agency	E-7	Ennis	E-4	Gardiner	E-5
Arlee	C-2	Big Timber	D-5	Cascade	C-4	Culbertson	B-10	Eureka	A-2	Geraldine	C-5
Ashland	E-8	Bigfork	B-2	Chester	A-5	Cut Bank	A-4	Fairfield	B-4	Glasgow	B-8
Augusta	C-4	Billings	E-7	Chinook	A-6	Deer Lodge	D-3	Fairview	B-10	Glendive	C-10
Baker	D-10	Black Eagle	C-4	Choteau	B-4	Denton	C-5	Florence	D-2	Great Falls	C-4
Ballantine	D-7	Boulder	D-4	Circle	C-9	Dillon	E-3	Forsyth	D-8	Hamilton	D-2
		Box Elder	B-5	Clinton	C-3	Drummond	D-3	Fort Belknap Agency	B-6	Hardin	E-7
		Bozeman	E-5	Clyde Park	D-5	Dutton	B-4	Fort Benton	B-5	Harlem	A-6
		Bridger	E-6	Colstrip	D-8	East Glacier Park		Frazer	B-8	Harlowton	D-6
		Broadus	E-9	Columbia Falls	B-2	Village	B-3	Frenchtown	C-2	Havre	A-6

NOTE: Maps are not always in alphabetical order.
See Page 1 for map location in this atlas.

Montana   61

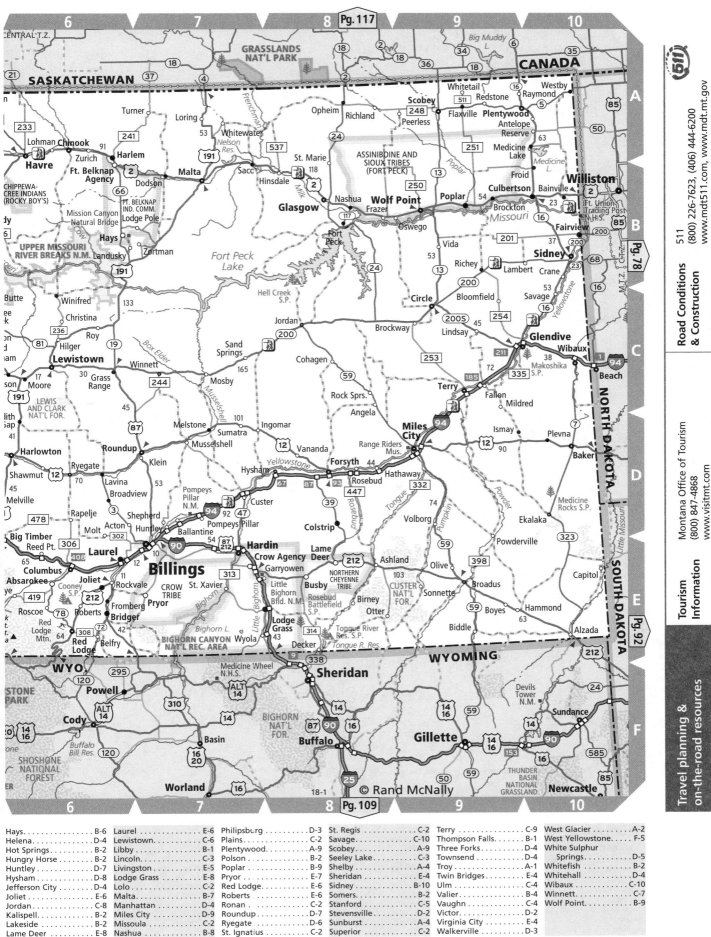

Hays B-6
Helena D-4
Hot Springs B-2
Hungry Horse B-2
Huntley D-7
Hysham D-8
Jefferson City D-4
Joliet E-6
Jordan C-8
Kalispell B-2
Lakeside B-2
Lame Deer E-8

Laurel E-6
Lewistown C-6
Libby B-1
Lincoln C-3
Livingston E-5
Lodge Grass E-8
Lolo C-2
Malta B-7
Manhattan D-4
Miles City D-9
Missoula C-2
Nashua B-8

Philipsburg D-3
Plains C-2
Plentywood A-9
Polson B-2
Poplar B-9
Pryor E-7
Red Lodge E-6
Roberts E-6
Ronan C-2
Roundup D-7
Ryegate D-6
St. Ignatius C-2

St. Regis C-2
Savage C-10
Scobey A-9
Seeley Lake C-3
Shelby A-4
Sheridan E-4
Sidney B-10
Somers B-2
Stanford C-5
Stevensville D-2
Sunburst A-4
Superior C-2

Terry C-9
Thompson Falls B-1
Three Forks D-4
Townsend D-4
Troy A-1
Twin Bridges E-4
Ulm C-4
Valier B-4
Vaughn C-4
Victor D-2
Virginia City E-4
Walkerville D-3

West Glacier A-2
West Yellowstone . . F-5
White Sulphur
  Springs D-5
Whitefish B-2
Whitehall D-4
Wibaux C-10
Winnett C-7
Wolf Point B-9

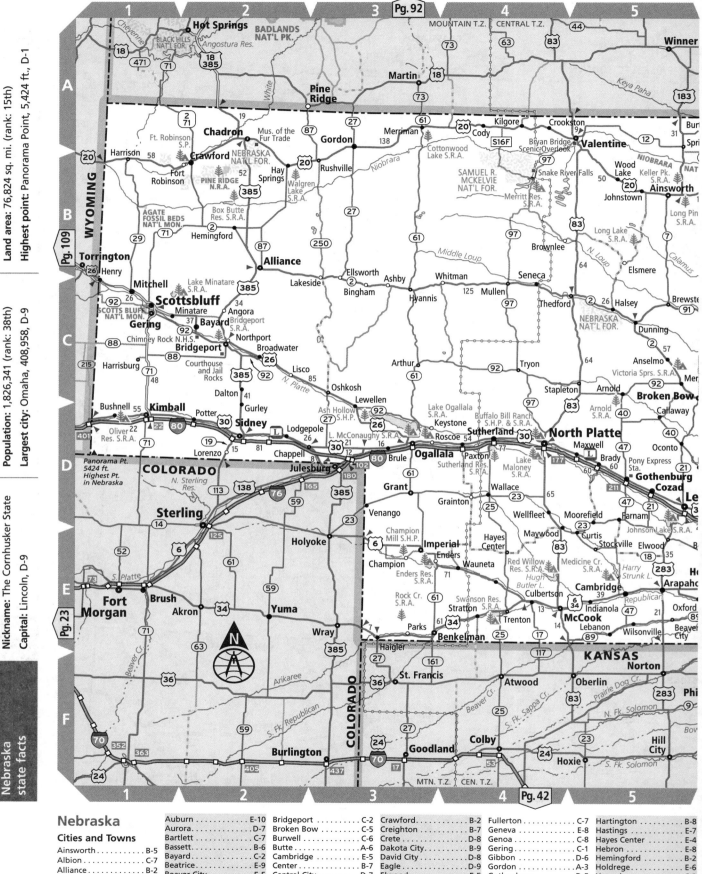

Pg. 92

Pg. 109

Pg. 23

Pg. 42

Land area: 76,824 sq. mi. (rank: 15th)
Highest point: Panorama Point, 5,424 ft., D-1

Population: 1,826,341 (rank: 38th)
Largest city: Omaha, 408,958, D-9

Nickname: The Cornhusker State
Capital: Lincoln, D-9

Nebraska state facts

Nebraska
Cities and Towns

Ainsworth	B-5	Auburn	E-10	Bridgeport	C-2
Albion	C-7	Aurora	D-7	Broken Bow	C-5
Alliance	B-2	Bartlett	C-7	Burwell	C-6
Alma	E-6	Bassett	B-6	Butte	A-6
Arapahoe	E-5	Bayard	C-2	Cambridge	E-5
Arthur	C-3	Beatrice	E-9	Center	B-7
Ashland	D-9	Beaver City	E-5	Central City	D-7
Atkinson	B-6	Bellevue	D-9	Chadron	A-2
		Benkelman	E-3	Chappell	D-2
		Blair	C-9	Clay Center	E-7
		Bloomfield	B-8	Columbus	C-8
		Brewster	C-5	Cozad	D-5

Crawford	B-2	Fullerton	C-7	Hartington	B-8
Creighton	B-7	Geneva	E-8	Hastings	E-7
Crete	D-8	Genoa	C-8	Hayes Center	E-4
Dakota City	B-9	Gering	C-1	Hebron	E-8
David City	D-8	Gibbon	D-6	Hemingford	B-2
Eagle	D-9	Gordon	A-3	Holdrege	E-6
Elwood	D-5	Gothenburg	D-5	Hyannis	C-3
Fairbury	E-8	Grand Island	D-7	Imperial	E-3
Falls City	E-10	Grant	D-3	Kearney	D-6
Franklin	E-7	Greeley	C-7	Kimball	D-1
Fremont	C-9	Harrisburg	C-1	Laurel	B-8
Friend	D-8	Harrison	B-1	Lexington	D-5

NOTE: Maps are not always in alphabetical order.
See Page 1 for map location in this atlas.

Nebraska   63

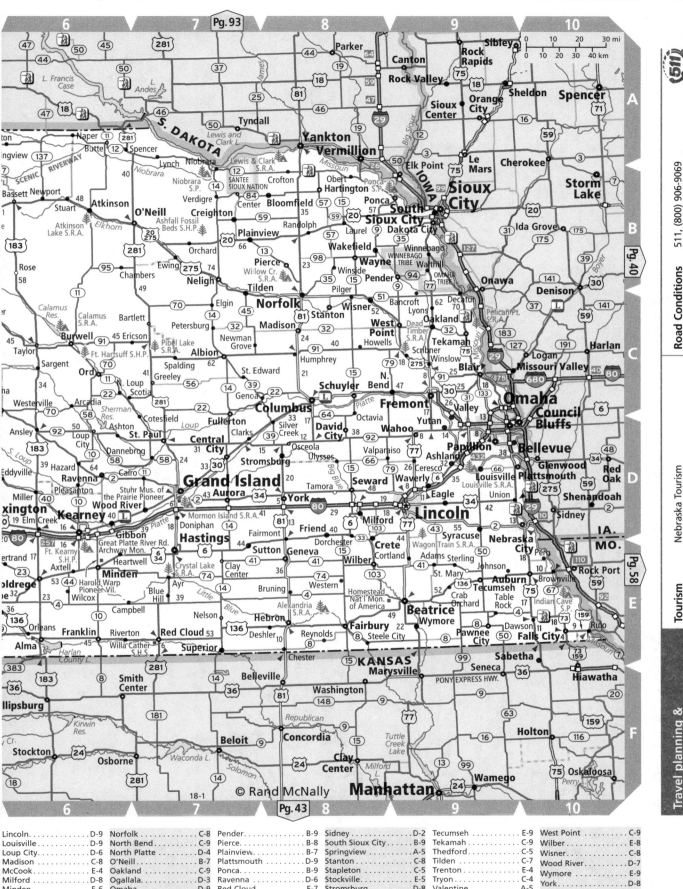

511 · (800) 906-9069
www.511.nebraska.gov
www.dor.state.ne.us

Road Conditions & Construction

Nebraska Tourism
(888) 444-1867, (402) 471-3796
www.visitnebraska.com

Tourism Information

Travel planning & on-the-road resources

Lincoln	D-9	Norfolk	C-8
Louisville	D-9	North Bend	C-9
Loup City	D-6	North Platte	D-4
Madison	C-8	O'Neill	B-7
McCook	E-4	Oakland	C-9
Milford	D-8	Ogallala	D-3
Minden	E-6	Omaha	D-9
Mitchell	C-1	Ord	C-6
Mullen	C-4	Osceola	D-8
Nebraska City	D-10	Oshkosh	C-3
Neligh	B-7	Papillion	D-9
Nelson	E-7	Pawnee City	E-9
Pender	B-9	Sidney	D-2	Tecumseh	E-9	West Point	C-9
Pierce	B-8	South Sioux City	B-9	Tekamah	C-9	Wilber	E-8
Plainview	B-7	Springview	A-5	Thedford	C-5	Wisner	C-8
Plattsmouth	D-9	Stanton	C-8	Tilden	C-7	Wood River	D-7
Ponca	B-9	Stapleton	C-5	Trenton	E-4	Wymore	E-9
Ravenna	D-6	Stockville	E-5	Tryon	C-4	York	D-8
Red Cloud	E-7	Stromsburg	D-8	Valentine	A-5	Yutan	D-9
Rushville	B-3	Superior	E-7	Valley	D-9		
St. Paul	D-7	Sutherland	D-4	Wahoo	D-9		
Schuyler	C-8	Sutton	E-7	Wakefield	B-8		
Scottsbluff	C-1	Syracuse	D-9	Waverly	D-9		
Seward	D-8	Taylor	C-6	Wayne	B-8		

© Rand McNally

Travel planning & on-the-road resources

Road Conditions & Construction
511, (603) 271-6862
www.nhtmc.com
www.nh.gov/dot

Tourism
N.H. Div. of Travel & Tourism
(603) 271-2665
www.visitnh.com

Information

New Hampshire state facts

Nickname: The Granite State
Capital: Concord, H-5
Population: 1,316,470 (rank: 42nd)
Largest city: Manchester, 109,565, H-5
Land area: 8,953 sq. mi. (rank: 44th)
Highest point: Mt. Washington, 6,288 ft., D-6

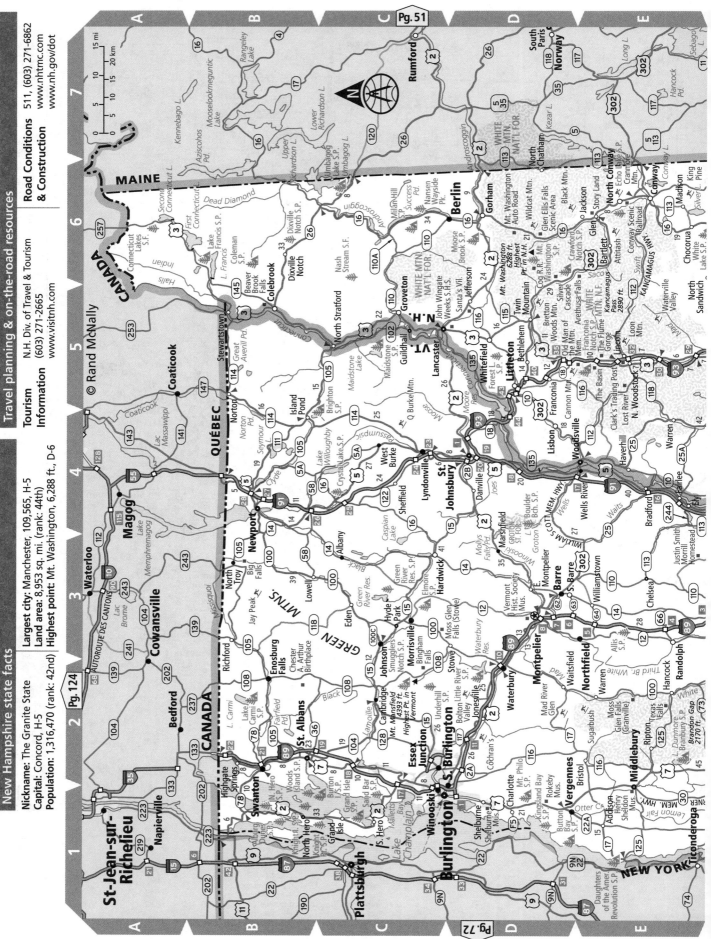

© Rand McNally

Pg. 51
Pg. 124
Pg. 72

NOTE: Maps are not always in alphabetical order.
See Page 1 for map location in this atlas.

New Hampshire • Vermont 65

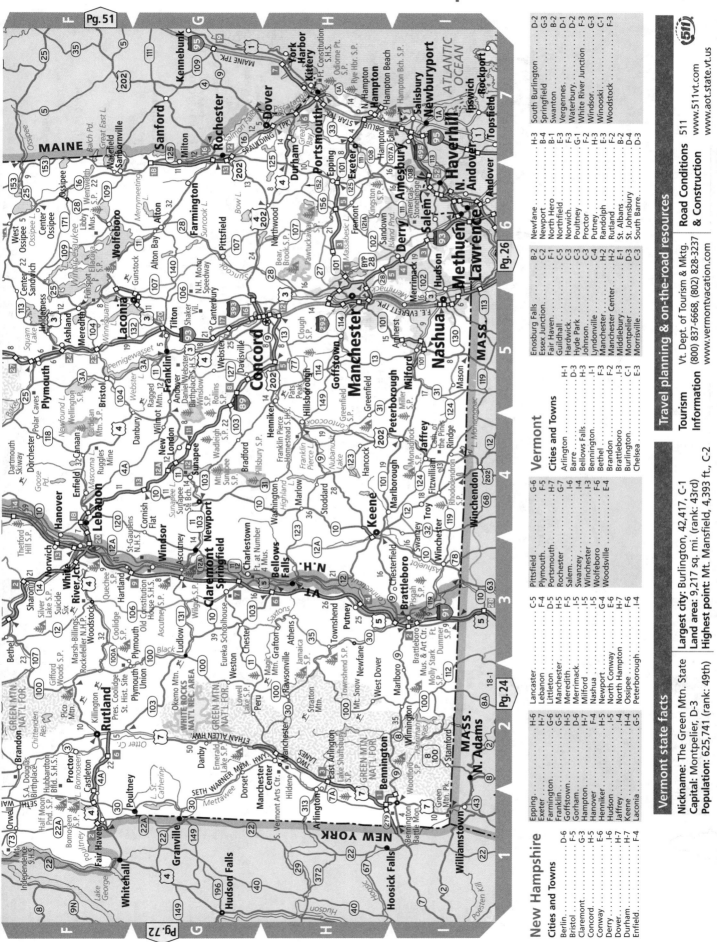

New Hampshire

Cities and Towns

Berlin	D-6
Bristol	F-5
Claremont	G-3
Concord	H-5
Conway	E-6
Derry	I-6
Dover	H-7
Durham	H-7
Enfield	F-4

Epping	H-6
Exeter	H-7
Farmington	G-6
Franklin	G-5
Goffstown	H-5
Gorham	D-6
Hampton	H-7
Hanover	F-4
Henniker	H-5
Hudson	I-6
Jaffrey	I-4
Keene	H-4
Laconia	G-5

Lancaster	H-6
Lebanon	F-4
Littleton	G-6
Manchester	H-5
Meredith	D-6
Merrimack	H-7
Milford	I-5
Nashua	I-5
Newport	G-4
North Conway	E-6
North Hampton	H-7
Ossipee	E-3
Peterborough	I-4

Pittsfield	C-5
Plymouth	F-4
Portsmouth	D-5
Rochester	F-5
Salem	I-6
Swanzey	I-4
Winchester	I-5
Wolfeboro	G-4
Woodsville	H-7

Vermont

Cities and Towns

Arlington	H-1
Barre	D-3
Bellows Falls	H-3
Bennington	I-1
Bethel	F-3
Brandon	I-3
Brattleboro	H-2
Burlington	C-1
Chelsea	E-3

Enosburg Falls	B-2
Essex Junction	C-2
Fair Haven	F-1
Guildhall	C-5
Hardwick	B-3
Hyde Park	C-3
Johnson	B-3
Lyndonville	B-4
Manchester	H-2
Manchester Center	I-1
Middlebury	I-3
Montpelier	C-1
Morrisville	E-3

Newfane	B-2
Newport	C-2
North Hero	F-1
Northfield	C-5
Norwich	E-3
Poultney	C-3
Proctor	C-4
Putney	H-2
Randolph	H-2
Rutland	E-1
St. Albans	F-2
St. Johnsbury	D-3
South Barre	C-3

South Burlington	D-2
Springfield	G-3
Swanton	B-1
Vergennes	D-1
Waterbury	D-2
White River Junction	F-3
Windsor	F-2
Winooski	H-3
Woodstock	F-3

Travel planning & on-the-road resources

Tourism Information	Vt. Dept. of Tourism & Mktg. (800) 837-6668, (802) 828-3237 www.vermontvacation.com	**Road Conditions & Construction**	511 www.511vt.com www.aot.state.vt.us

Vermont state facts

Nickname: The Green Mtn. State
Capital: Montpelier, D-3
Population: 625,741 (rank: 49th)

Largest city: Burlington, 42,417, C-1
Land area: 9,217 sq. mi. (rank: 43rd)
Highest point: Mt. Mansfield, 4,393 ft., C-2

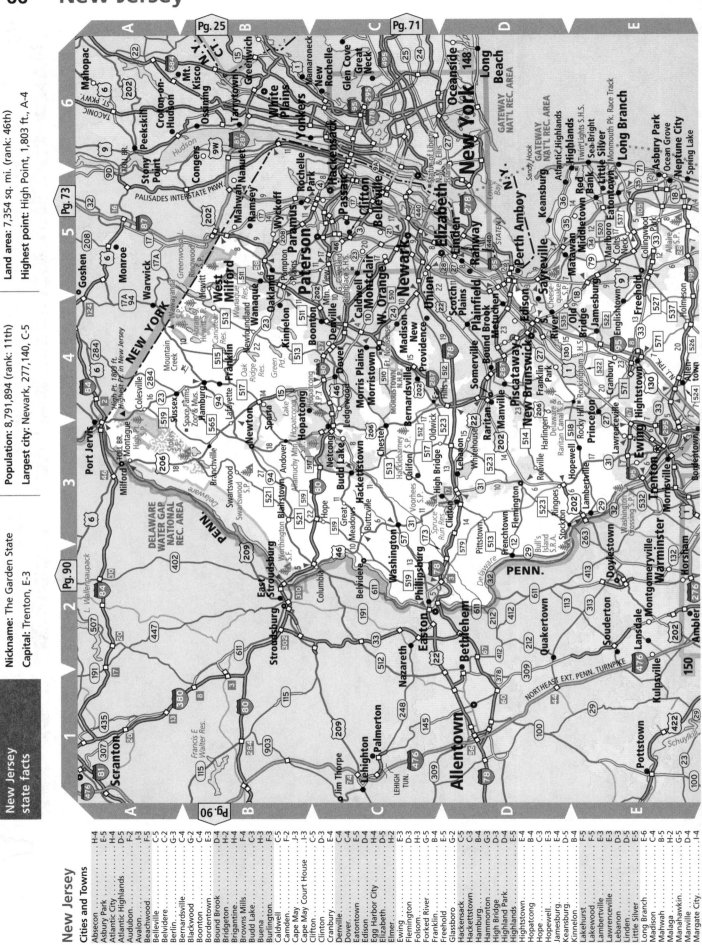

New Jersey
state facts

Nickname: The Garden State
Capital: Trenton, E-3

Population: 8,791,894 (rank: 11th)
Largest city: Newark, 277,140, C-5

Land area: 7,354 sq. mi. (rank: 46th)
Highest point: High Point, 1,803 ft., A-4

New Jersey

Cities and Towns

Absecon H-4
Asbury Park E-5
Atlantic City H-4
Atlantic Highlands D-5
Audubon F-2
Avalon I-3
Beachwood F-5
Belleville C-5
Belvidere C-2
Berlin G-3
Bernardsville D-4
Blackwood G-2
Boonton C-4
Bordentown E-3
Bridgeton H-2
Brigantine H-4
Browns Mills F-4
Budd Lake C-3
Buena H-3
Burlington F-3
Caldwell C-5
Camden F-2
Cape May J-3
Cape May Court House I-3
Clifton C-5
Cranbury E-4
Denville C-4
Dover C-4
Eatontown E-5
Edison D-4
Egg Harbor City H-4
Elizabeth D-5
Elmer H-2
Ewing E-3
Flemington D-3
Folsom H-3
Forked River G-5
Franklin B-4
Freehold E-5
Glassboro G-2
Hackensack C-5
Hackettstown C-3
Hamburg B-4
Hammonton G-3
High Bridge D-3
Highland Park D-4
Highlands D-5
Hightstown E-4
Hopatcong C-4
Hopewell E-3
Jamesburg E-4
Keansburg D-5
Kinnelon C-4
Lakehurst F-5
Lakewood F-5
Lambertville E-3
Lawrenceville E-3
Lebanon D-3
Linden D-5
Little Silver E-5
Long Branch E-6
Madison C-4
Mahwah B-5
Malaga H-2
Manahawkin G-5
Manville D-4
Margate City I-4

NOTE: Maps are not always in alphabetical order.
See Page 1 for map location in this atlas.

New Jersey   67

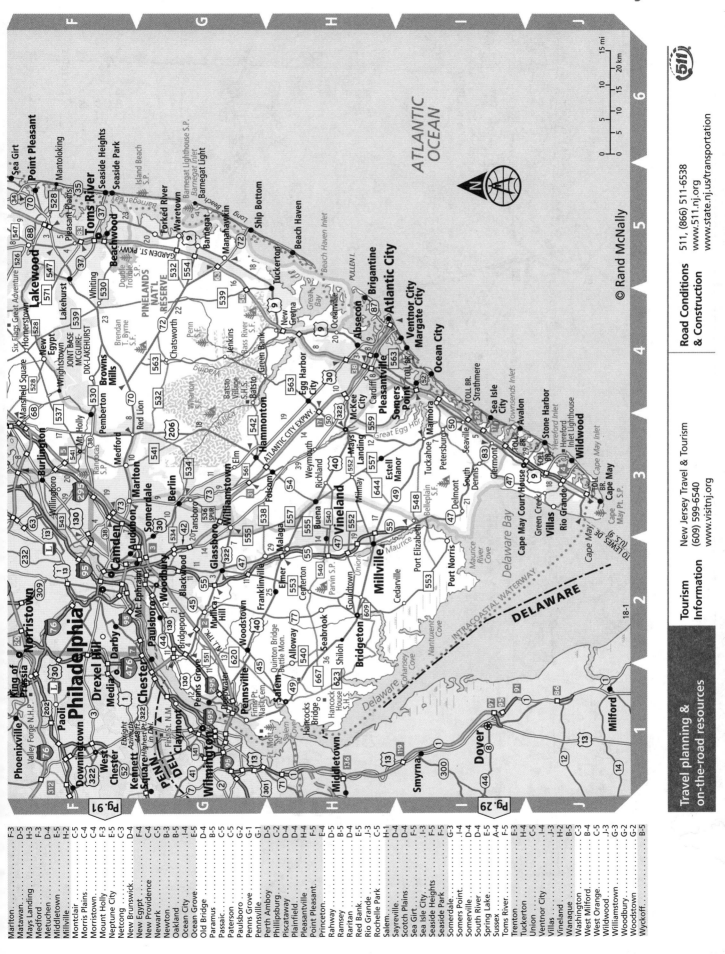

ATLANTIC OCEAN

© Rand McNally

DELAWARE

| Road Conditions & Construction | 511, (866) 511-6538 www.511.nj.org www.state.nj.us/transportation |
| Tourism Information | New Jersey Travel & Tourism (609) 599-6540 www.visitnj.org |

Travel planning & on-the-road resources

Marlton F-3
Matawan D-5
Mays Landing H-3
Medford F-3
Metuchen D-4
Middletown E-5
Millville H-2
Montclair C-5
Morris Plains C-4
Morristown C-4
Mount Holly F-3
Neptune City E-5
Netcong C-4
New Brunswick ... D-4
New Egypt E-5
New Providence ... C-5
Newark C-5
Oakland B-3
Ocean City I-4
Ocean Grove E-5
Old Bridge D-4
Paramus B-5
Passaic C-5
Paterson C-5
Paulsboro G-2
Penns Grove G-1
Pennsville G-1
Perth Amboy D-5
Phillipsburg C-2
Piscataway D-4
Plainfield C-4
Pleasantville H-4
Point Pleasant ... F-5
Princeton E-4
Rahway D-5
Ramsey B-5
Raritan D-4
Red Bank E-5
Rio Grande J-3
Rochelle Park C-5
Salem G-1
Sayreville D-5
Scotch Plains C-5
Sea Girt E-5
Sea Isle City I-3
Seaside Heights .. F-5
Seaside Park F-5
Somerdale G-3
Somers Point I-4
Somerville D-4
South River D-5
Spring Lake E-5
Sussex A-4
Toms River F-5
Tuckerton G-5
Union C-5
Ventnor City I-4
Villas J-3
Vineland H-2
Wanaque B-5
Washington C-3
West Milford B-4
West Orange C-5
Wildwood J-3
Williamstown G-2
Woodbury G-2
Woodstown G-2
Wyckoff B-5

Nickname: Land of Enchantment

Capital: Santa Fe, C-4

Population: 2,059,179 (rank: 36th)

Largest city: Albuquerque, 545,852, D-3

Land area: 121,298 sq. mi. (rank: 5th)

Highest point: Wheeler Peak, 13,161 ft., B-5

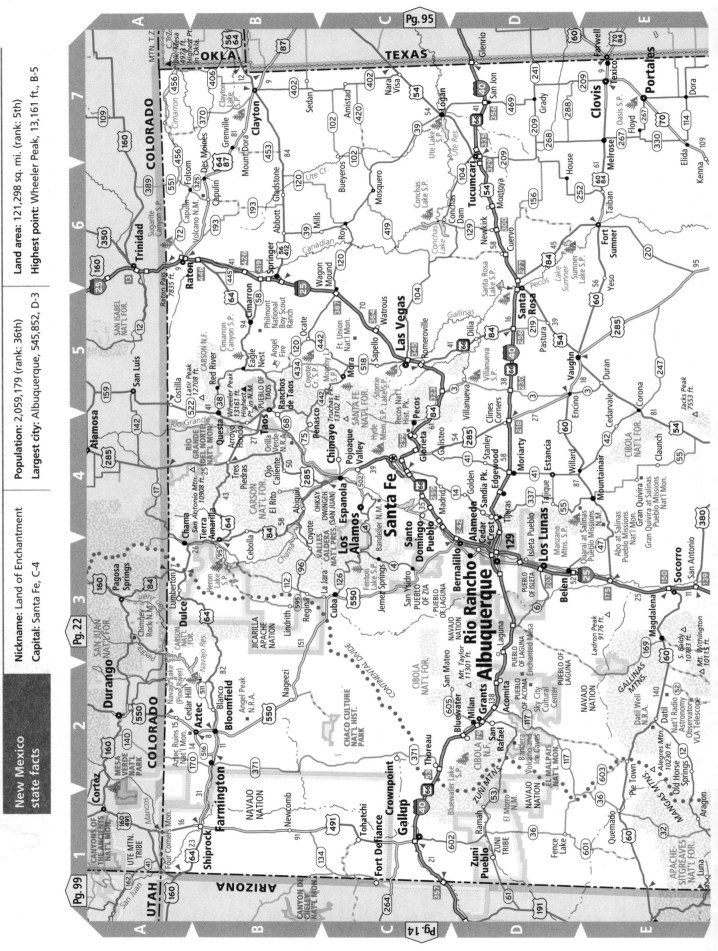

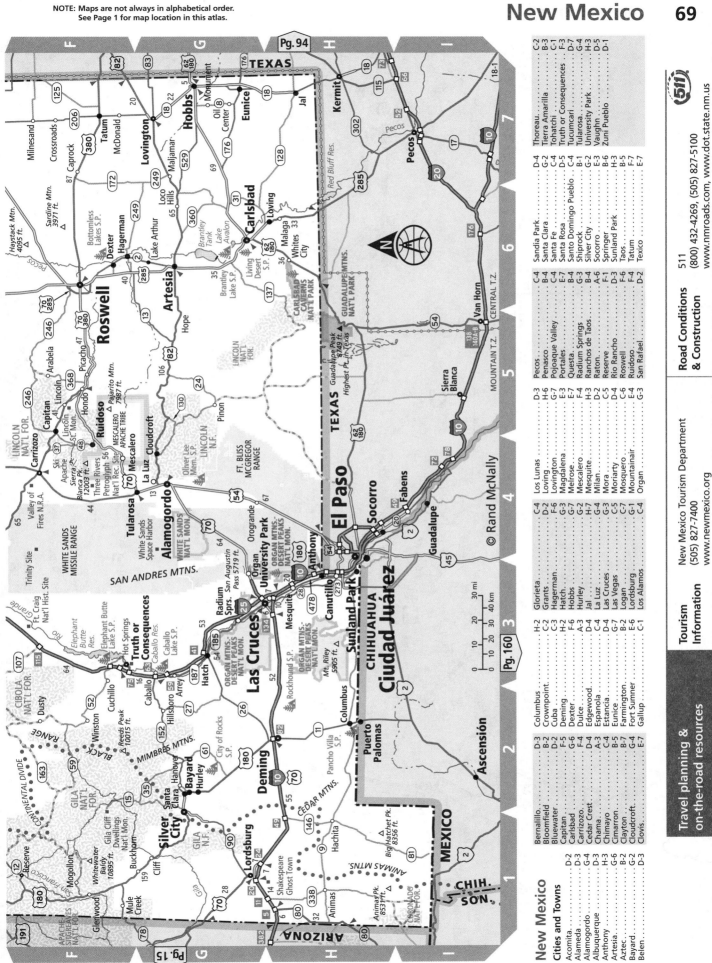

more map Pg.72

New York state facts

Nickname: The Empire State

Capital: Albany, F-11

Population: 19,378,102 (rank: 3rd)

Largest city: New York, 8,175,133, J-1

Land area: 47,126 sq. mi. (rank: 30th)

Highest point: Mount Marcy, 5,344 ft., C-11

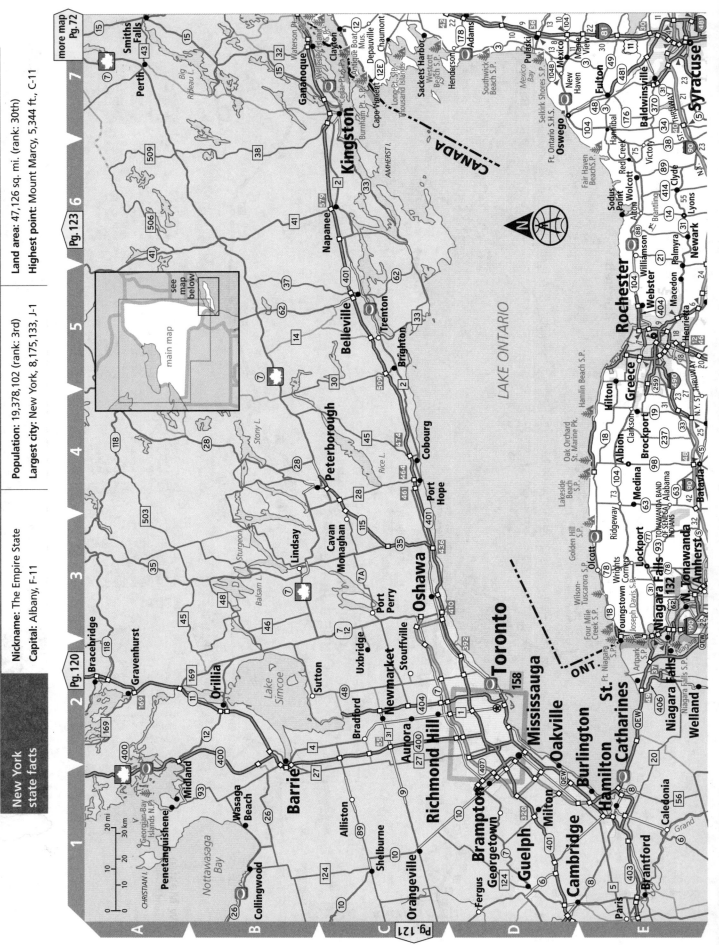

NOTE: Maps are not always in alphabetical order.
See Page 1 for map location in this atlas.

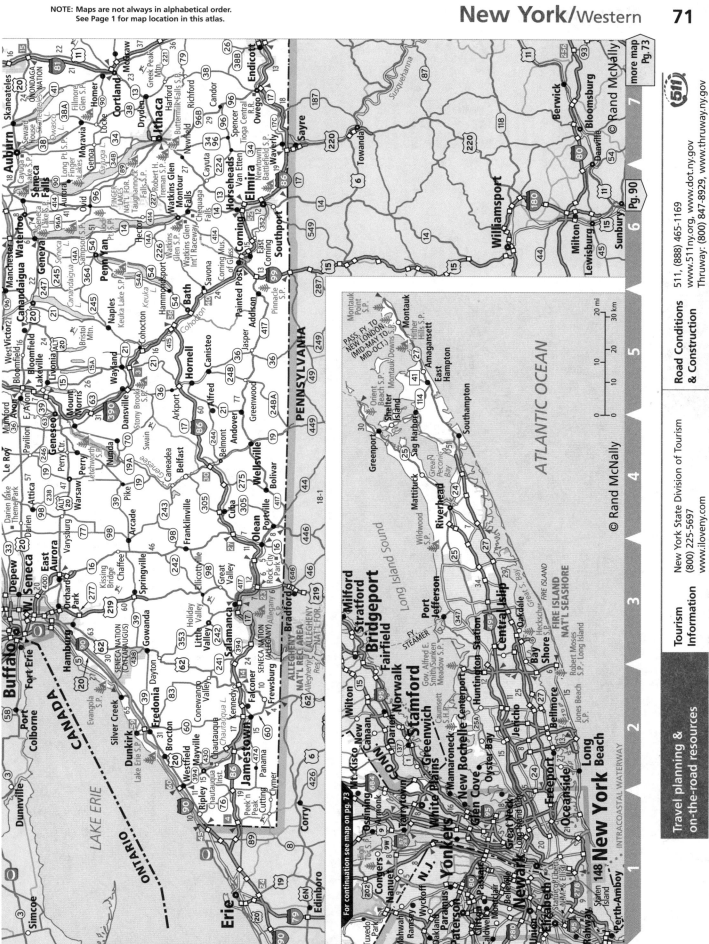

For continuation see map on pg. 73

Tourism Information	New York State Division of Tourism (800) 225-5697 www.iloveny.com	Road Conditions & Construction	511, (888) 465-1169 www.511ny.org, www.dot.ny.gov Thruway: (800) 847-8929, www.thruway.ny.gov

Travel planning & on-the-road resources

© Rand McNally

New York state facts

Nickname: The Empire State
Capital: Albany, F-11

Population: 19,378,102 (rank: 3rd)
Largest city: New York, 8,175,133, J-1

Land area: 47,126 sq. mi. (rank: 30th)
Highest point: Mount Marcy, 5,344 ft., C-11

more map
Pg.70

New York

Cities and Towns

Place	Grid
Adams	D-7
Adams Center	D-8
Addison	G-5
Albany	F-11
Albion	E-4
Alexandria Bay	B-8
Alfred	G-5
Amagansett	J-2
Amenia	H-12
Amherst	E-3
Amsterdam	F-11
Arcade	F-4
Andover	G-5
Arkport	G-5
Armonk	I-11
Attica	F-4
Auburn	F-7
Avon	F-5
Bainbridge	G-8
Baldwinsville	E-7
Ballston Spa	F-10
Batavia	E-4
Bath	G-5
Bay Shore	J-3
Beacon	I-11
Belfast	G-4
Bellmore	J-2
Belmont	G-4
Binghamton	H-7
Bolivar	H-4
Bolton Landing	D-11
Brewster	I-12
Brockport	E-4
Brocton	F-3
Buffalo	E-3
Cadyville	B-11
Cairo	G-11
Cambridge	E-12
Camden	E-8
Canajoharie	F-9
Canandaigua	F-6
Canastota	E-8
Candor	G-7
Canisteo	G-5
Canton	C-7
Carthage	D-8
Catskill	G-11
Cayuta	G-6
Cazenovia	F-8
Centerport	I-2
Central Islip	J-3
Champlain	A-12
Chestertown	D-11
Claverack	G-11
Clayton	C-7
Clinton	E-9
Clyde	F-6
Cobleskill	F-10
Cohocton	G-5
Cohoes	F-11
Congers	I-11
Cooperstown	F-9
Corinth	E-11
Corning	G-6
Cornwall-on-Hudson	I-11
Cortland	G-7
Croton Falls	I-12
Croton-on-Hudson	I-11
Crown Point	C-12
Le Roy	E-4
Liberty	H-10
Little Falls	E-9
Little Valley	G-3
Livingston Manor	H-9
Livonia	F-5
Loch Sheldrake	H-10
Lockport	E-3
Long Beach	J-2
Lowville	D-8
Lyons	G-5
Macedon	F-5
Mahopac	I-11
Malone	B-8
Mamaroneck	J-11
Manchester	F-6
Massena	B-8
Mattituck	I-3
Mayville	F-2
McGraw	G-7
Mechanicville	F-11
Medina	E-4
Mexico	E-7
Middleburgh	F-10
Middletown	I-10
Millbrook	H-11
Millerton	H-12
Monroe	I-11
Montauk	I-5
Monticello	H-10
Montour Falls	G-6
Moravia	F-7
Mount Kisco	I-11
Mount Morris	F-4
Naples	F-5
New Berlin	F-9
New Hartford	E-9
New Lebanon	G-12
New Paltz	I-11
New Rochelle	J-1
New Windsor	I-11
New York	J-1
New York Mills	E-8
Newark	F-6
Newburgh	I-11
Niagara Falls	E-3
North Tonawanda	E-3
Northville	E-10
Norwich	F-8
Norwood	B-8
Nunda	F-4
Oakdale	J-3
Oceanside	J-2
Ogdensburg	B-8
Olcott	E-3
Old Forge	D-9
Olean	H-3
Oneida	E-8
Oneonta	G-9
Orchard Park	F-3
Ossining	I-11
Oswego	E-7
Oxford	G-8
Oyster Bay	I-2
Painted Post	G-6
Palmyra	F-6
Pawling	I-12
Peekskill	I-11
Penn Yan	F-6
Perry	F-4
Plattsburgh	A-12
Port Henry	C-12
Port Jefferson	I-3

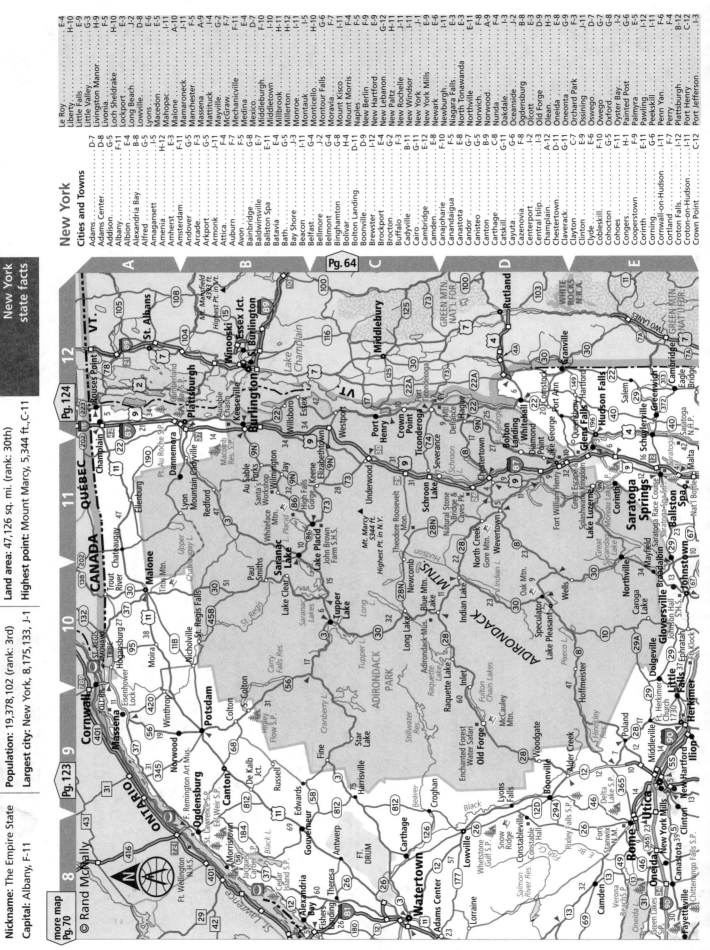

© Rand McNally

NOTE: Maps are not always in alphabetical order.
See Page 1 for map location in this atlas.

New York/Eastern   73

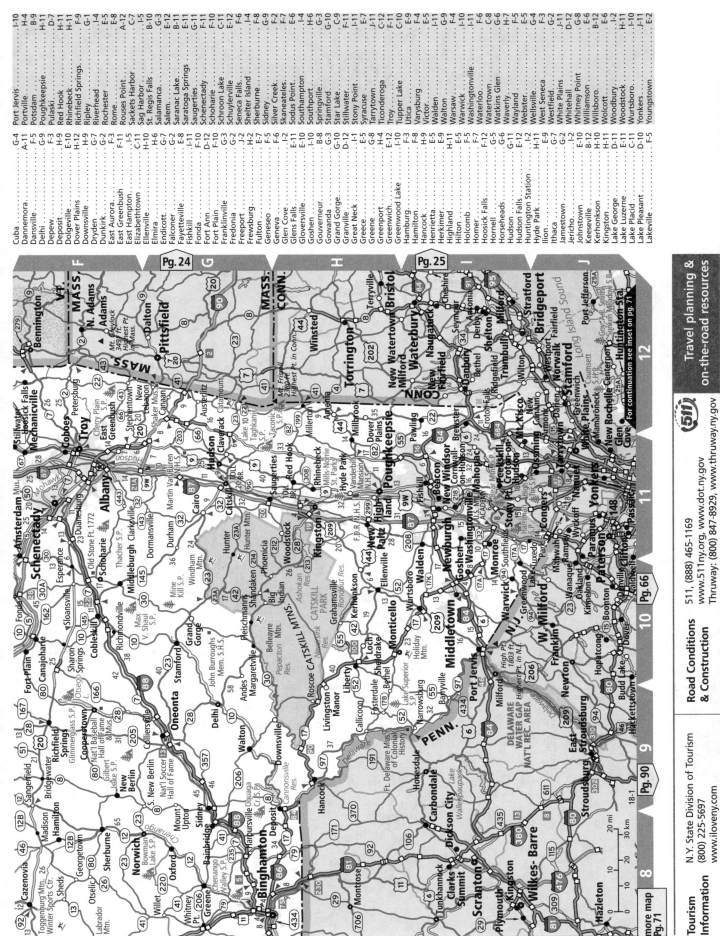

Cuba ... G-4
Dannemora ... A-11
Dansville ... F-5
Delhi ... G-9
Depew ... F-3
Deposit ... H-9
Dolgeville ... E-10
Dover Plains ... H-12
Downsville ... H-9
Dryden ... G-7
Dunkirk ... G-2
East Aurora ... F-3
East Greenbush ... F-11
East Hampton ... I-5
Elizabethtown ... C-11
Ellenville ... H-10
Elmira ... H-6
Endicott ... G-7
Falconer ... E-8
Fayetteville ... I-11
Fishkill ... F-10
Fonda ... D-12
Fort Ann ... F-10
Fort Plain ... F-10
Franklinville ... G-3
Fredonia ... G-2
Freeport ... J-2
Frewsburg ... H-2
Fulton ... E-7
Geneseo ... F-5
Geneva ... F-6
Glen Cove ... I-2
Glens Falls ... E-11
Gloversville ... E-10
Goshen ... I-10
Gouverneur ... B-8
Gowanda ... G-3
Grand Gorge ... G-10
Granville ... D-12
Great Neck ... I-1
Greece ... E-5
Greene ... G-8
Greenport ... H-4
Greenwich ... E-12
Greenwood Lake ... I-10
Hamburg ... F-3
Hamilton ... F-8
Hancock ... H-9
Henrietta ... E-5
Herkimer ... E-9
Highland ... H-11
Hilton ... E-5
Holcomb ... F-5
Homer ... F-7
Hoosick Falls ... F-12
Hornell ... G-5
Horseheads ... G-6
Hudson ... G-11
Hudson Falls ... E-12
Huntington Station ... J-2
Hyde Park ... H-11
Ilion ... E-9
Ithaca ... G-7
Jamestown ... H-2
Jericho ... J-2
Johnstown ... E-10
Keeseville ... B-12
Kerhonkson ... H-10
Kingston ... H-11
Lake George ... D-11
Lake Luzerne ... E-11
Lake Placid ... C-11
Lake Pleasant ... D-10
Lakeville ... F-5

Port Jervis ... I-10
Portville ... H-4
Potsdam ... B-9
Poughkeepsie ... H-11
Pulaski ... D-7
Red Hook ... H-11
Rhinebeck ... H-11
Richfield Springs ... F-9
Ripley ... G-1
Riverhead ... I-4
Rochester ... E-5
Rome ... E-8
Rouses Point ... A-12
Sackets Harbor ... C-7
Sag Harbor ... I-5
St. Regis Falls ... B-10
Salamanca ... G-3
Salem ... E-12
Saranac Lake ... B-11
Saratoga Springs ... E-11
Saugerties ... G-11
Schenectady ... E-11
Schoharie ... F-10
Schroon Lake ... C-11
Schuylerville ... E-11
Seneca Falls ... F-6
Shelter Island ... I-4
Sherburne ... F-8
Sidney ... G-9
Silver Creek ... G-2
Skaneateles ... F-7
Sodus Point ... E-6
Southampton ... I-4
Southport ... H-6
Springville ... G-3
Stamford ... G-10
Star Lake ... C-9
Stillwater ... E-11
Stony Point ... I-1
Syracuse ... E-7
Tarrytown ... I-2
Ticonderoga ... C-12
Tivoli ... H-11
Tupper Lake ... C-10
Utica ... E-9
Varysburg ... F-4
Victor ... E-5
Walden ... H-10
Walton ... G-9
Warsaw ... F-4
Warwick ... I-10
Washingtonville ... H-11
Waterloo ... F-6
Watertown ... C-8
Watkins Glen ... G-6
Waverly ... H-7
Wayland ... G-5
Webster ... E-5
Wellsville ... H-4
West Seneca ... F-3
Westfield ... H-1
White Plains ... I-2
Whitehall ... D-12
Whitney Point ... G-8
Williamson ... E-6
Willsboro ... B-12
Wolcott ... E-6
Woodbury ... I-2
Woodstock ... H-11
Wurtsboro ... I-10
Yonkers ... J-11
Youngstown ... E-2

Travel planning & on-the-road resources

Tourism Information
N.Y. State Division of Tourism
(800) 225-5697
www.iloveny.com

Road Conditions & Construction
511, (888) 465-1169
www.511ny.org, www.dot.ny.gov
Thruway: (800) 847-8929, www.thruway.ny.gov

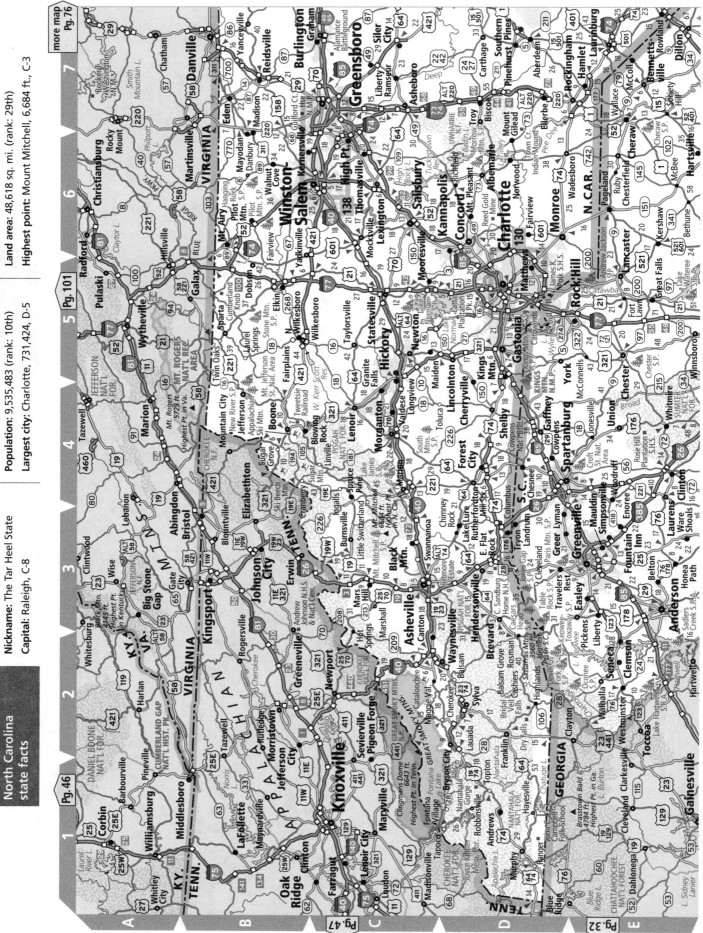

NOTE: Maps are not always in alphabetical order.
See Page 1 for map location in this atlas.

North Carolina • South Carolina/Western

75

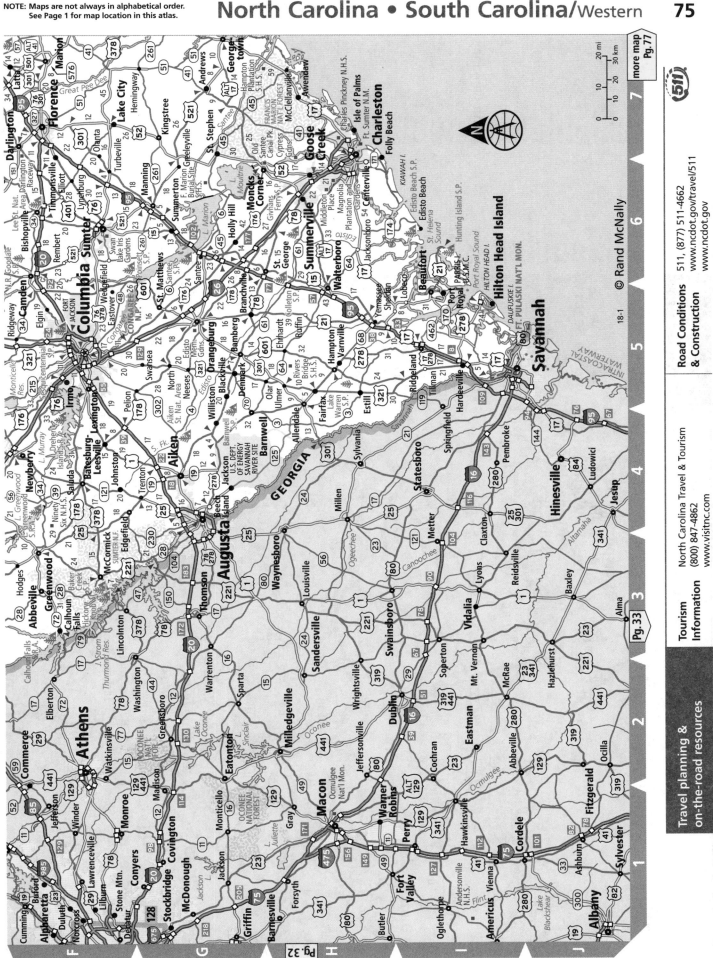

more map
Pg. 77

© Rand McNally

511

Pg. 33
Pg. 32

Road Conditions & Construction
511, (877) 511-4662
www.ncdot.gov/travel/511
www.ncdot.gov

Tourism Information
North Carolina Travel & Tourism
(800) 847-4862
www.visitnc.com

Travel planning & on-the-road resources

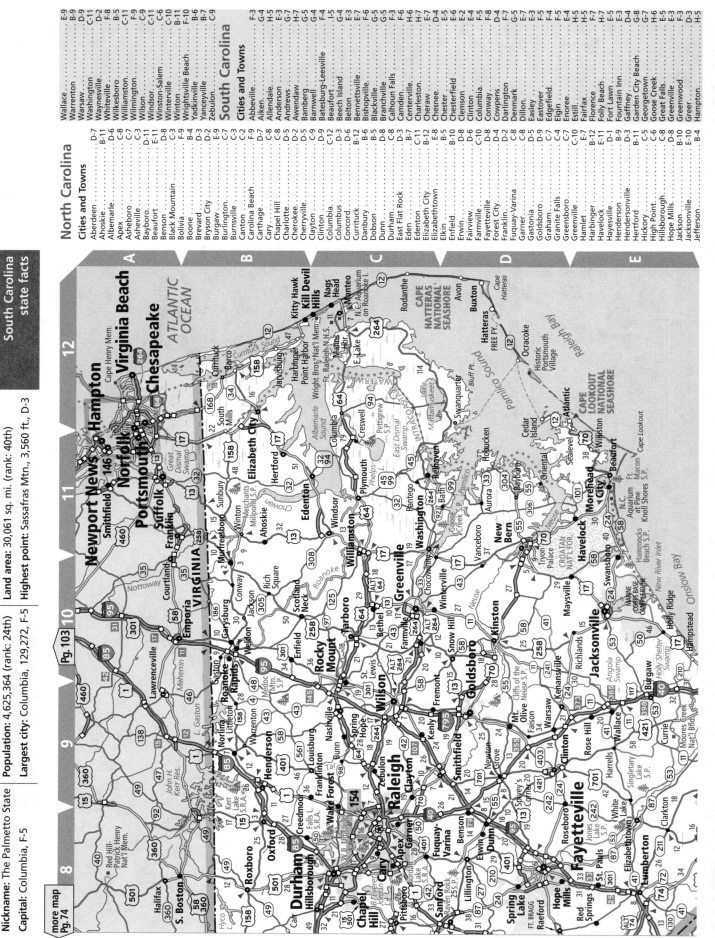

South Carolina state facts

Nickname: The Palmetto State
Capital: Columbia, F-5
Population: 4,625,364 (rank: 24th)
Largest city: Columbia, 129,272, F-5
Land area: 30,061 sq. mi. (rank: 40th)
Highest point: Sassafras Mtn., 3,560 ft., D-3

more map Pg. 74

North Carolina

Cities and Towns

Aberdeen D-7
Ahoskie B-11
Albemarle D-6
Apex C-8
Asheboro C-7
Asheville C-3
Bayboro D-11
Beaufort E-11
Benson D-8
Black Mountain C-3
Bolivia F-9
Boone B-4
Brevard D-3
Bryson City D-2
Burgaw E-9
Burlington C-7
Burnsville C-2
Canton F-9
Carolina Beach D-7
Carthage C-8
Cary D-5
Chapel Hill H-7
Charlotte D-5
Cherokee D-2
Cherryville C-9
Clayton C-9
Clinton D-9
Columbia C-12
Columbus D-3
Concord D-6
Currituck B-6
Danbury B-5
Dobson D-8
Dunn D-3
Durham B-7
East Flat Rock C-11
Eden B-12
Edenton E-8
Elizabeth City B-5
Elizabethtown B-10
Elkin D-8
Enfield D-6
Erwin C-10
Fairview D-2
Farmville C-8
Fayetteville D-5
Forest City C-7
Franklin C-4
Fuquay-Varina C-10
Garner D-5
Gastonia E-7
Goldsboro D-9
Graham C-7
Granite Falls C-4
Greensboro C-7
Greenville C-10
Hamlet E-7
Harbinger B-12
Havelock E-11
Hayesville B-9
Henderson D-3
Hendersonville B-11
Hertford C-5
Hickory C-6
High Point C-8
Hillsborough D-8
Hope Mills E-10
Jackson B-10
Jacksonville E-10
Jefferson B-4

South Carolina

Cities and Towns

Abbeville F-3
Aiken G-4
Allendale H-5
Anderson E-3
Andrews G-7
Awendaw H-7
Bamberg G-5
Barnwell G-4
Batesburg-Leesville . F-4
Beaufort J-5
Beech Island G-4
Belton E-3
Bennettsville E-7
Bishopville F-6
Blacksburg G-5
Blackville G-4
Branchville H-6
Calhoun Falls H-7
Camden D-4
Centerville E-6
Charleston E-2
Chesnee F-5
Chester F-8
Chesterfield F-7
Clemson E-3
Clinton F-4
Columbia H-5
Conway F-7
Cowpens E-3
Darlington F-4
Denmark G-9
Dillon E-7
Easley E-3
Eastover F-4
Edgefield E-4
Elgin E-5
Enoree D-7
Estill H-5
Fairfax F-7
Florence B-12
Folly Beach E-11
Fort Lawn B-9
Fort Mill D-3
Fountain Inn B-11
Gaffney D-4
Garden City Beach ... G-8
Georgetown G-7
Goose Creek H-6
Great Falls E-5
Greenville E-5
Greenwood B-10
Greer D-3
Hampton H-5

NOTE: Maps are not always in alphabetical order.
See Page 1 for map location in this atlas.

North Carolina • South Carolina/Eastern — 77

Place	Grid	Place	Grid
Hardeeville	I-5	Kannapolis	D-6
Hartsville	E-6	Kenansville	D-9
Hilton Head Island	J-5	Kill Devil Hills	B-6
Holly Hill	G-6	Kings Mountain	C-12
Honea Path	E-3	Kinston	D-10
Irmo	F-5	Kitty Hawk	B-12
Isle of Palms	H-7	Laurinburg	E-7
Jackson	G-4	Lenoir	C-4
Johnston	F-4	Lexington	C-6
Jonesville	E-4	Lillington	C-7
Kershaw	E-6	Lincolnton	D-8
Kingstree	G-7	Longview	D-5
Lake City	F-7	Louisburg	C-9
Lancaster	E-5	Lumberton	E-8
Landrum	D-3	Maiden	C-12
Latta	E-8	Manteo	C-4
Laurens	E-4	Marion	C-3
Lexington	F-5	Marshall	D-5
Liberty	E-3	Matthews	B-6
Little River	F-8	Mayodan	C-6
Loris	F-8	Mocksville	D-6
Lyman	D-3	Monroe	C-5
Manning	G-6	Mooresville	G-6
Marion	F-7	Morehead City	E-11
Mauldin	E-3	Morganton	C-4
McBee	E-6	Mount Airy	B-6
McColl	E-7	Mount Olive	D-9
McCormick	F-3	Murfreesboro	B-10
Moncks Corner	G-8	Murphy	D-1
Murrells Inlet	G-8	Nags Head	C-12
Myrtle Beach	F-8	Nashville	G-8
North	G-5	New Bern	D-11
North Myrtle Beach	F-8	Newton	C-5
Orangeburg	G-5	North Wilkesboro	B-5
Pageland	E-6	Oak Island	F-9
Pickens	E-3	Oxford	B-8
Port Royal	I-5	Pinehurst	D-7
Rock Hill	E-5	Pittsboro	C-8
St. George	H-6	Plymouth	C-11
St. Matthews	G-7	Raeford	D-8
St. Stephen	G-7	Raleigh	C-8
Saluda	F-4	Red Springs	E-8
Santee	G-6	Reidsville	B-7
Seneca	E-2	Roanoke Rapids	B-10
Simpsonville	E-3	Robbinsville	D-1
Socastee	G-8	Rockingham	E-7
Society Hill	E-7	Rocky Mount	C-9
Spartanburg	D-4	Roxboro	B-8
Summerton	G-6	Rutherfordton	D-4
Summerville	H-6	Salisbury	C-6
Sumter	F-6	Sanford	D-8
Timmonsville	F-7	Scotland Neck	B-10
Travelers Rest	D-3	Shallotte	F-9
Turbeville	F-6	Shelby	D-4
Union	E-4	Siler City	C-7
Varnville	H-5	Smithfield	D-9
Walhalla	E-2	Snow Hill	D-10
Walterboro	H-5	Southern Pines	D-7
Ware Shoals	E-3	Sparta	B-5
Westminster	E-2	Spring Lake	E-4
Whitmire	E-4	Statesville	C-5
Williston	G-4	Swannanoa	C-3
Winnsboro	E-5	Swanquarter	D-12
Woodruff	E-4	Sylva	D-2
Yemassee	H-5	Tabor City	F-8
York	D-5	Tarboro	C-10
		Taylorsville	C-5
		Thomasville	C-6
		Troy	D-7
		Valdese	C-4
		Wadesboro	D-6
		Wake Forest	C-9

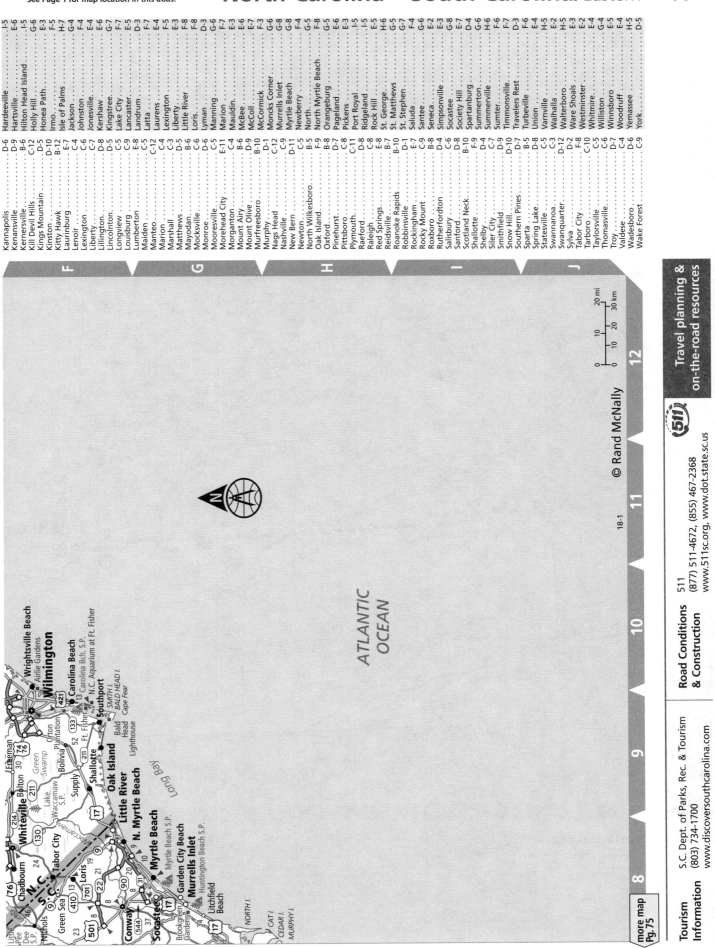

© Rand McNally

more map Pg.75

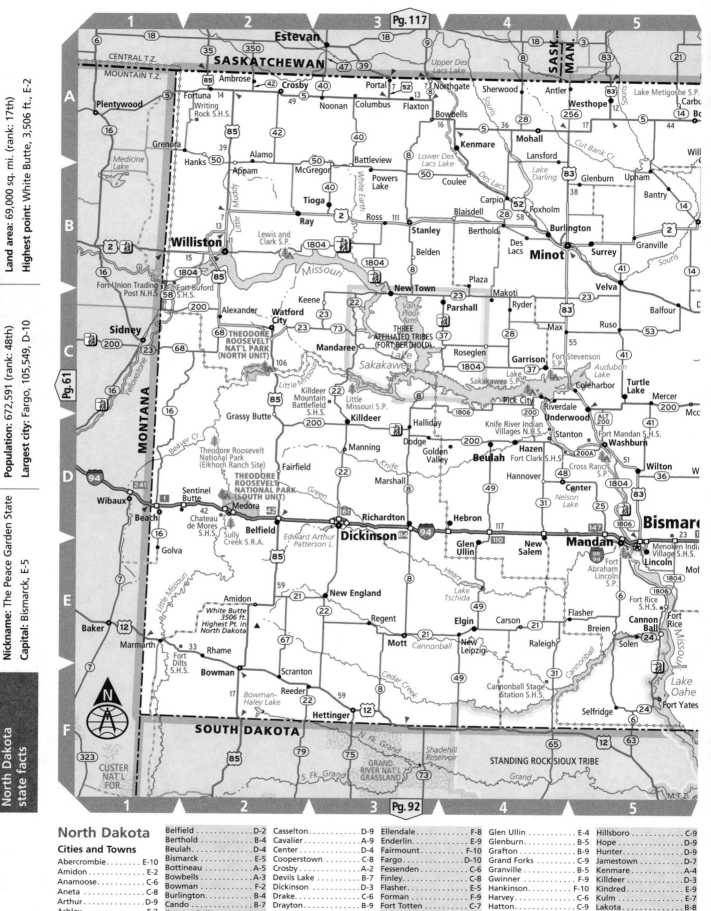

North Dakota state facts

Nickname: The Peace Garden State
Capital: Bismarck, E-5

Population: 672,591 (rank: 48th)
Largest city: Fargo, 105,549, D-10

Land area: 69,000 sq. mi. (rank: 17th)
Highest point: White Butte, 3,506 ft., E-2

North Dakota

Cities and Towns

Abercrombie E-10
Amidon E-2
Anamoose C-6
Aneta C-8
Arthur D-9
Ashley F-7
Beach D-1
Belcourt A-6

Belfield D-2
Berthold B-4
Beulah D-4
Bismarck E-5
Bottineau A-5
Bowbells A-3
Bowman F-2
Burlington B-4
Cando B-7
Cannon Ball E-5
Carrington C-7
Carson E-4

Casselton D-9
Cavalier A-9
Center D-4
Cooperstown C-8
Crosby A-2
Devils Lake B-7
Dickinson D-3
Drake C-6
Drayton B-9
Dunseith A-6
Edgeley E-7
Elgin E-4

Ellendale F-8
Enderlin E-8
Fairmount F-10
Fargo D-10
Fessenden C-6
Finley C-8
Flasher E-5
Forman F-9
Fort Totten C-7
Fort Yates F-5
Gackle E-7
Garrison C-4

Glen Ullin E-4
Glenburn B-5
Grafton B-9
Grand Forks C-9
Granville B-5
Gwinner F-9
Hankinson F-10
Harvey C-6
Hatton C-9
Hazen D-4
Hebron D-4
Hettinger F-3

Hillsboro C-9
Hope D-9
Hunter D-9
Jamestown D-7
Kenmare A-4
Killdeer D-3
Kindred E-9
Kulm E-7
Lakota B-8
Lamoure E-8
Langdon A-8
Larimore C-9

NOTE: Maps are not always in alphabetical order.
See Page 1 for map location in this atlas.

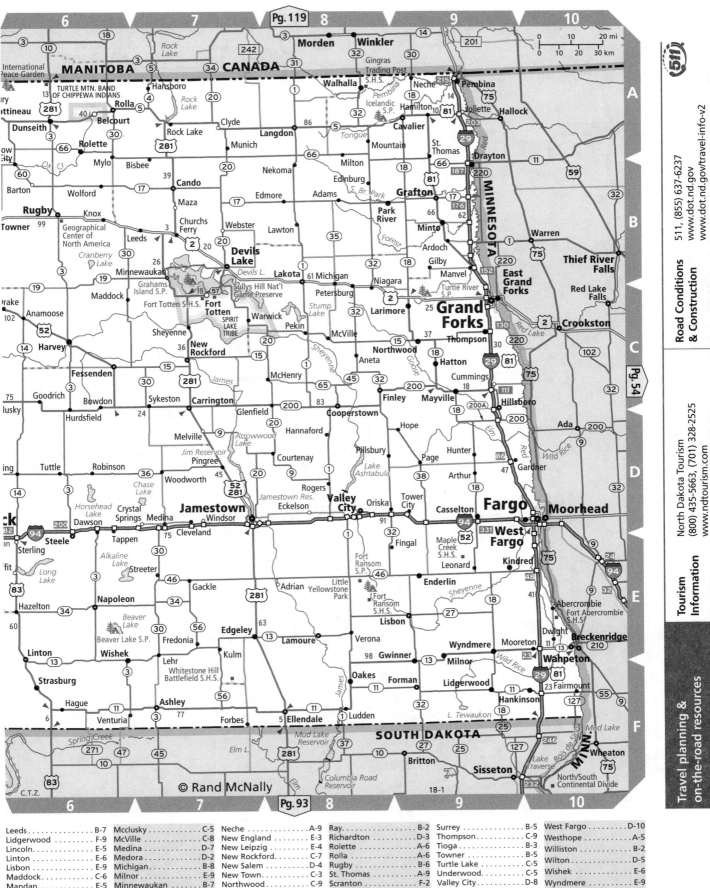

© Rand McNally

Leeds B-7	Mcclusky C-5	Neche A-9	Ray B-2	Surrey B-5
Lidgerwood F-9	McVille C-8	New England E-3	Richardton D-3	Thompson C-9
Lincoln E-5	Medina D-7	New Leipzig E-4	Rolette A-6	Tioga B-3
Linton E-6	Medora D-2	New Rockford C-7	Rolla A-6	Towner B-5
Lisbon E-9	Michigan B-8	New Salem D-4	Rugby B-6	Turtle Lake C-5
Maddock C-6	Milnor E-9	New Town C-3	St. Thomas A-9	Underwood C-5
Mandan E-5	Minnewaukan B-7	Northwood C-9	Scranton F-2	Valley City D-8
Mandaree C-3	Minot B-4	Oakes F-8	Sheyenne C-7	Velva B-5
Manning D-3	Minto B-9	Park River B-8	Stanley B-3	Wahpeton E-10
Manvel B-9	Mohall A-4	Parshall C-4	Stanton D-4	Walhalla A-8
Max C-4	Mott E-3	Pembina A-9	Steele D-6	Washburn D-5
Mayville C-9	Napoleon E-6	Powers Lake B-3	Strasburg F-6	Watford City C-2
				West Fargo D-10
				Westhope A-5
				Williston B-2
				Wilton D-5
				Wishek E-6
				Wyndmere E-9

511, (855) 637-6237
www.dot.nd.gov
www.dot.nd.gov/travel-info-v2

Road Conditions & Construction

North Dakota Tourism
(800) 435-5663, (701) 328-2525
www.ndtourism.com

Tourism Information

Travel planning & on-the-road resources

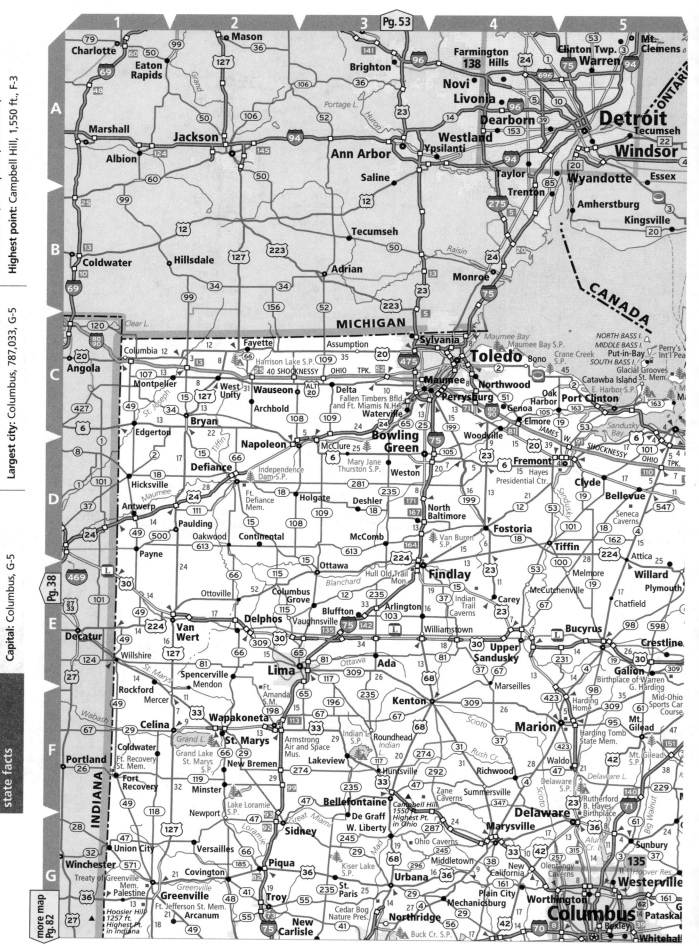

Pg. 53

Land area: 40,861 sq. mi. (rank: 35th)
Highest point: Campbell Hill, 1,550 ft., F-3

Population: 11,536,504 (rank: 7th)
Largest city: Columbus, 787,033, G-5

Nickname: The Buckeye State
Capital: Columbus, G-5

Ohio state facts

more map Pg. 82

NOTE: Maps are not always in alphabetical order.
See Page 1 for map location in this atlas.

© Rand McNally 18-1

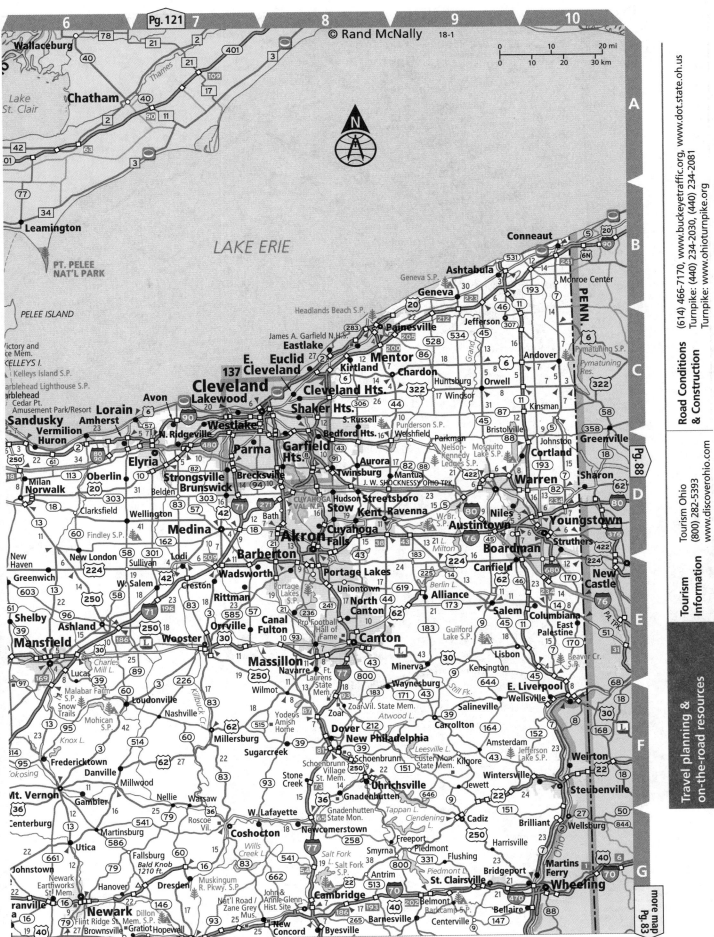

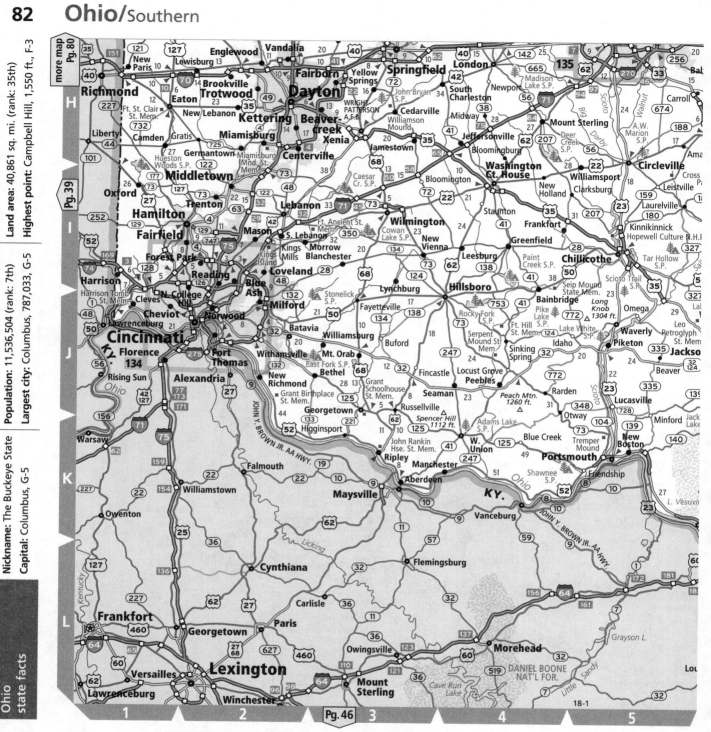

Ohio

Nickname: The Buckeye State
Capital: Columbus, G-5

Population: 11,536,504 (rank: 7th)
Largest city: Columbus, 787,033, G-5

Land area: 40,861 sq. mi. (rank: 35th)
Highest point: Campbell Hill, 1,550 ft., F-3

Ohio state facts

Cities and Towns

Aberdeen K-3	Bellefontaine F-3	Canal Fulton E-8	Covington G-2	Fostoria D-4	Jefferson C-9
Ada E-3	Bellevue D-5	Canfield E-9	Crestline E-5	Fredericktown F-6	Johnstown G-5
Akron D-8	Belmont G-9	Canton E-8	Creston E-7	Fremont D-5	Kent D-8
Alliance E-9	Belpre I-8	Carey E-4	Crooksville H-7	Galion E-5	Kenton F-4
Amherst D-6	Bethel J-3	Carroll H-5	Cuyahoga Falls D-8	Gallipolis K-7	Kettering H-2
Antwerp D-1	Bexley G-5	Carrollton F-9	Dayton H-2	Gambier F-6	Kirtland C-8
Arcanum G-2	Bidwell J-6	Cedarville H-3	Defiance D-2	Garfield Heights C-8	Lakewood C-7
Archbold C-2	Blanchester I-3	Celina F-2	Delaware G-5	Geneva B-9	Lancaster H-6
Ashland E-6	Blue Ash I-2	Centerville H-2	Delphos E-2	Genoa C-4	Lebanon I-2
Ashtabula B-9	Bluffton E-3	Chardon C-8	Delta C-3	Georgetown J-3	Lewisburg H-2
Athens I-7	Boardman E-10	Cheviot J-1	Dover F-8	Germantown H-2	Lima E-3
Aurora D-8	Boston Heights D-8	Chillicothe I-5	East Cleveland C-8	Glouster I-7	Lisbon E-9
Austintown D-9	Bowling Green D-3	Cincinnati J-2	East Liverpool F-10	Granville G-6	Lodi E-7
Avon D-7	Brecksville D-8	Circleville H-5	East Palestine E-10	Greenfield I-4	Logan I-6
Baltimore H-6	Bridgeport G-10	Cleveland C-7	Eastlake C-8	Greenville G-1	London H-4
Barberton E-8	Brilliant G-10	Cleveland Heights . . . C-8	Eaton H-1	Greenwich E-6	Lorain C-7
Barnesville G-9	Brookville H-2	Cleves J-1	Edgerton C-1	Hamilton I-2	Loudonville F-6
Batavia J-2	Brunswick D-7	Clyde D-5	Elyria D-7	Harrison I-1	Loveland I-2
Beavercreek H-3	Bryan C-1	Coldwater F-1	Englewood H-2	Hicksville D-1	Lucasville J-5
Bedford Heights D-8	Bucyrus E-5	Columbiana E-10	Euclid C-8	Hillsboro J-4	Manchester K-4
Bellaire G-9	Byesville G-8	Columbus G-5	Fairborn H-3	Hudson D-8	Mansfield E-6
	Cadiz G-9	Columbus Grove . . . E-3	Fairfield I-2	Huron D-6	Mantua D-8
	Caldwell H-8	Conneaut B-10	Findlay E-3	Ironton K-5	Marietta I-8
	Cambridge G-8	Cortland D-9	Forest Park I-2	Jackson J-6	Marion F-5
	Camden H-1	Coshocton G-7		Jamestown H-3	Martins Ferry G-10

NOTE: Maps are not always in alphabetical order.
See Page 1 for map location in this atlas.

Ohio/Southern   83

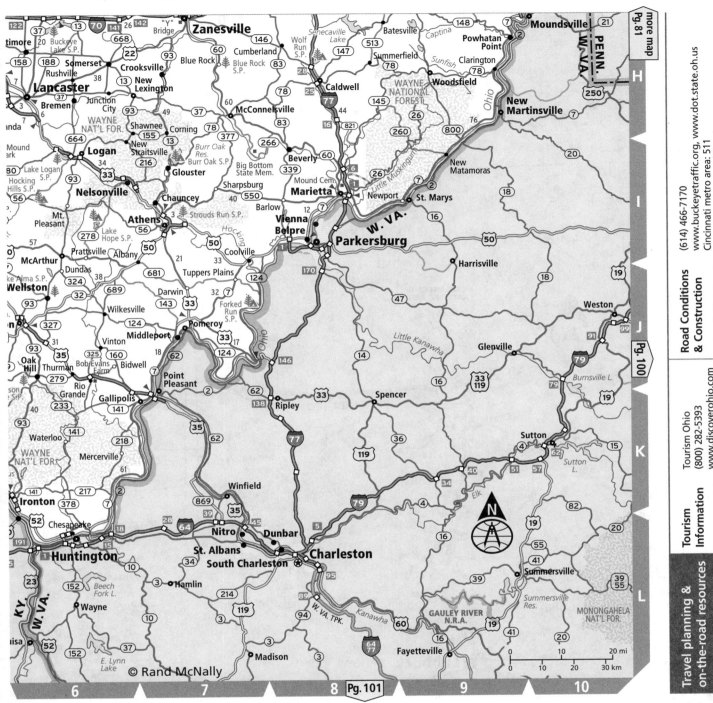

(614) 466-7170
www.buckeyetraffic.org, www.dot.state.oh.us
Cincinnati metro area: 511

Road Conditions & Construction

Tourism Ohio
(800) 282-5393
www.discoverohio.com

Tourism Information

Travel planning & on-the-road resources

Marysville G-4
Mason I-2
Massillon E-8
Maumee C-3
McArthur I-6
McComb D-3
McConnelsville H-7
Mechanicsburg G-4
Medina D-7
Mendon F-2
Mentor C-8
Miamisburg H-2
Middleport J-7
Middletown I-2
Milford J-2
Millersburg F-7
Minerva E-9
Minster F-2
Montpelier C-2
Mount Gilead F-5
Mount Orab J-3
Mount Sterling H-4
Mount Vernon F-6
Napoleon D-3
Nelsonville I-6

New Boston K-5
New Bremen F-2
New Carlisle G-3
New Concord G-7
New Lebanon H-2
New Lexington H-6
New London D-6
New Paris H-1
New Philadelphia F-8
New Richmond J-2
Newark G-6
Newcomerstown G-8
Niles D-9
North Baltimore D-3
North Canton E-8
North College Hill I-2
North Ridgeville D-7
Northridge G-3
Northwood C-4
Norwalk D-6
Norwood J-2
Oak Harbor C-5
Oak Hill J-6
Oberlin D-6
Orrville E-7

Orwell C-9
Ottawa E-3
Oxford I-1
Painesville C-8
Parma D-7
Pataskala G-6
Paulding D-2
Peebles J-4
Perrysburg C-4
Piketon J-5
Piqua G-2
Plain City G-4
Plymouth E-6
Pomeroy J-7
Port Clinton C-5
Portage Lakes E-8
Portsmouth K-5
Powhatan Point H-9
Ravenna D-8
Reading I-2
Richwood F-4
Ripley K-3
Rittman E-7
St. Clairsville G-9
St. Marys F-2

St. Paris G-3
Salem E-9
Sandusky C-5
Shaker Heights C-8
Shelby E-6
Sidney G-2
Somerset H-6
South Charleston H-3
South Lebanon I-2
South Russell C-8
Spencerville E-2
Springfield H-3
Steubenville F-10
Stow D-8
Streetsboro D-8
Strongsville D-7
Struthers D-10
Sugarcreek F-8
Sunbury G-5
Sylvania C-3
Tiffin D-4
Toledo C-4
Trenton I-2
Trotwood H-2
Troy G-2

Twinsburg D-8
Uhrichsville F-8
Union City G-1
Uniontown E-8
Upper Sandusky E-4
Urbana G-3
Utica G-6
Van Wert E-2
Vandalia H-2
Vermilion C-6
Versailles G-2
Wadsworth E-7
Wapakoneta F-2
Warren D-9
Washington
  Court House I-4
Waterville C-3
Wauseon C-3
Waverly J-5
Wellington D-6
Wellston J-6
Wellsville F-10
West Lafayette G-7
West Liberty G-3
West Salem E-7

West Union K-4
West Unity C-2
Westerville G-5
Westlake C-7
Weston D-3
Whitehall G-5
Willard D-5
Williamsburg J-3
Wilmington I-3
Wintersville F-10
Withamsville J-2
Woodsfield H-9
Woodville C-4
Wooster E-7
Worthington G-5
Xenia H-3
Yellow Springs H-3
Youngstown D-10
Zanesville H-7

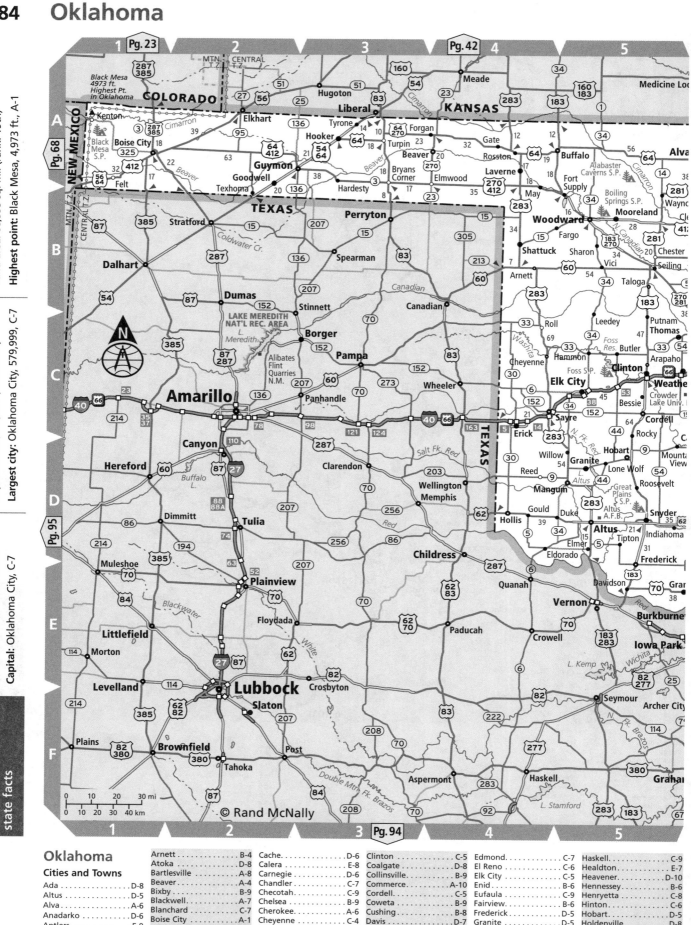

Pg. 23 · Pg. 42 · Pg. 68 · Pg. 95 · Pg. 94

Oklahoma state facts

Land area: 68,595 sq. mi. (rank: 19th)

Highest point: Black Mesa, 4,973 ft., A-1

Population: 3,751,351 (rank: 28th)

Largest city: Oklahoma City, 579,999, C-7

Nickname: The Sooner State

Capital: Oklahoma City, C-7

Oklahoma

Cities and Towns

Ada D-8
Altus D-5
Alva A-6
Anadarko D-6
Antlers E-9
Apache D-6
Arapaho C-5
Ardmore E-7

Arnett B-4
Atoka D-8
Bartlesville A-8
Beaver A-4
Bixby B-9
Blackwell A-7
Blanchard C-7
Boise City A-1
Bristow C-8
Broken Arrow B-9
Broken Bow E-10
Buffalo A-4

Cache D-6
Calera E-8
Carnegie D-6
Chandler C-7
Checotah C-9
Chelsea B-9
Cherokee A-6
Cheyenne C-4
Chickasha D-6
Chouteau B-9
Claremore B-9
Cleveland B-8

Clinton C-5
Coalgate D-8
Collinsville B-9
Commerce A-10
Cordell C-5
Coweta B-9
Cushing B-8
Davis D-7
Dewey A-8
Drumright B-8
Duncan D-6
Durant E-8

Edmond C-7
El Reno C-6
Elk City C-5
Enid B-6
Eufaula C-9
Fairview B-6
Frederick D-5
Granite D-5
Grove A-10
Guthrie B-7
Guymon A-2
Harrah C-7

Haskell C-9
Healdton E-7
Heavener D-10
Hennessey B-6
Henryetta C-8
Hinton C-6
Hobart D-5
Holdenville D-8
Hollis D-4
Hominy B-8
Hooker A-3
Hugo E-9

© Rand McNally

NOTE: Maps are not always in alphabetical order.
See Page 1 for map location in this atlas.

Oklahoma 85

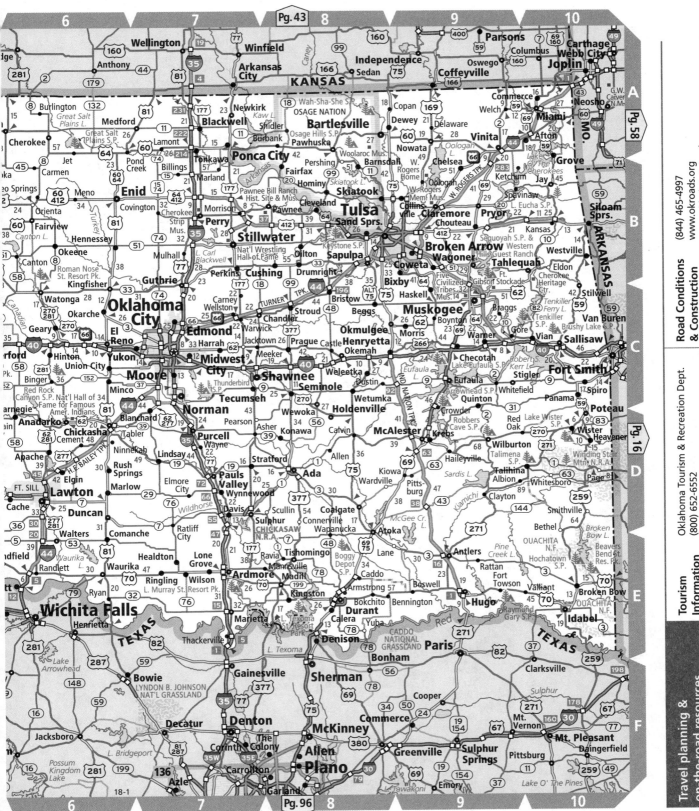

Pg. 43

Pg. 58

Pg. 16

Pg. 96

Road Conditions & Construction
(844) 465-4997
www.okroads.org
www.okladot.state.ok.us

Tourism Information
Oklahoma Tourism & Recreation Dept.
(800) 652-6552
www.travelok.com

Travel planning & on-the-road resources

Idabel	E-10	Medford	A-7	Pauls Valley	D-7	Sand Springs	B-8	Tahlequah	B-10	Westville	B-10
Jay	B-10	Miami	A-10	Pawhuska	A-8	Sapulpa	B-8	Taloga	B-5	Wewoka	C-8
Kingfisher	C-6	Midwest City	C-7	Pawnee	B-8	Sayre	C-4	Tecumseh	C-7	Wilburton	D-9
Krebs	D-9	Minco	C-7	Perkins	B-7	Seminole	C-8	Tishomingo	E-8	Wilson	E-7
Lawton	D-6	Moore	C-7	Perry	B-7	Shawnee	C-7	Tonkawa	A-7	Woodward	B-5
Lindsay	D-7	Muskogee	C-9	Picher	A-10	Skiatook	B-8	Tulsa	B-8	Wynnewood	D-7
Lone Grove	E-7	Newkirk	A-7	Ponca City	A-7	Spiro	C-10	Vinita	A-9	Yukon	C-7
Madill	E-8	Norman	C-7	Poteau	D-10	Stigler	C-9	Wagoner	B-9		
Mangum	D-5	Nowata	A-9	Prague	C-8	Stillwater	B-7	Walters	E-6		
Marietta	E-7	Okemah	C-7	Pryor	B-9	Stilwell	C-10	Watonga	C-6		
Marlow	D-6	Oklahoma City	C-7	Purcell	D-7	Stroud	C-8	Waurika	E-6		
McAlester	D-9	Okmulgee	C-8	Sallisaw	C-10	Sulphur	D-7	Weatherford	C-5		

Oregon
Cities and Towns

Albany C-2
Amity C-2
Ashland G-3
Astoria A-2
Athena B-7
Baker City C-8
Bandon E-1
Beaverton B-3
Bend D-4
Boardman B-6
Brookings G-1
Bunker Hill E-1
Burns E-7
Cannon Beach A-2
Canyon City D-7
Canyonville F-2
Cave Junction G-2
Central Point G-2
Clatskanie A-2
Condon B-5
Coos Bay E-1
Coquille E-1
Corvallis C-2
Cottage Grove E-2
Dallas C-2
Eagle Point F-3
Elgin B-8
Enterprise B-8
Estacada B-3
Eugene D-2
Florence D-1
Fossil C-5
Gladstone B-3
Glide E-2
Gold Beach F-1
Grants Pass F-2
Heppner B-6
Hermiston B-6
Hillsboro B-3
Hood River B-4
Jacksonville G-2
John Day D-7
Junction City D-2
Klamath Falls G-4
La Grande B-8
La Pine E-4
Lakeside E-1
Lakeview G-5
Lebanon C-3
Lincoln City C-1
Madras C-4
McMinnville B-2
Medford G-3
Mill City C-3
Milton-Freewater A-7
Molalla C-3
Monmouth C-2
Moro B-5
Myrtle Creek F-2
Myrtle Point F-1
Newberg B-3
Newport C-1
North Bend E-1
Nyssa D-9
Oakridge E-3
Ontario D-9
Oregon City B-3
Pendleton B-7
Philomath C-2
Phoenix G-3
Pilot Rock B-7
Portland B-3
Prineville D-5
Rainier A-3
Redmond D-4
Reedsport E-1
Rockaway Beach B-2
Roseburg E-2
St. Helens B-3
Salem C-2
Sandy B-3
Scappoose B-3
Seaside A-2
Silverton C-3
Springfield D-2
Stayton C-3
Sublimity C-3
Sutherlin E-2
Sweet Home D-3
The Dalles B-4
Tigard B-3
Tillamook B-2
Toledo C-2
Umatilla A-6
Union B-8
Vale D-9
Veneta D-2
Vernonia A-2
Waldport D-1
Warm Springs C-4
Warrenton A-2
Winston E-2
Woodburn C-3

Oregon state facts

Land area: 95,988 sq. mi. (rank: 10th)

Highest point: Mount Hood, 11,239 ft., B-4

Population: 3,831,074 (rank: 27th)

Largest city: Portland, 583,776, B-3

Nickname: The Beaver State

Capital: Salem, C-2

Pg. 104

Pg. 18

NOTE: Maps are not always in alphabetical order.
See Page 1 for map location in this atlas.

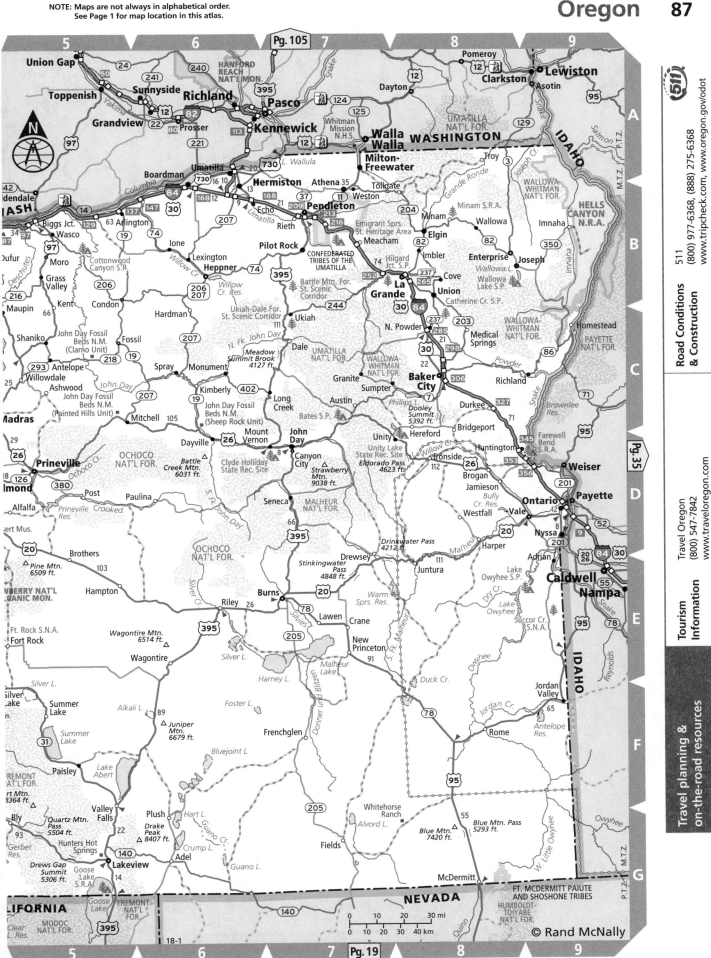

Road Conditions & Construction

511
(800) 977-6368, (888) 275-6368
www.tripcheck.com, www.oregon.gov/odot

Tourism Information

Travel Oregon
(800) 547-7842
www.traveloregon.com

Travel planning & on-the-road resources

© Rand McNally

more map
Pg. 90

Pennsylvania
state facts

Nickname: The Keystone State

Capital: Harrisburg, G-9

Population: 12,702,379 (rank: 6th)

Largest city: Philadelphia, 1,526,006, H-13

Land area: 44,743 sq. mi. (rank: 32nd)

Highest point: Mount Davis, 3,213 ft, I-4

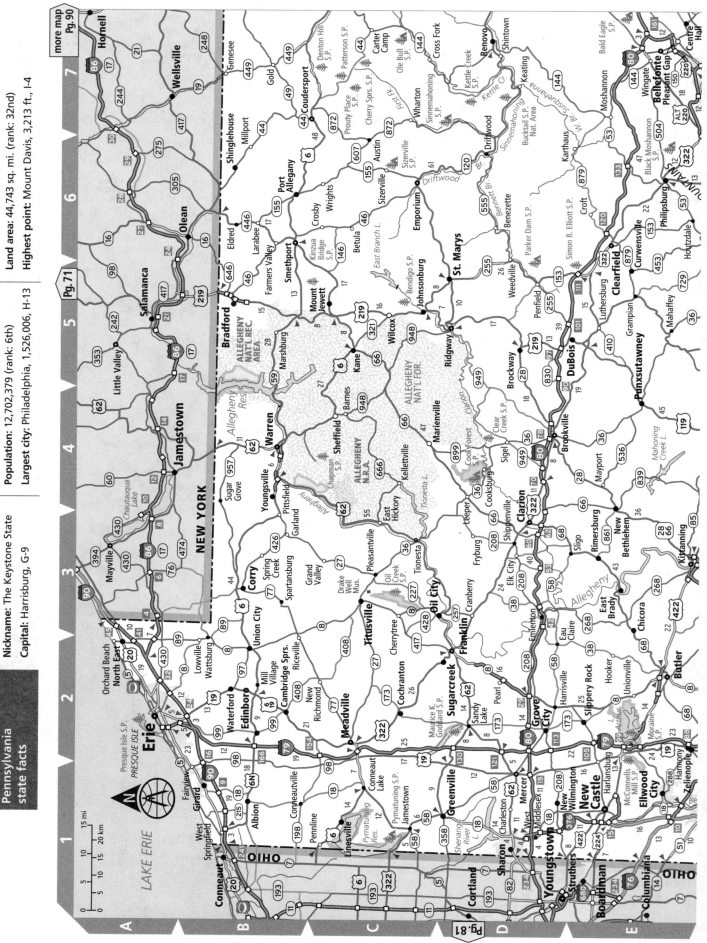

Pg. 71

Pg. 81

NOTE: Maps are not always in alphabetical order. See Page 1 for map location in this atlas.

Pennsylvania/Western 89

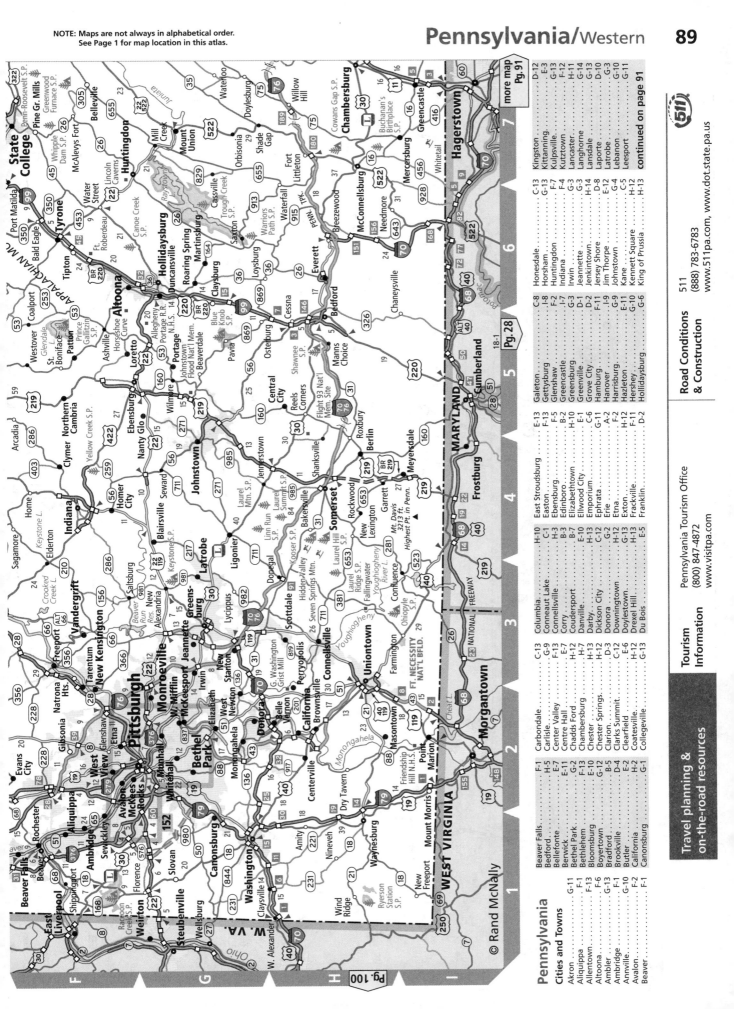

more map Pg. 91

continued on page 91

Pg. 28

Pg.100

Pennsylvania
Cities and Towns

Akron	G-11
Aliquippa	F-1
Allentown	F-13
Altoona	F-6
Ambler	G-13
Ambridge	F-1
Annville	G-10
Avalon	F-2
Beaver	F-1

Beaver Falls	F-1
Bedford	H-5
Bellefonte	E-7
Berwick	E-11
Bethel Park	G-2
Bethlehem	F-13
Bloomsburg	E-10
Boyertown	G-12
Bradford	D-3
Brookville	B-5
Butler	D-4
California	H-2
Canonsburg	G-1

Carbondale	F-1
Carlisle	H-5
Center Valley	E-7
Centre Hall	E-7
Chadds Ford	G-2
Chambersburg	H-7
Chester	H-13
Chester Springs	G-12
Clarion	D-3
Clarks Summit	E-6
Clearfield	E-2
Coatesville	H-12
Collegeville	G-13

Columbia	C-13
Conneaut Lake	G-9
Connellsville	H-3
Corry	E-7
Coudersport	H-7
Danville	H-13
Darby	H-13
Dickson City	E-12
Donora	D-3
Downingtown	G-12
Doylestown	H-12
Drexel Hill	H-13
Du Bois	D-2

East Stroudsburg	H-10
Easton	C-1
Ebensburg	H-3
Edinboro	B-3
Elizabethtown	B-7
Ellwood City	E-10
Emporium	H-13
Ephrata	C-12
Erie	G-2
Exton	A-2
Frackville	G-13
Franklin	E-5

Galeton	E-13
Gettysburg	F-13
Glenshaw	F-5
Greencastle	B-2
Greensburg	G-3
Greenville	E-1
Grove City	C-6
Hamburg	G-11
Hanover	F-11
Harrisburg	F-2
Hazleton	E-11
Hershey	F-11
Hollidaysburg	D-2

Honesdale	C-8
Horsham	G-13
Huntingdon	F-7
Indiana	F-4
Irwin	G-3
Jeannette	G-3
Jenkintown	H-14
Jersey Shore	D-8
Jim Thorpe	F-11
Johnstown	I-9
Kane	E-12
Kennett Square	E-11
King of Prussia	G-6

Kingston	D-12
Kittanning	G-13
Kulpsville	F-7
Kutztown	F-4
Lancaster	G-3
Langhorne	G-3
Lansdale	G-10
Laporte	D-10
Latrobe	G-3
Lebanon	G-10
Leesport	G-11

Travel planning & on-the-road resources

Tourism Information	Road Conditions & Construction
Pennsylvania Tourism Office (800) 847-4872 www.visitpa.com	511 (888) 783-6783 www.511pa.com, www.dot.state.pa.us

© Rand McNally

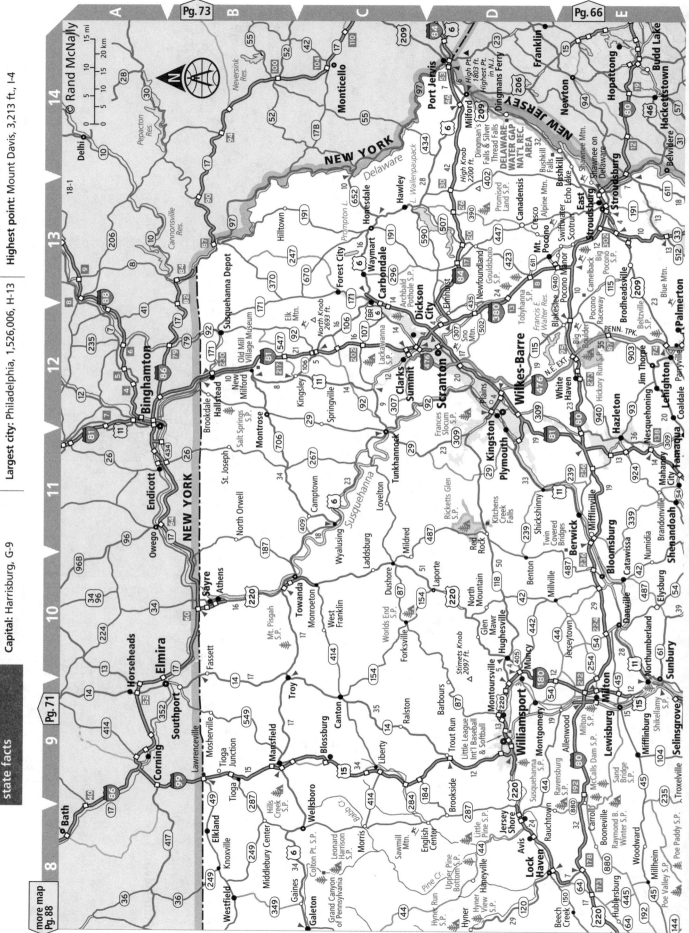

© Rand McNally

15 mi

20 km

Pennsylvania state facts

Nickname: The Keystone State
Capital: Harrisburg, G-9

Population: 12,702,379 (rank: 6th)
Largest city: Philadelphia, 1,526,006, H-13

Land area: 44,743 sq. mi. (rank: 32nd)
Highest point: Mount Davis, 3,213 ft., I-4

NEW YORK

NEW JERSEY

DELAWARE WATER GAP NAT'L REC. AREA

more map Pg. 88
Pg. 71

NOTE: Maps are not always in alphabetical order.
See Page 1 for map location in this atlas.

Pennsylvania/Eastern **91**

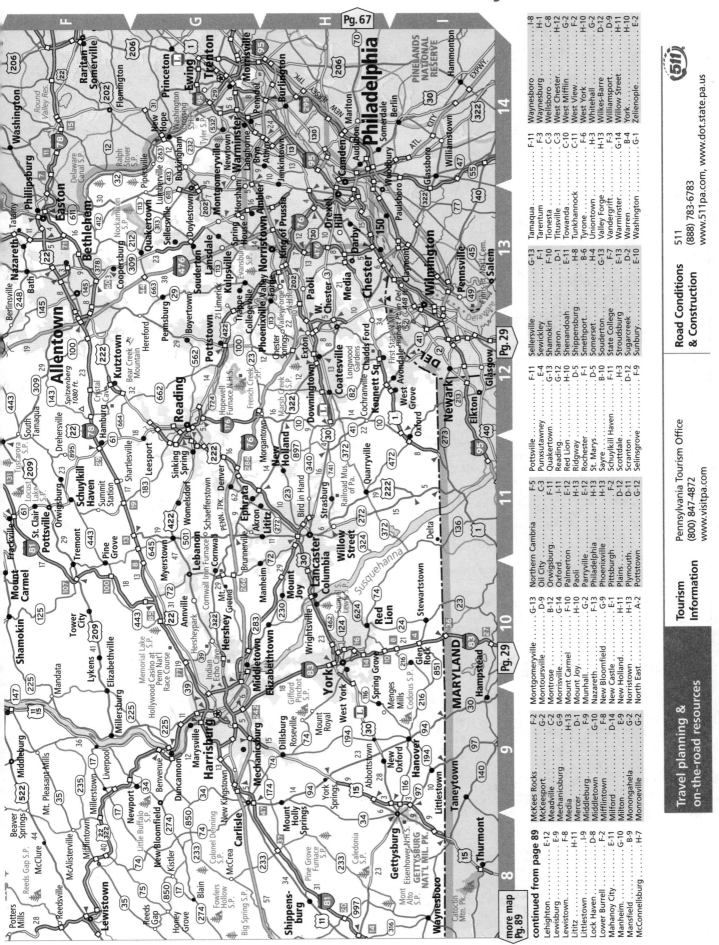

Waynesboro	F-11
Waynesburg	F-3
Wellsboro	C-3
West Chester	C-3
West Mifflin	C-10
West View	C-11
West York	H-8
Whitehall	F-6
Wilkes-Barre	H-3
Williamsport	D-12
Willow Street	D-9
York	F-3
Zelienople	G-14
	B-4
	E-2

Tamaqua	G-13
Tarentum	F-1
Tionesta	F-10
Titusville	D-1
Towanda	E-11
Tunkhannock	H-8
Tyrone	B-6
Uniontown	F-1
Valley Forge	H-4
Vandergrift	G-13
Warminster	F-7
Warren	E-13
Washington	D-11
	D-2
	E-10

Sellersville	F-11
Sewickley	E-4
Shamokin	G-13
Sharon	D-1
Shenandoah	H-10
Shippensburg	D-5
Smethport	F-1
Somerset	B-10
Souderton	F-11
State College	H-3
Stroudsburg	D-12
Sugarcreek	G-12
Sunbury	F-9

Pottsville	F-5
Punxsutawney	C-3
Quakertown	F-11
Reading	J-1
Red Lion	E-12
Ridgway	H-13
Rochester	E-2
St. Marys	H-13
Sayre	H-13
Schuylkill Haven	F-2
Scottdale	D-12
Scranton	D-11
Selinsgrove	G-12

Northern Cambria	G-13
Oil City	D-9
Orwigsburg	B-12
Oxford	G-14
Palmerton	F-10
Paoli	E-12
Parryville	E-12
Philadelphia	H-13
Phoenixville	F-13
Pittsburgh	G-9
Plains	E-1
Plymouth	H-11
Pottstown	H-13

Montgomeryville	F-2
Montoursville	G-2
Montrose	C-2
Morrisville	H-13
Mount Carmel	D-1
Mount Joy	E-10
Munhall	F-9
Nazareth	G-10
New Bloomfield	F-8
New Castle	E-1
New Holland	E-9
Norristown	G-2
North East	A-2

McKees Rocks	F-2
McKeesport	G-2
Meadville	C-2
Mechanicsburg	H-13
Media	D-1
Mercer	H-11
Middleburg	F-9
Middletown	G-10
Milford	F-2
Milton	D-14
Monongahela	G-2
Monroeville	H-7

continued from page 89
Lehighton	E-12
Lewisburg	E-9
Lewistown	F-8
Lititz	H-11
Littlestown	I-9
Lock Haven	D-8
Lower Burrell	F-2
Mahanoy City	E-11
Manheim	G-10
Mansfield	B-9
McConnellsburg	H-7

more map
Pg. 89

Travel planning & on-the-road resources

Tourism Information
Pennsylvania Tourism Office
(800) 847-4872
www.visitpa.com

Road Conditions & Construction
511
(888) 783-6783
www.511pa.com, www.dot.state.pa.us

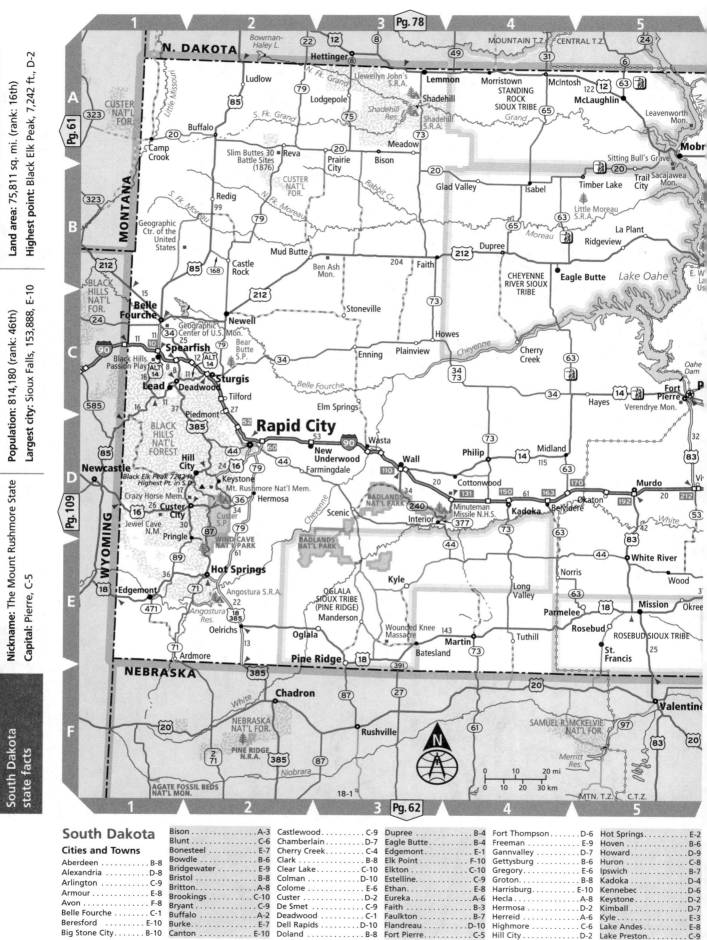

South Dakota state facts

Nickname: The Mount Rushmore State

Capital: Pierre, C-5

Population: 814,180 (rank: 46th)

Largest city: Sioux Falls, 153,888, E-10

Land area: 75,811 sq. mi. (rank: 16th)

Highest point: Black Elk Peak, 7,242 ft., D-2

South Dakota

Cities and Towns

Aberdeen	B-8	Bison	A-3
Alexandria	D-8	Blunt	C-6
Arlington	C-9	Bonesteel	E-7
Armour	E-8	Bowdle	B-6
Avon	F-8	Bridgewater	E-9
Belle Fourche	C-1	Bristol	B-8
Beresford	E-10	Britton	A-8
Big Stone City	B-10	Bryant	C-9
		Buffalo	A-2
		Burke	E-7
		Canton	E-10

Castlewood	C-9	Dupree	B-4
Chamberlain	D-7	Eagle Butte	B-4
Cherry Creek	C-4	Edgemont	E-1
Clark	B-8	Elk Point	F-10
Clear Lake	C-10	Elkton	C-10
Colman	D-10	Estelline	C-9
Colome	E-6	Ethan	E-8
Custer	D-2	Eureka	A-6
De Smet	C-9	Faith	B-3
Deadwood	C-1	Faulkton	B-7
Dell Rapids	D-10	Flandreau	D-10
Doland	B-8	Fort Pierre	C-5

Fort Thompson	D-6	Hot Springs	E-2
Freeman	E-9	Hoven	B-6
Gannvalley	D-7	Howard	D-9
Gettysburg	B-6	Huron	C-8
Gregory	E-6	Ipswich	B-7
Groton	B-8	Kadoka	D-4
Harrisburg	E-10	Kennebec	D-6
Hecla	A-8	Keystone	D-2
Herreid	A-6	Kimball	D-7
Hermosa	D-2	Kyle	E-3
Highmore	C-6	Lake Andes	E-8
Hill City	D-2	Lake Preston	C-9

NOTE: Maps are not always in alphabetical order.
See Page 1 for map location in this atlas.

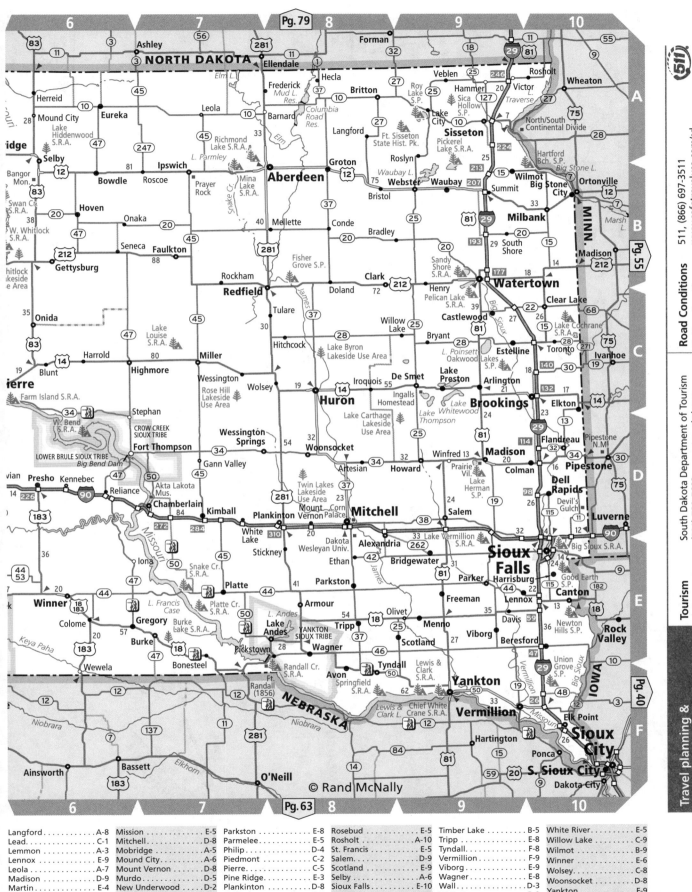

Road Conditions & Construction

511, (866) 697-3511
www.safetraveluSA.com/sd
www.sddot.com

Tourism Information

South Dakota Department of Tourism
(800) 732-5682; www.travelsd.com,
www.travelsouthdakota.com

Travel planning & on-the-road resources

Langford A-8	Mission E-5	Parkston E-8	Rosebud E-5	Timber Lake B-5	White River E-5
Lead C-1	Mitchell D-8	Parmelee E-5	Rosholt A-10	Tripp E-8	Willow Lake C-9
Lemmon A-3	Mobridge A-5	Philip D-4	St. Francis E-5	Tyndall F-8	Wilmot B-9
Lennox E-9	Mound City A-6	Piedmont C-2	Salem D-9	Vermillion F-9	Winner E-6
Leola A-7	Mount Vernon . . . D-8	Pierre D-6	Scotland E-9	Viborg E-9	Wolsey C-8
Madison D-9	Murdo D-5	Pine Ridge E-3	Selby A-6	Wagner E-8	Woonsocket D-8
Martin E-4	New Underwood . . D-2	Plankinton D-8	Sioux Falls E-10	Wall D-3	Yankton F-9
McIntosh A-4	Newell C-2	Platte E-7	Sisseton A-9	Watertown B-9	
McLaughlin A-5	Oglala E-3	Presho D-6	Spearfish C-1	Waubay B-9	
Menno E-9	Olivet E-9	Rapid City D-2	Stickney E-8	Webster B-9	
Milbank B-10	Onida C-6	Redfield B-8	Sturgis C-2	Wessington Springs . D-7	
Miller C-7	Parker E-9	Roscoe B-7	Summit B-9	White Lake D-7	

Texas
state facts

Nickname: The Lone Star State

Capital: Austin, E-9

Population: 25,145,561 (rank: 2nd)

Largest city: Houston, 2,099,451, F-11

Land area: 261,231 sq. mi. (rank: 2nd)

Highest point: Guadalupe Peak, 8,749 ft., C-2

For continuation see inset on pg. 95

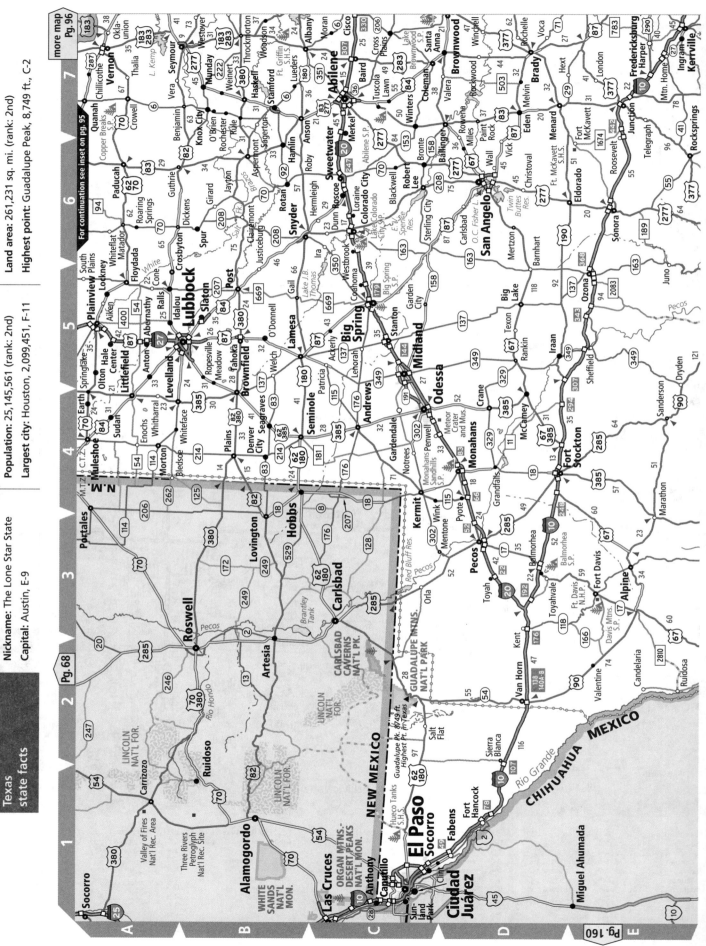

Pg. 68

Pg. 160

NOTE: Maps are not always in alphabetical order.
See Page 1 for map location in this atlas.

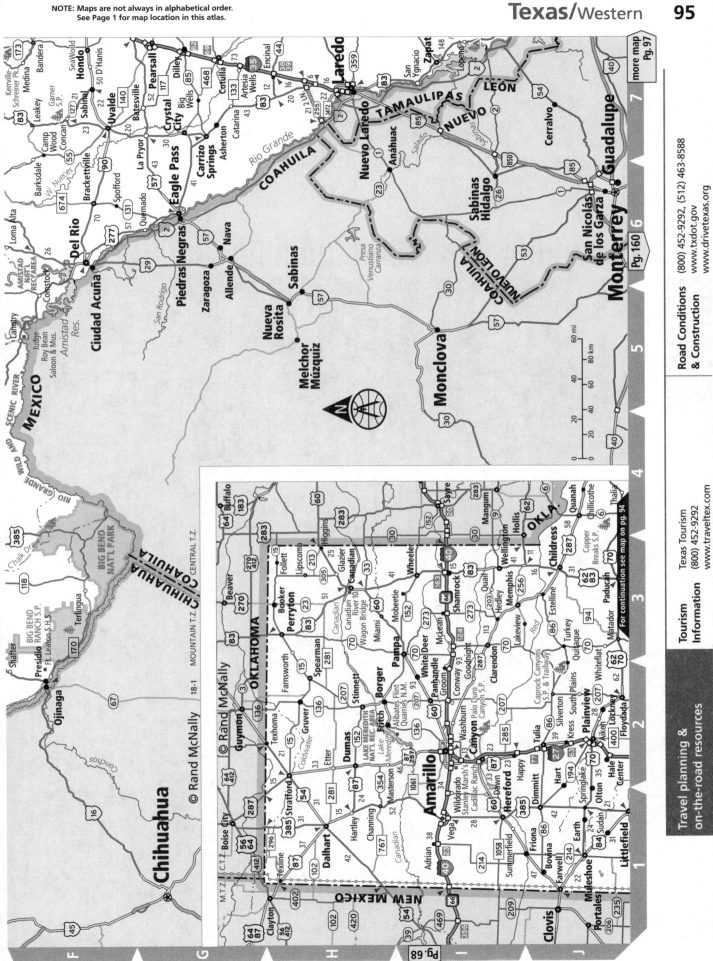

© Rand McNally

© Rand McNally

more map Pg. 97

Pg. 160

For continuation see map on pg. 94

BIG BEND NAT'L PARK

BIG BEND RANCH S.P.

AMISTAD NAT'L REC. AREA

LAKE MEREDITH NAT'L REC. AREA

Palo Duro Canyon S.P.

Caprock Canyons S.P. & Trailway

MEXICO

CHIHUAHUA

COAHUILA

NUEVO LEÓN

TAMAULIPAS

LEÓN

NEW MEXICO

OKLAHOMA

OKLA.

Road Conditions & Construction
(800) 452-9292, (512) 463-8588
www.txdot.gov
www.drivetexas.org

Tourism Information
Texas Tourism
(800) 452-9292
www.traveltex.com

Travel planning & on-the-road resources

Texas state facts

Nickname: The Lone Star State
Capital: Austin, E-9

Population: 25,145,561 (rank: 2nd)
Largest city: Houston, 2,099,451, F-11

Land area: 261,231 sq. mi. (rank: 2nd)
Highest point: Guadalupe Peak, 8,749 ft., C-2

Texas

Cities and Towns

Abilene	C-7	Johnson City	E-8
Albany	B-7	Jourdanton	G-8
Alice	H-8	Junction	E-7
Allen	B-10	Karnes City	G-9
Alpine	E-3	Kaufman	C-10
Alvin	F-11	Kermit	C-4
Amarillo	I-2	Kerrville	E-7
Anahuac	F-12	Kingsville	H-9
Anderson	E-10	Kingwood	F-11
Angleton	F-11	Kountze	E-12
Anson	C-4	La Grange	E-10
Archer City	B-7	La Porte	F-11
Arlington	D-8	Lake Jackson	F-11
Aspermont	B-9	Lamesa	B-5
Athens	C-10	Lampasas	D-8
Austin	E-9	Laredo	H-7
Baird	C-7	Leakey	F-7
Ballinger	D-7	Levelland	A-4
Bandera	F-7	Liberty	E-12
Bastrop	E-9	Linden	B-12
Baytown	F-11	Lipscomb	H-3
Beaumont	E-12	Littlefield	A-4
Beeville	G-9	Livingston	E-11
Bellville	E-10	Llano	E-8
Belton	D-9	Lockhart	F-9
Benjamin	B-7	Longview	C-11
Big Lake	D-5	Lubbock	B-5
Big Spring	C-5	Lufkin	D-11
Boerne	F-8	Madisonville	D-10
Bonham	A-10	Marlin	D-9
Borger	I-3	Marshall	B-11
Brackettville	F-6	Matador	B-5
Brady	D-7	McAllen	J-8
Breckenridge	C-8	McKinney	B-10
Brownfield	B-4	Memphis	I-3
Brownsville	J-9	Menard	D-7
Brownwood	D-7	Mentone	C-3
Bryan	E-10	Mercedes	J-9
Burnet	E-8	Meridian	D-9
Caldwell	E-10	Mertzon	D-6
Cameron	D-9	Miami	H-3
Canadian	H-3	Midland	C-5
Canton	C-10	Mineral Wells	C-8
Canyon	I-2	Mission	J-8
Carrizo Springs	G-7	Monahans	C-4
Carthage	C-12	Montague	B-9
Cedar Park	E-9	Morton	A-4
Center	C-12	Mount Pleasant	B-11
Centerville	D-10	Mount Vernon	B-11
Channing	H-1	Muleshoe	A-3
Childress	I-3	Nacogdoches	D-11
Clarendon	I-3	New Braunfels	F-8
Clarksville	A-11	Odessa	C-4
Cleburne	C-9	Orange	E-12
Coldspring	E-11	Ozona	D-6
Coleman	D-7	Paducah	I-3
College Station	E-10	Paint Rock	D-7
Colorado City	C-6	Palestine	C-11
Columbus	F-10	Palo Pinto	C-8
Comanche	C-8	Pampa	H-2
Conroe	E-11	Panhandle	I-2
Cooper	B-11	Paris	A-11
Copperas Cove	D-9	Pearsall	G-7
Corpus Christi	H-9	Pecos	C-3
Corinth	C-10	Perryton	H-2
Corsicana	C-10	Pharr	J-8
Cotulla	G-7	Pittsburg	B-11
Crane	D-4	Plains	B-4
		Plainview	A-4
		Plano	B-10
		Port Arthur	E-12
		Port Lavaca	G-10
		Post	B-5

NOTE: Maps are not always in alphabetical order.
See Page 1 for map location in this atlas.

Crockett ... D-11
Crosbyton ... A-5
Crowell ... A-7
Crystal City ... G-7
Cuero ... F-9
Daingerfield ... B-11
Dalhart ... H-1
Dallas ... B-10
Decatur ... B-9
Del Rio ... F-6
Denison ... A-10
Denton ... B-9
Dickens ... F-11
Dickinson ... J-1
Dimmitt ... J-9
Donna ... H-2
Dumas ... G-6
Eagle Pass ... C-8
Eastland ... I-8
Edinburg ... G-10
Edna ... C-1
El Paso ... D-6
Eldorado ... B-10
Emory ... C-10
Ennis ... C-10
Fairfield ... H-8
Falfurrias ... J-1
Farwell ... A-5
Floresville ... E-3
Floydada ... D-4
Fort Davis ... B-9
Fort Stockton ... D-10
Fort Worth ... E-8
Franklin ... B-5
Fredericksburg ... A-9
Gail ... F-12
Gainesville ... C-5
Galveston ... D-9
Garden City ... G-8
Gatesville ... E-9
George West ... E-9
Georgetown ... B-11
Giddings ... C-9
Gilmer ... D-8
Glen Rose ... G-9
Goldthwaite ... B-8
Goliad ... C-9
Gonzales ... B-10
Graham ... D-10
Granbury ... F-11
Greenville ... F-10
Groesbeck ... B-7
Groveton ... D-8
Guthrie ... D-9
Hallettsville ... J-9
Hamilton ... B-7
Harker Heights ... C-11
Harlingen ... F-7
Haskell ... D-2
Hebbronville ... G-9
Hemphill ... D-9
Hempstead ... B-9
Henderson ... E-11
Henrietta ... A-8
Hereford ... I-1
Hillsboro ... C-9
Hondo ... F-7
Houston ... F-11
Huntsville ... B-8
Jacksboro ... B-8
Jacksonville ... C-11
Jasper ... A-8
Jayton ... I-3
Jefferson ... D-12

Quanah ... J-4
Quitman ... B-11
Rankin ... D-5
Raymondville ... G-9
Refugio ... F-11
Richmond ... I-8
Rio Grande City ... C-6
Robert Lee ... H-9
Robstown ... B-6
Roby ... E-6
Rockport ... B-10
Rocksprings ... F-11
Rockwall ... C-11
Rosenberg ... D-6
Round Rock ... C-8
Rusk ... I-8
San Angelo ... G-10
San Antonio ... C-1
San Augustine ... H-8
San Benito ... D-6
San Diego ... B-10
San Marcos ... C-10
San Saba ... C-10
Sanderson ... H-8
Sarita ... J-1
Seguin ... A-5
Seminole ... E-3
Seymour ... D-4
Sherman ... B-9
Sierra Blanca ... D-10
Silverton ... E-8
Sinton ... B-5
Snyder ... A-9
Socorro ... F-12
Sonora ... C-5
Spearman ... D-9
Spring ... G-8
Stanton ... E-9
Stephenville ... E-9
Sterling City ... B-11
Stinnett ... C-9
Stratford ... D-8
Sugar Land ... G-9
Sulphur Springs ... B-8
Sweetwater ... C-9
Tahoka ... B-10
Taylor ... D-10
Temple ... F-11
Terrell ... F-10
Texarkana ... B-7
Texas City ... D-8
The Colony ... D-9
The Woodlands ... J-9
Throckmorton ... B-7
Tilden ... C-11
Tulia ... F-7
Tyler ... D-2
Uvalde ... G-9
Van Horn ... D-9
Vega ... B-9
Victoria ... E-11
Waco ... A-8
Waxahachie ... I-1
Weatherford ... C-9
Wellington ... F-7
Weslaco ... F-11
Wharton ... B-8
Wheeler ... B-8
Wichita Falls ... C-11
Woodville ... A-8
Zapata ... I-3
... D-12
... B-6
... B-12

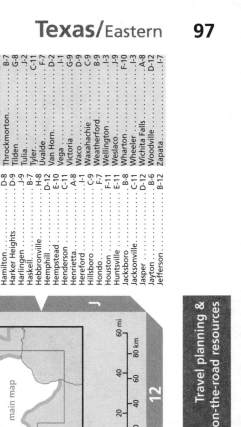

© Rand McNally

60 mi
0 20 40 60 80 km

see map on pg. 95
main map

Utah
state facts

Nickname: The Beehive State
Capital: Salt Lake City, C-4

Population: 2,763,885 (rank: 34th)
Largest city: Salt Lake City, 186,440, C-4

Land area: 82,169 sq. mi. (rank: 12th)
Highest point: Kings Peak, 13,528 ft., C-5

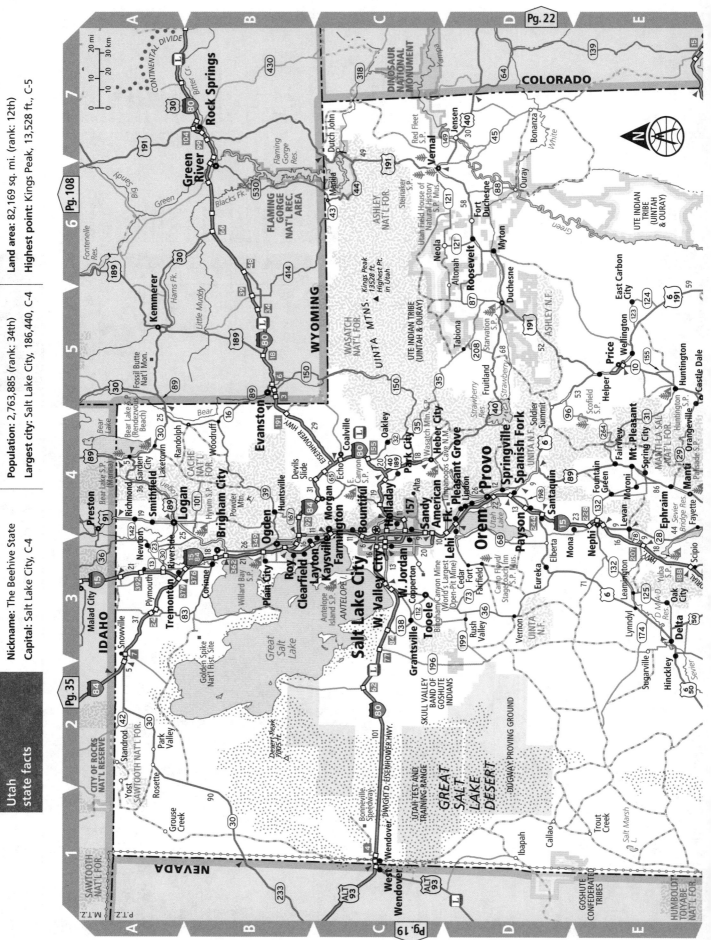

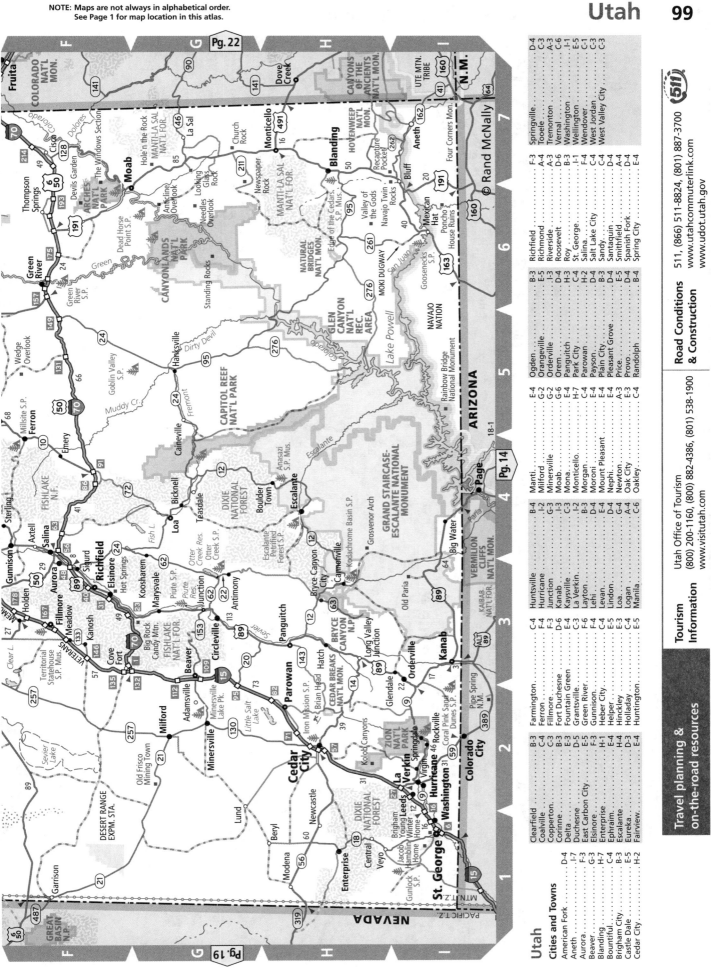

more map Pg. 102
Pg. 89
Pg. 81
Pg. 82
Pg. 46

Virginia state facts

Nickname: Old Dominion
Capital: Richmond, G-11

Population: 8,001,024 (rank: 12th)
Largest city: Virginia Beach, 437,994, H-13

Land area: 39,490 sq. mi. (rank: 36th)
Highest point: Mount Rogers, 5,729 ft., I-4

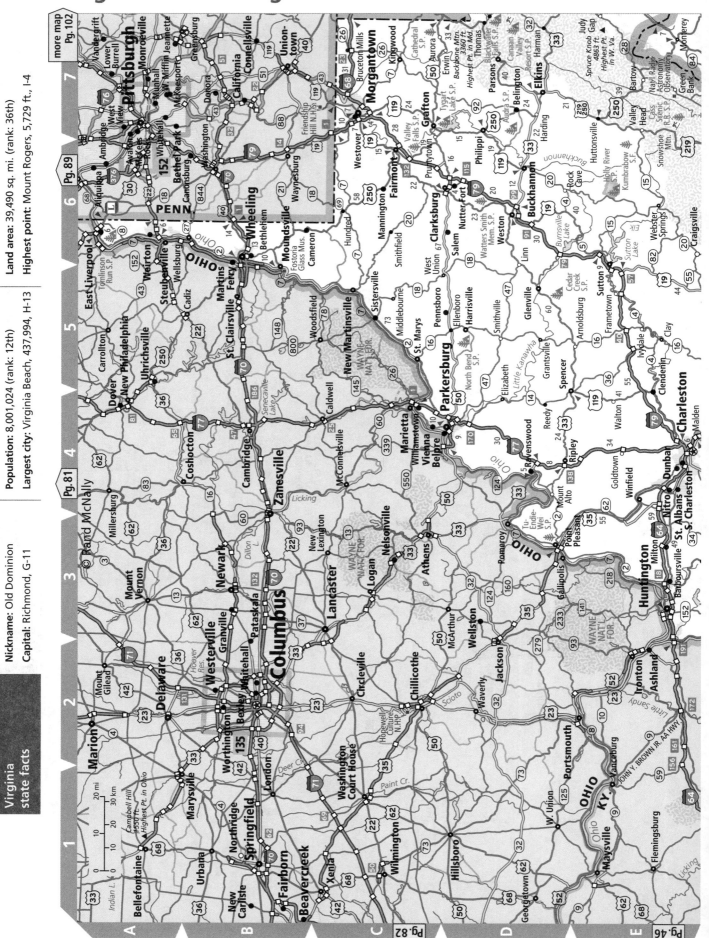

© Rand McNally

NOTE: Maps are not always in alphabetical order.
See Page 1 for map location in this atlas.

Virginia • West Virginia/Western   **101**

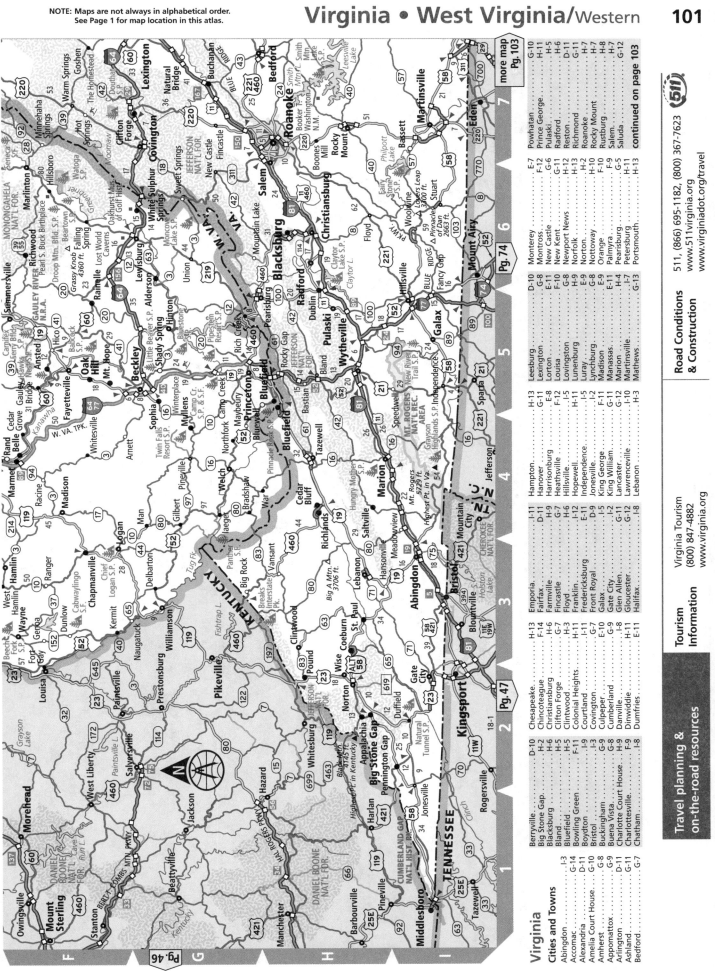

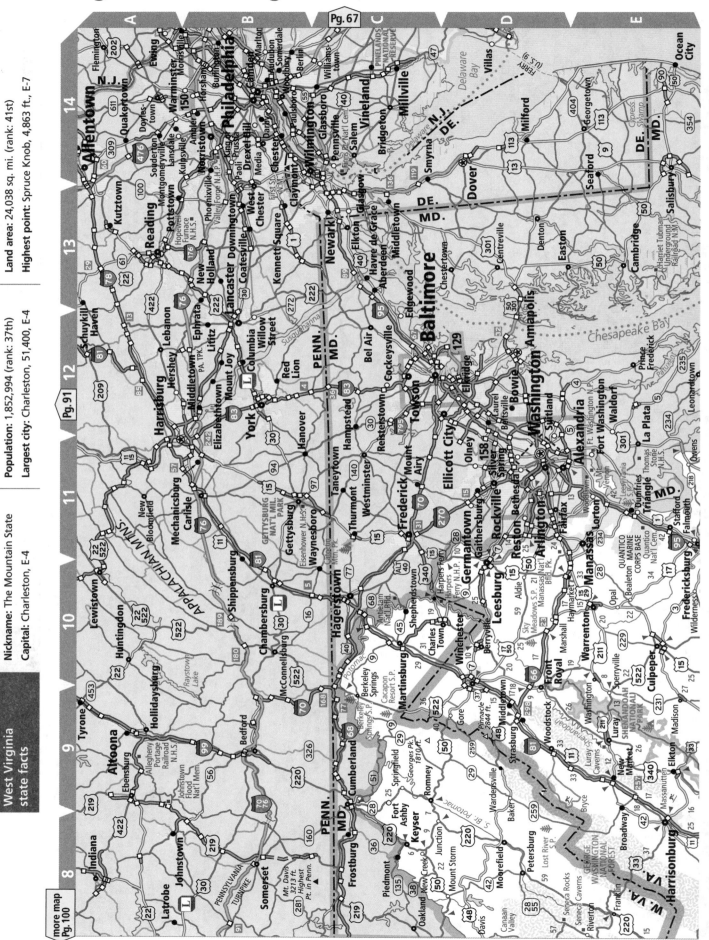

West Virginia state facts

Nickname: The Mountain State

Capital: Charleston, E-4

Population: 1,852,994 (rank: 37th)

Largest city: Charleston, 51,400, E-4

Land area: 24,038 sq. mi. (rank: 41st)

Highest point: Spruce Knob, 4,863 ft., E-7

more map Pg. 100
Pg. 91
Pg. 67

NOTE: Maps are not always in alphabetical order.
See Page 1 for map location in this atlas.

Virginia • West Virginia/Eastern **103**

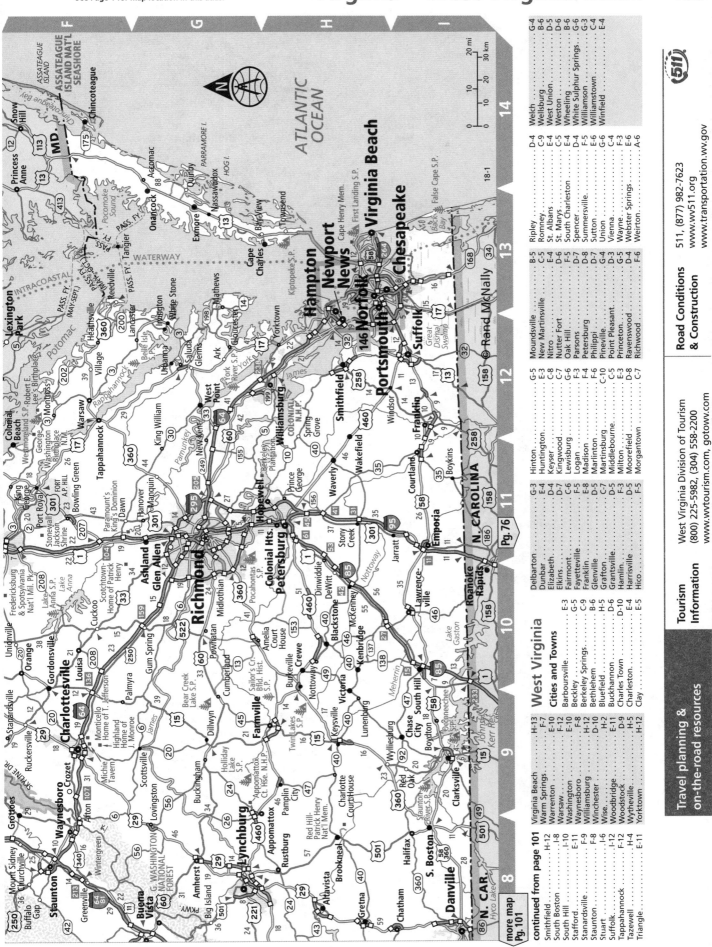

Welch	G-4
Wellsburg	B-6
West Union	D-5
Weston	D-6
Wheeling	B-6
White Sulphur Springs	G-6
Williamson	F-5
Williamstown	C-4
Winfield	E-4

Ripley	B-5
Romney	C-9
St. Albans	E-4
St. Marys	C-5
South Charleston	E-4
Spencer	D-4
Summersville	F-5
Sutton	E-6
Union	G-6
Vienna	C-4
Wayne	G-3
Webster Springs	E-6
Weirton	A-6

Moundsville	B-6
New Martinsville	B-6
Nitro	E-4
Nutter Fort	D-6
Oak Hill	G-6
Parsons	D-7
Petersburg	D-8
Philippi	D-7
Pineville	G-4
Point Pleasant	C-3
Princeton	G-5
Ravenswood	C-4
Richwood	E-6

Corresponding code listings:
Moundsville	G-5
New Martinsville	E-3
Nitro	C-8
Nutter Fort	C-7
Oak Hill	G-6
Parsons	F-5
Petersburg	F-4
Philippi	E-8
Pineville	F-6
Point Pleasant	C-7
Princeton	C-5
Ravenswood	E-3
Richwood	D-8
Morgantown	C-7

Hinton	G-3
Huntington	E-4
Keyser	D-4
Kingwood	D-7
Lewisburg	C-6
Logan	F-5
Madison	E-8
Marlinton	D-5
Martinsburg	C-7
Middlebourne	D-5
Milton	F-3
Moorefield	D-5
Morgantown	F-5

Delbarton	G-5
Dunbar	E-4
Elizabeth	D-4
Elkins	E-3
Fairmont	G-5
Fayetteville	C-9
Franklin	E-8
Glenville	D-5
Grafton	H-5
Grantsville	D-6
Hamlin	C-5
Harrisville	E-4
Hico	E-5

West Virginia

Cities and Towns

Barboursville	E-3
Beckley	G-5
Berkeley Springs	C-9
Bethlehem	B-6
Bluefield	H-5
Buckhannon	E-11
Charles Town	D-10
Charleston	E-4
Clay	H-12

continued from page 101

Smithfield	H-13
South Boston	F-7
South Hill	E-10
Stafford	E-12
Stanardsville	E-10
Staunton	E-11
Stuart	F-9
Suffolk	F-8
Tappahannock	D-10
Tazewell	I-6
Triangle	I-12

Virginia Beach	H-12
Warm Springs	I-8
Warrenton	E-10
Warsaw	E-10
Washington	F-8
Waynesboro	F-9
Williamsburg	F-8
Winchester	H-2
Wise	I-6
Woodbridge	I-12
Woodstock	F-12
Wytheville	H-4
Yorktown	E-11

more map
Pg. 101

Road Conditions & Construction
511, (877) 982-7623
www.wv511.org
www.transportation.wv.gov

Tourism Information
West Virginia Division of Tourism
(800) 225-5982, (304) 558-2200
www.wvtourism.com, gotowv.com

Travel planning & on-the-road resources

© Rand McNally

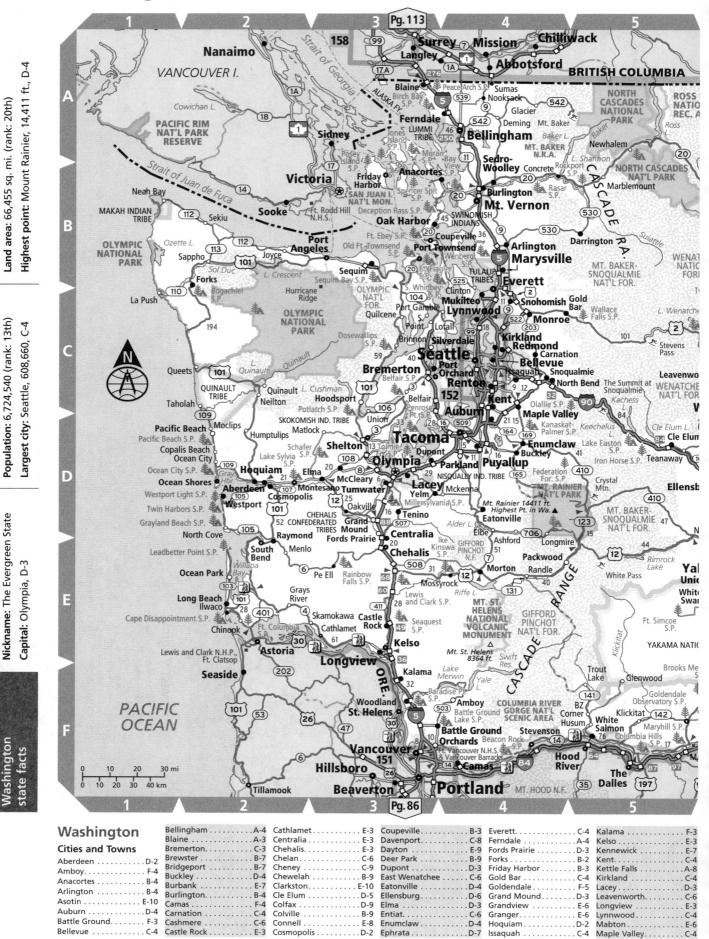

Pg. 113

Pg. 86

Washington

Cities and Towns

Aberdeen D-2	Cathlamet E-3	Coupeville B-3	Everett C-4	Kalama F-3
Amboy F-4	Centralia E-3	Davenport C-8	Ferndale A-4	Kelso E-3
Anacortes B-4	Chehalis E-3	Dayton E-9	Fords Prairie D-3	Kennewick E-7
Arlington B-4	Chelan C-6	Deer Park B-9	Forks B-2	Kent C-4
Asotin E-10	Cheney C-9	Dupont D-3	Friday Harbor B-3	Kettle Falls A-8
Auburn D-4	Chewelah B-9	East Wenatchee C-6	Gold Bar C-4	Kirkland C-4
Battle Ground F-3	Clarkston E-10	Eatonville D-4	Goldendale F-5	Lacey D-3
Bellevue C-4	Cle Elum D-5	Ellensburg D-6	Grand Mound D-3	Leavenworth C-6
Bellingham A-4	Colfax D-9	Elma D-3	Grandview E-6	Longview E-3
Blaine A-3	Colville B-9	Entiat C-6	Granger E-6	Lynnwood C-4
Bremerton C-3	Connell E-8	Enumclaw D-4	Hoquiam D-2	Mabton E-6
Brewster B-7	Cosmopolis D-2	Ephrata D-7	Issaquah C-4	Maple Valley C-4
Bridgeport B-7				
Buckley D-4				
Burbank E-7				
Burlington B-4				
Camas F-4				
Carnation C-4				
Cashmere C-6				
Castle Rock E-3				

NOTE: Maps are not always in alphabetical order.
See Page 1 for map location in this atlas.

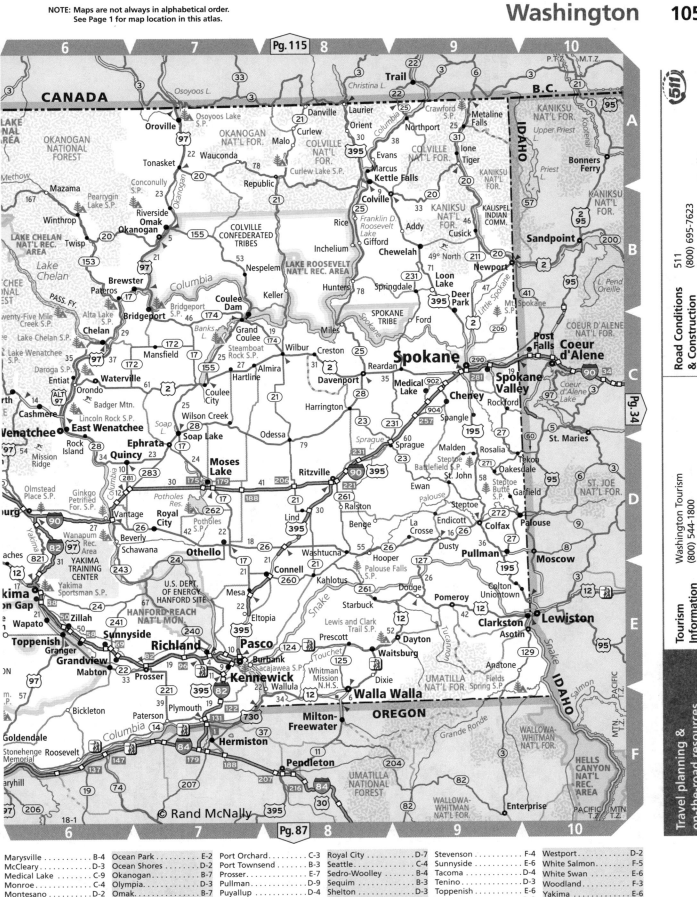

© Rand McNally

Marysville B-4	Ocean Park E-2	Port Orchard C-3
McCleary D-3	Ocean Shores D-2	Port Townsend C-3
Medical Lake C-9	Okanogan B-7	Prosser E-7
Monroe C-4	Olympia D-3	Pullman D-9
Montesano D-2	Omak B-7	Puyallup D-4
Morton E-4	Orchards F-3	Quincy D-6
Moses Lake D-7	Oroville A-7	Raymond E-2
Mount Vernon B-4	Othello D-7	Redmond C-4
Mukilteo C-4	Parkland D-4	Renton C-4
Newport B-9	Pasco E-7	Republic A-8
North Bend C-4	Pomeroy E-9	Richland E-7
Oak Harbor B-3	Port Angeles B-3	Ritzville D-8

Royal City D-7	Stevenson F-4	Westport D-2
Seattle C-4	Sunnyside E-6	White Salmon F-5
Sedro-Woolley B-4	Tacoma D-4	White Swan E-6
Sequim B-3	Tenino D-3	Woodland F-3
Shelton D-3	Toppenish E-6	Yakima E-6
Silverdale C-3	Tumwater D-3	Yelm D-3
Snohomish C-4	Union Gap E-6	Zillah E-6
Snoqualmie C-4	Vancouver F-3	
Soap Lake C-7	Walla Walla F-8	
South Bend E-2	Wapato E-6	
Spokane C-9	Waterville C-6	
Spokane Valley C-9	Wenatchee C-6	

511
Road Conditions & Construction
511
(800) 695-7623
www.wsdot.wa.gov/traffic

Tourism Information
Washington Tourism
(800) 544-1800
www.experiencewa.com

Travel planning & on-the-road resources

Wisconsin state facts

Nickname: The Badger State

Capital: Madison, G-4

Population: 5,686,986 (rank: 20th)

Largest city: Milwaukee, 594,833, G-6

Land area: 54,158 sq. mi. (rank: 25th)

Highest point: Timms Hill, 1,951 ft., D-4

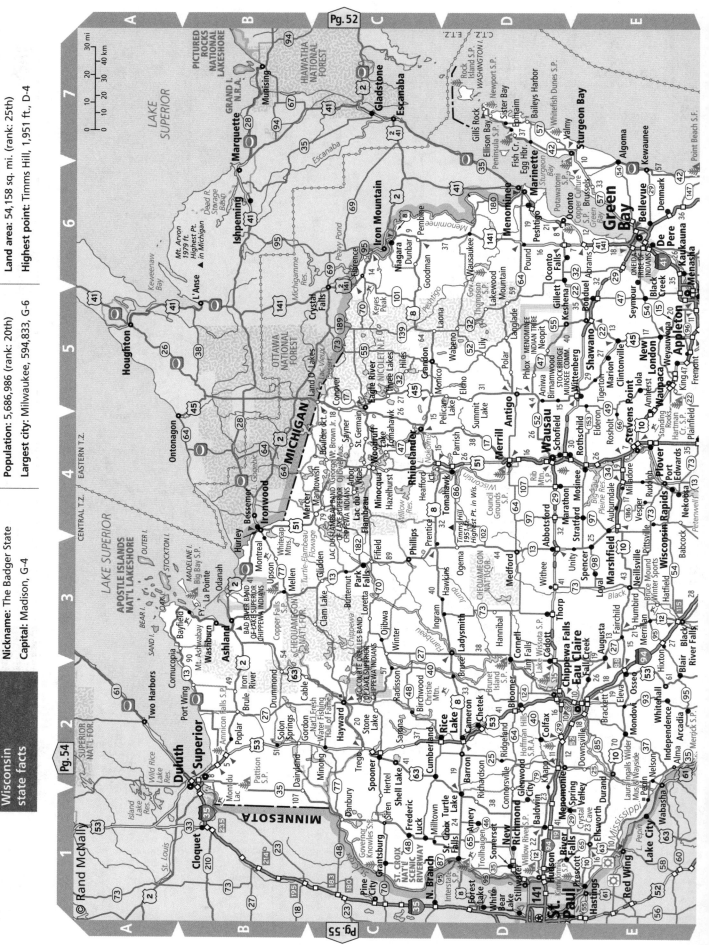

© Rand McNally

NOTE: Maps are not always in alphabetical order.
See Page 1 for map location in this atlas.

Wisconsin 107

Wisconsin

Cities and Towns

Antigo	D-5
Appleton	E-5
Arbor Vitae	C-4
Ashland	B-3
Baraboo	G-4
Barron	D-2
Beaver Dam	E-6
Beloit	H-5
Black River Falls	E-3
Bonduel	E-5
Chilton	F-6
Chippewa Falls	D-4
Darlington	H-4
De Pere	E-6
Dodgeville	G-4
Eau Claire	E-2
Elkhorn	H-5
Ellsworth	D-2
Fond du Lac	E-1
Fort Atkinson	E-6
Franklin	H-5
Grafton	E-3
Green Bay	E-6
Hartford	F-6
Hayward	D-4
Hudson	H-4
Janesville	G-4
Jefferson	E-2
Juneau	H-5
Kaukauna	F-5
Kenosha	E-1
Kewaunee	F-5
La Crosse	G-6
Ladysmith	G-6
Lancaster	G-6
Madison	G-6
Manitowoc	C-2
Marinette	D-1
Marshfield	H-5
Mauston	F-4
Medford	D-3
Menasha	G-5
Menomonee Falls	H-6
Menomonie	H-6
Mequon	G-6
Merrill	F-2
Middleton	D-3
Milwaukee	H-3
Monroe	G-4
Neenah	F-6
Neillsville	D-6
New Berlin	E-4
New Richmond	F-4
Oconomowoc	D-3
Oconto	E-5
Onalaska	D-2
Oshkosh	G-6
Peshtigo	D-4
Pewaukee	G-4
Plover	G-6
Port Washington	H-4
Portage	F-5
Prairie du Chien	E-3
Racine	G-6
Rhinelander	D-1
Rice Lake	G-5
Richland Center	D-2
River Falls	D-1
Rothschild	F-5
Sauk City	G-4
Shawano	E-5
Sheboygan	E-4
South Milwaukee	G-6
Sparta	G-4
Stevens Point	E-4
Stoughton	G-5
Sturgeon Bay	H-6
Sun Prairie	C-4
Superior	D-2
Thiensville	B-2
Two Rivers	D-1
Viroqua	G-4
Washburn	E-5
Watertown	F-6
Waukesha	G-6
Waupaca	F-3
Waupun	E-4
Wausau	G-5
Wautoma	E-7
West Bend	G-5
Whitefish Bay	B-2
Whitewater	G-6
Wisconsin Dells	F-6
Wisconsin Rapids	F-3
	B-3

Travel planning & on-the-road resources

Tourism Information	Wisconsin Department of Tourism	(800) 432-8747, (608) 266-2161
	www.travelwisconsin.com	
Road Conditions & Construction	511	(866) 511-9472
		www.511wi.gov

Wyoming

Cities and Towns

Afton D-1
Albin F-9
Alpine C-1
Baggs G-5
Bairoil E-5
Bar Nunn D-6
Basin B-4
Beulah A-9
Big Horn A-6
Big Piney D-2
Bondurant C-2
Buffalo B-6
Burlington B-4
Burns F-9
Carpenter G-9
Casper D-6
Centennial F-7
Cheyenne F-8
Chugwater F-8
Clearmont A-6
Cody A-3
Cokeville E-1
Daniel D-2
Dayton A-5
Deaver A-4
Diamondville F-2
Douglas D-7
Dubois C-3
Eden E-3
Edgerton C-6
Elk Mountain F-6
Evanston F-1
Evansville D-6
Farson E-3
Fort Bridger F-2
Fort Laramie E-8
Fort Washakie D-4
Freedom D-1
Garland A-4
Gillette B-7
Glendo D-8
Granger F-2
Green River F-3
Greybull B-4
Guernsey E-8
Hanna E-6
Horse Creek F-8
Hudson D-4
Hulett A-8
Jackson C-1
Jeffrey City D-5
Kaycee C-6
Kemmerer E-2
Kinnear D-4
La Barge E-2
LaGrange F-9
Lander D-4
Laramie F-7
Linch C-6
Lingle E-9
Lovell A-4
Lucerne C-4
Lusk D-8
Lyman F-2
Manderson B-5
Manville D-8
Marbleton D-2
McFadden F-7
Medicine Bow E-6
Meeteetse B-4
Midwest C-6
Moorcroft B-8
Moose C-2
Mountain View F-2
Newcastle B-9
Opal F-2
Osage B-8
Pavillion C-4
Pine Bluffs F-9
Pinedale D-2
Powell A-4
Ranchester A-5
Rawlins F-5
Riverton D-4
Rock River F-7
Rock Springs F-3
Saratoga F-6
Sheridan A-6
Shoshoni C-4
Sinclair F-5
Smoot D-1
Sundance B-8
Superior F-3
Ten Sleep B-5
Teton Village C-1
Thayne D-1
Thermopolis C-4
Torrington E-9
Upton B-8
Wamsutter F-5
Wheatland E-8
Worland B-5
Wright C-7

Wyoming state facts

Land area: 97,093 sq. mi. (rank: 9th)

Highest point: Gannett Peak, 13,804 ft., C-3

Population: 563,626 (rank: 50th)

Largest city: Cheyenne, 59,466, F-8

Nickname: The Equality State

Capital: Cheyenne, F-8

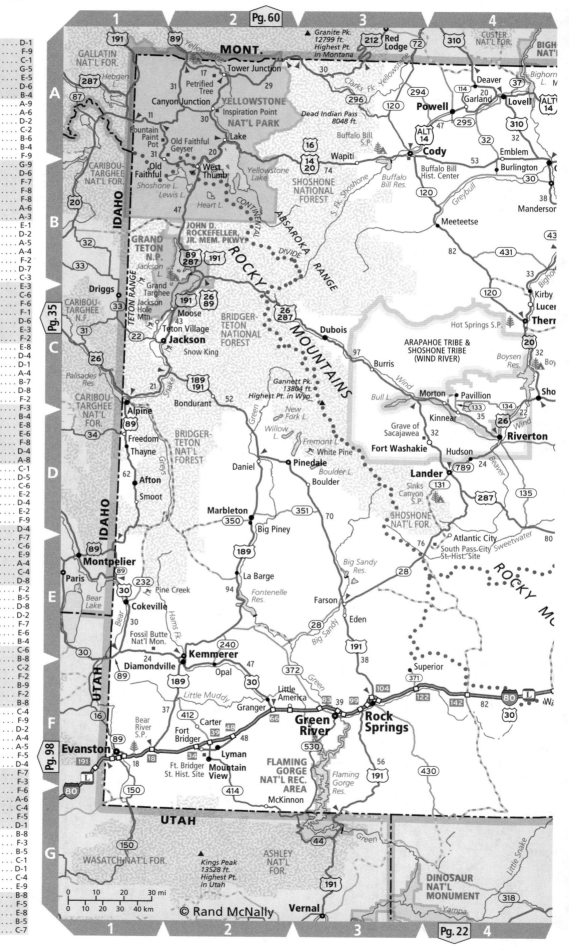

© Rand McNally

NOTE: Maps are not always in alphabetical order.
See Page 1 for map location in this atlas.

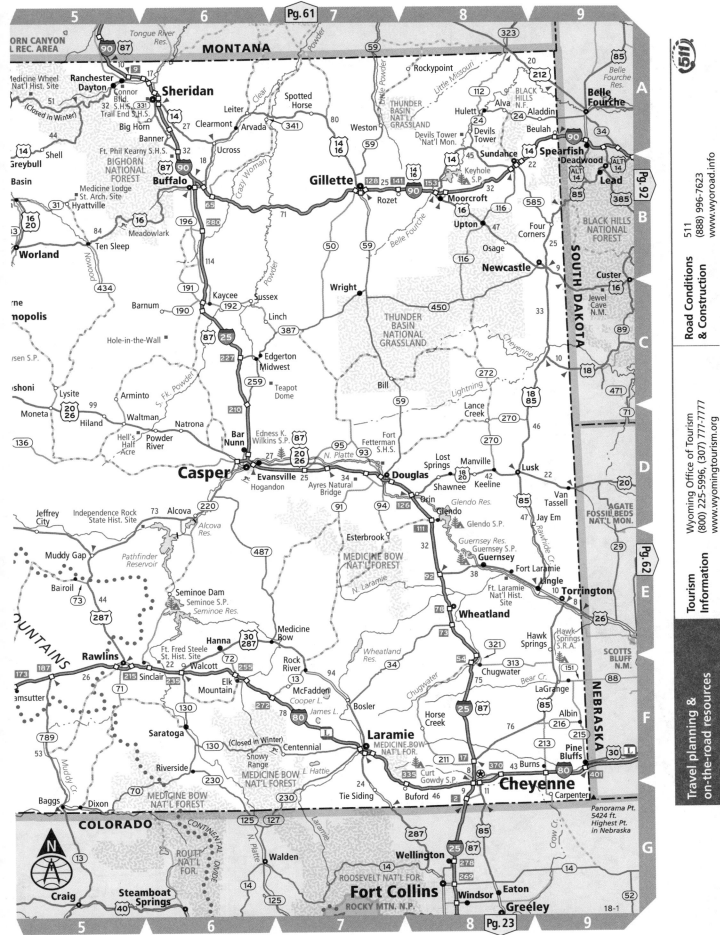

511

Road Conditions & Construction

511
(888) 996-7623
www.wyoroad.info

Tourism Information

Wyoming Office of Tourism
(800) 225-5996, (307) 777-7777
www.wyomingtourism.org

Travel planning & on-the-road resources

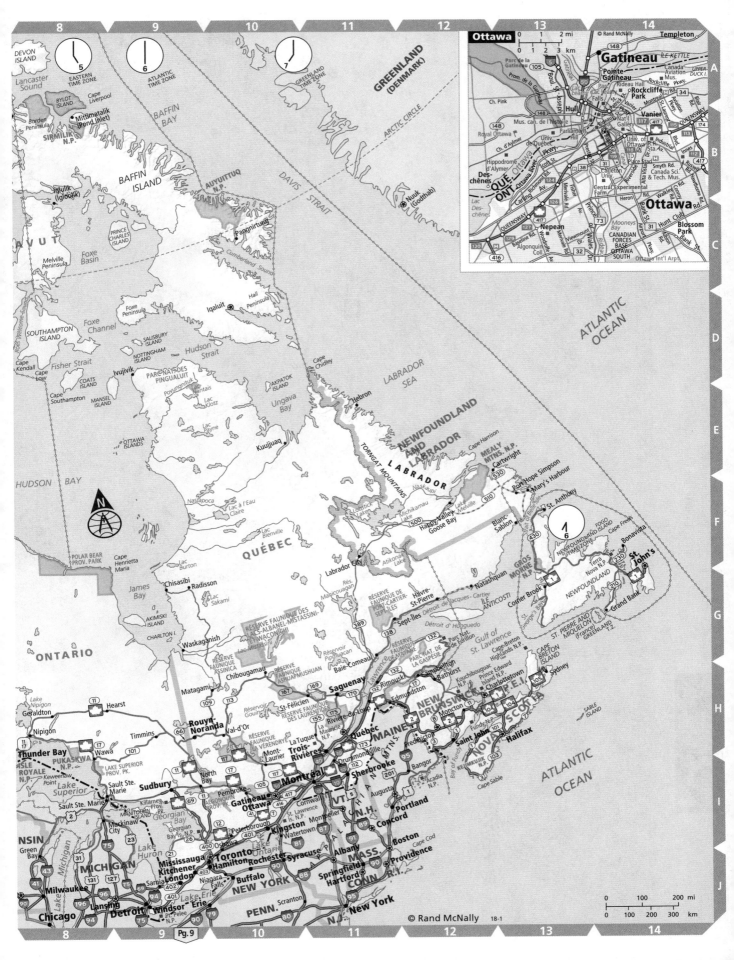

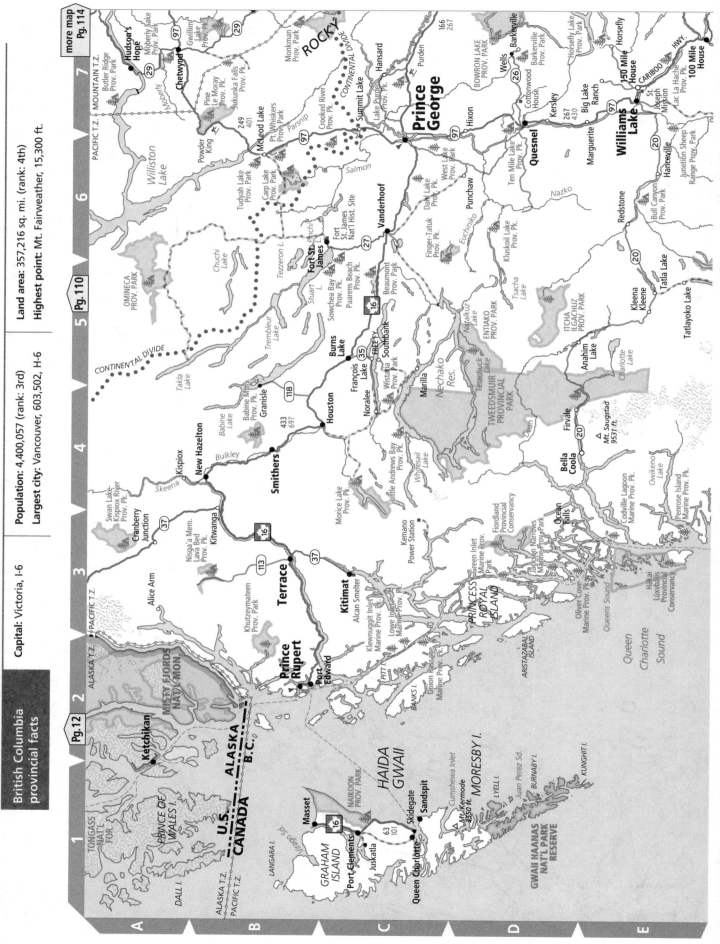

more map Pg. 114

Pg. 110

Pg. 12

British Columbia provincial facts

Capital: Victoria, I-6

Population: 4,400,057 (rank: 3rd)
Largest city: Vancouver, 603,502, H-6

Land area: 357,216 sq. mi. (rank: 4th)
Highest point: Mt. Fairweather, 15,300 ft.

Hudson's Hope
Chetwynd
Prince George
Quesnel
Williams Lake
100 Mile House
150 Mile House
Vanderhoof
Fort St. James
Burns Lake
Houston
New Hazelton
Smithers
Terrace
Prince Rupert
Kitimat
Port Edward
Bella Coola
Anahim Lake
Ketchikan
Masset
Port Clements
Queen Charlotte
Skidegate
Sandspit

ROCKY
CONTINENTAL DIVIDE
Williston Lake
OMINECA PROV. PARK
Takla Lake
Trembleur Lake
Babine Lake
HAIDA GWAII
GRAHAM ISLAND
MORESBY I.
MISTY FJORDS NAT'L MON.
PRINCE OF WALES I.
TONGASS NAT'L FOR.
TWEEDSMUIR PROVINCIAL PARK
Nechako Res.
PRINCESS ROYAL ISLAND
Queen Charlotte Sound
GWAII HAANAS NAT'L PARK RESERVE

Mt. Saugstad 9531 ft.
Mt. Kermode 3550 ft.

U.S.
CANADA
ALASKA
B.C.

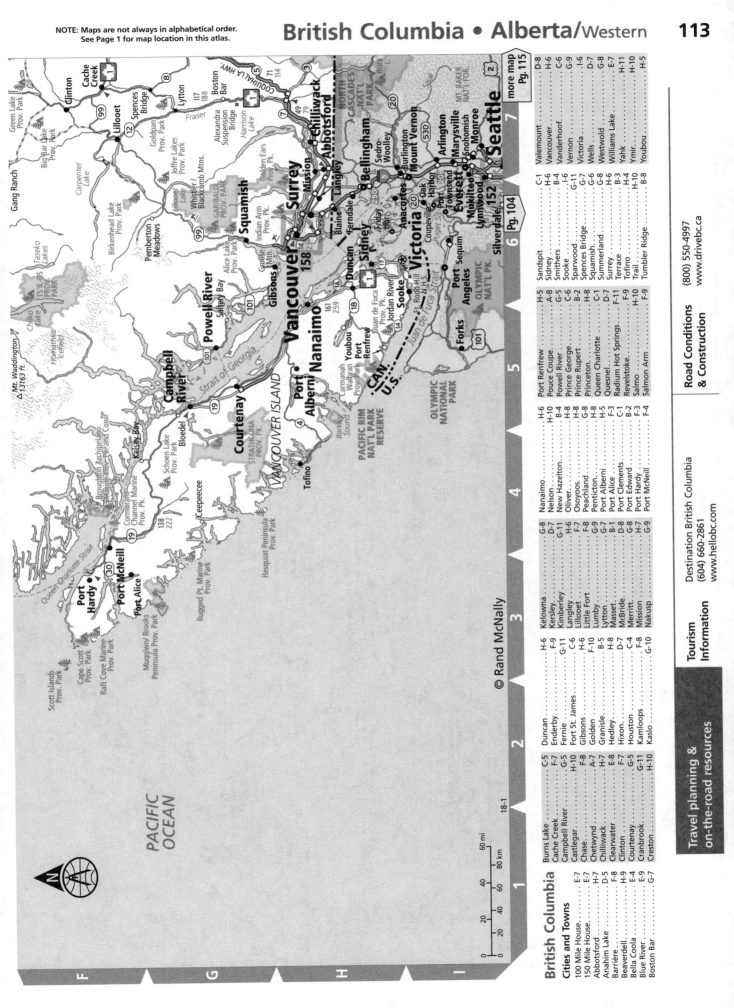

NOTE: Maps are not always in alphabetical order.
See Page 1 for map location in this atlas.

more map Pg. 115

Pg. 104

© Rand McNally

British Columbia
Cities and Towns

100 Mile House	E-7
150 Mile House	E-7
Abbotsford	H-7
Anahim Lake	D-5
Barrière	H-9
Beaverdell	E-4
Bella Coola	E-4
Blue River	E-9
Boston Bar	G-7
Burns Lake	C-5
Cache Creek	F-7
Campbell River	G-5
Castlegar	H-10
Chase	F-8
Chetwynd	A-7
Chilliwack	H-7
Clearwater	E-8
Clinton	F-7
Courtenay	G-5
Cranbrook	G-11
Creston	G-7
Duncan	H-6
Enderby	F-9
Fernie	G-11
Fort St. James	H-10
Gibsons	F-8
Golden	A-7
Granisle	H-7
Hedley	E-8
Hixon	F-7
Houston	C-4
Kamloops	G-11
Kaslo	H-10
Kelowna	G-8
Kersley	D-7
Kimberley	G-11
Langley	H-6
Lillooet	F-7
Little Fort	F-10
Lumby	F-9
Lytton	H-8
Masset	B-5
McBride	D-7
Merritt	C-4
Mission	F-8
Nakusp	G-10
Nanaimo	G-8
Nelson	D-7
New Hazelton	G-11
Oliver	H-6
Osoyoos	F-7
Peachland	F-8
Penticton	G-9
Port Alberni	G-7
Port Alice	B-1
Port Clements	D-8
Port Edward	H-7
Port McNeill	G-9
Port Renfrew	H-5
Pouce Coupe	H-10
Powell River	B-4
Prince George	H-8
Prince Rupert	G-8
Princeton	H-8
Queen Charlotte	H-5
Quesnel	F-3
Radium Hot Springs	C-1
Revelstoke	B-2
Salmo	F-3
Salmon Arm	F-4
Sandspit	H-5
Sidney	A-8
Smithers	G-5
Sooke	C-6
Sparwood	B-2
Spences Bridge	H-8
Squamish	C-1
Summerland	D-7
Surrey	H-6
Terrace	B-3
Tofino	H-4
Trail	H-10
Tumbler Ridge	B-8
Valemount	D-8
Vancouver	H-6
Vanderhoof	B-4
Vernon	G-9
Victoria	I-6
Wells	D-7
Westwold	G-8
Williams Lake	H-6
Yahk	E-7
Ymir	H-11
Youbou	H-10

Tourism Information
Destination British Columbia
(604) 660-2861
www.hellobc.com

Road Conditions & Construction
(800) 550-4997
www.drivebc.ca

Travel planning & on-the-road resources

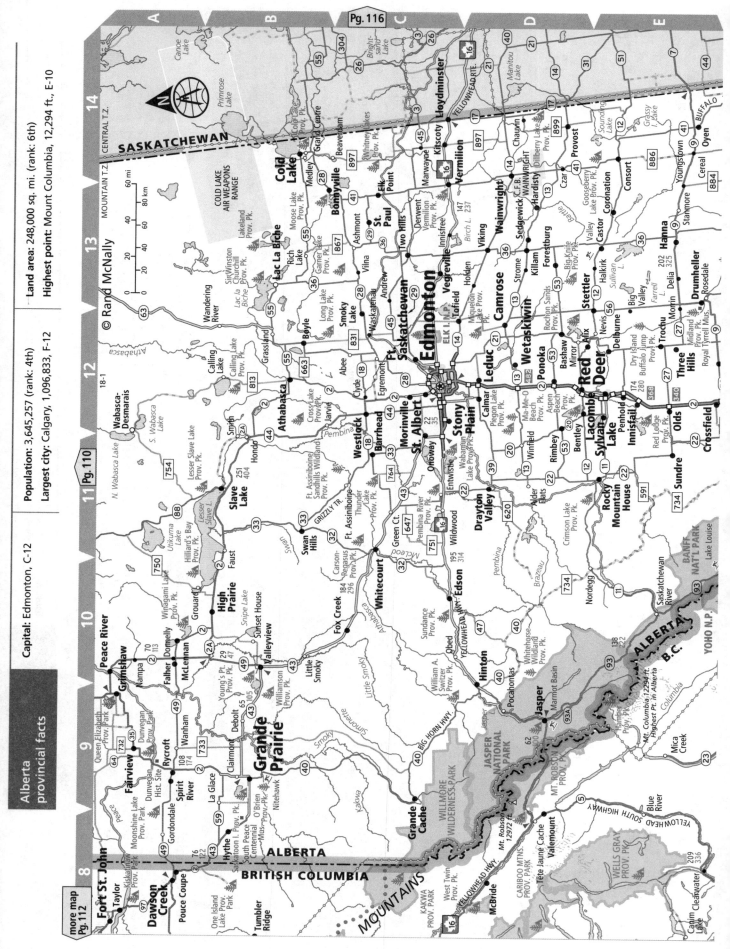

Pg. 116

Pg. 110

Alberta
provincial facts

Capital: Edmonton, C-12

Population: 3,645,257 (rank: 4th)
Largest city: Calgary, 1,096,833, F-12

Land area: 248,000 sq. mi. (rank: 6th)
Highest point: Mount Columbia, 12,294 ft., E-10

© Rand McNally

more map
Pg.112

NOTE: Maps are not always in alphabetical order.
See Page 1 for map location in this atlas.

British Columbia • Alberta/Eastern   115

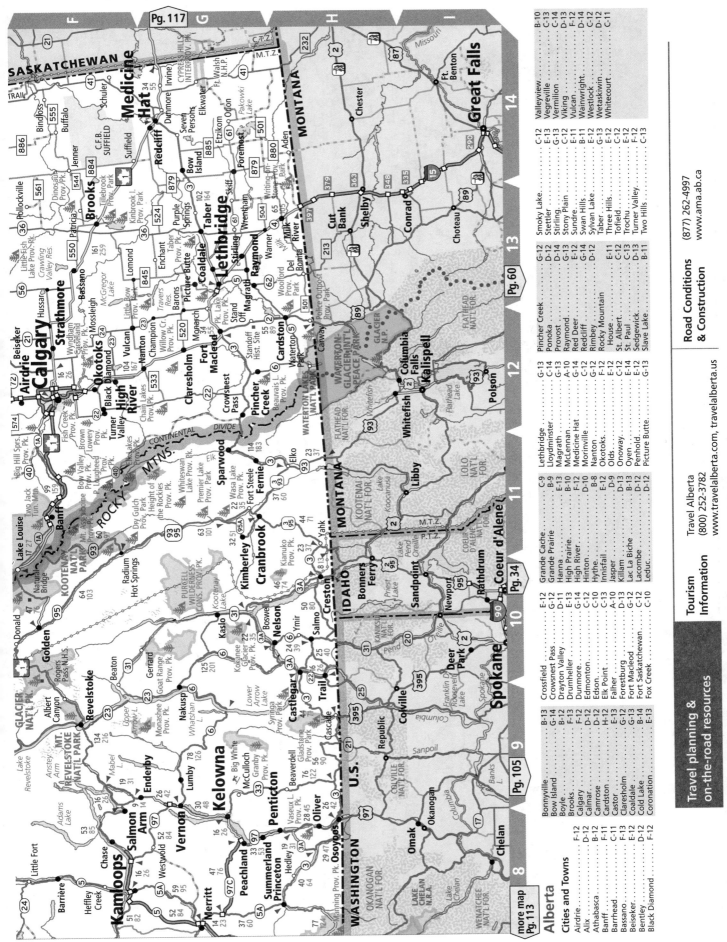

Pg. 117 · Pg. 60 · Pg. 34 · Pg. 105 · more map Pg. 113

Alberta

Cities and Towns

Airdrie	F-12
Alix	D-12
Athabasca	B-12
Barrhead	C-11
Bassano	F-13
Beiseker	E-12
Bentley	D-12
Black Diamond	F-12
Bonnyville	B-13
Bow Island	G-14
Boyle	B-12
Brooks	F-13
Calgary	F-12
Calmar	D-12
Camrose	C-12
Cardston	H-12
Castor	D-12
Claresholm	G-12
Coaldale	G-13
Cold Lake	B-14
Coronation	E-13
Crossfield	E-12
Crowsnest Pass	G-12
Drayton Valley	D-11
Drumheller	E-12
Dunmore	G-14
Edmonton	C-12
Edson	C-10
Elk Point	C-13
Falher	A-10
Forestburg	D-13
Fort Macleod	G-13
Fort Saskatchewan	C-12
Fox Creek	C-10
Grande Cache	C-9
Grande Prairie	B-9
Hanna	E-13
High Prairie	B-10
High River	F-12
Hinton	D-10
Hythe	B-8
Innisfail	E-12
Jasper	D-9
Killam	D-13
Lac La Biche	B-12
Lacombe	D-12
Leduc	C-12
Lethbridge	G-13
Lloydminster	C-14
Magrath	G-13
McLennan	B-10
Medicine Hat	F-13
Morinville	C-12
Nanton	F-12
Okotoks	F-12
Olds	E-12
Onoway	C-11
Oyen	E-14
Penhold	D-12
Picture Butte	G-13
Pincher Creek	G-13
Ponoka	D-12
Provost	D-14
Raymond	G-13
Red Deer	D-12
Redcliff	F-13
Rimbey	D-12
Rocky Mountain House	E-11
St. Albert	C-12
St. Paul	C-13
Sedgewick	D-13
Slave Lake	B-11
Smoky Lake	C-12
Stettler	D-12
Stirling	G-13
Stony Plain	C-12
Sundre	E-11
Swan Hills	B-11
Sylvan Lake	D-12
Taber	G-13
Three Hills	E-12
Tofield	C-12
Trochu	E-12
Turner Valley	F-12
Two Hills	C-13
Valleyview	B-10
Vegreville	C-13
Vermilion	C-14
Viking	C-13
Vulcan	F-12
Wainwright	D-13
Westlock	C-12
Wetaskiwin	D-12
Whitecourt	C-11

Tourism Information
Travel Alberta
(800) 252-3782
www.travelalberta.com, travelalberta.us

Road Conditions & Construction
(877) 262-4997
www.ama.ab.ca

Travel planning & on-the-road resources

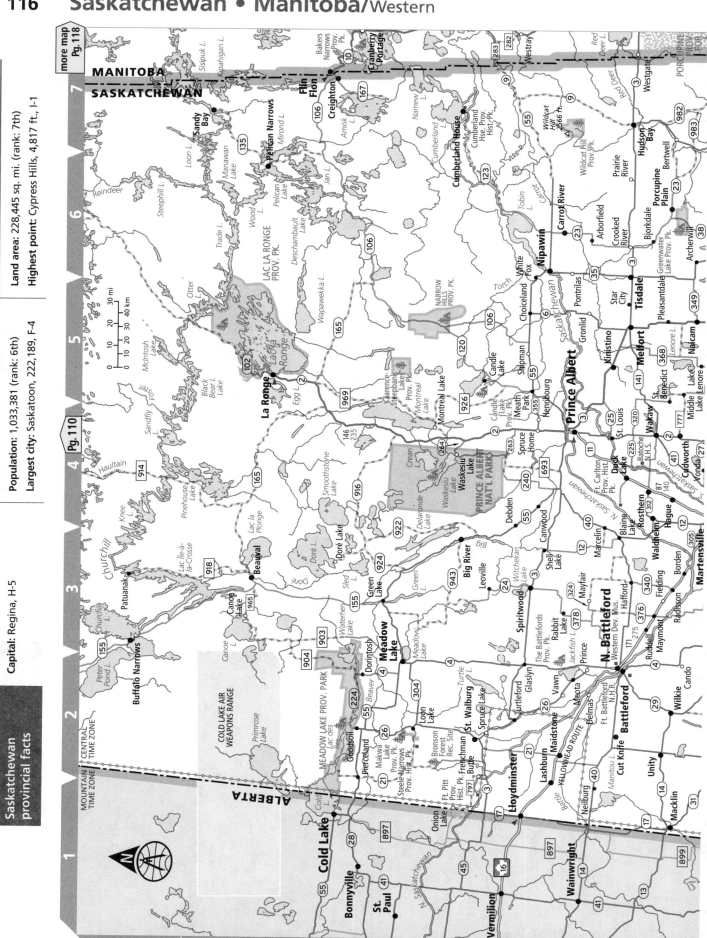

more map Pg. 118

Saskatchewan provincial facts

Land area: 228,445 sq. mi. (rank: 7th)

Highest point: Cypress Hills, 4,817 ft., I-1

Population: 1,033,381 (rank: 6th)

Largest city: Saskatoon, 222,189, F-4

Capital: Regina, H-5

MOUNTAIN TIME ZONE
CENTRAL TIME ZONE

MANITOBA
SASKATCHEWAN

ALBERTA

Pg. 110

Pg. 114

NOTE: Maps are not always in alphabetical order.
See Page 1 for map location in this atlas.

Saskatchewan • Manitoba/Western   117

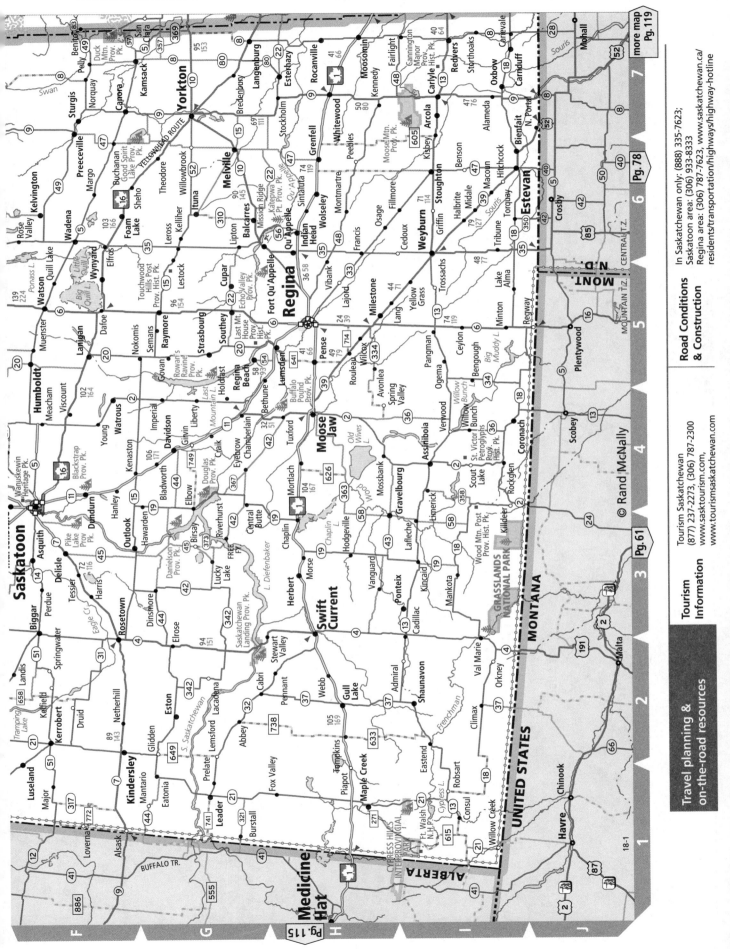

more map Pg. 119

Pg. 78

Pg. 61

Pg. 115

Tourism
Information

Tourism Saskatchewan
(877) 237-2273, (306) 787-2300
www.sasktourism.com,
www.tourismsaskatchewan.com

Road Conditions
& Construction

In Saskatchewan only: (888) 335-7623;
Saskatoon area: (306) 933-8333
Regina area: (306) 787-7623, www.saskatchewan.ca/
residents/transportation/highways/highway-hotline

Travel planning &
on-the-road resources

© Rand McNally

Manitoba provincial facts

Capital: Winnipeg, H-11
Land area: 213,729 sq. mi. (rank: 8th)
Population: 1,208,268 (rank: 5th)
Largest city: Winnipeg, 663,617, H-11
Highest point: Baldy Mountain, 2,730 ft., G-8

Saskatchewan
Cities and Towns

Arcola	I-7
Asquith	F-3
Assiniboia	I-4
Avonlea	G-6
Balcarres	G-6
Battleford	E-2
Beauval	B-3
Bethune	G-5
Bienfait	I-6
Big River	D-3
Biggar	F-3
Blaine Lake	F-3
Buffalo Narrows	A-3
Cabri	G-2
Canora	F-7
Canwood	D-4
Carlyle	I-7
Carnduff	I-7
Carrot River	D-6
Central Butte	G-4
Choiceland	D-5
Coronach	I-4
Craik	G-4
Creighton	C-7
Cudworth	E-4
Cumberland House	D-7
Cupar	G-5
Cut Knife	E-2
Davidson	G-4
Debden	D-4
Delisle	F-3
Duck Lake	E-4
Dundurn	F-4
Eastend	I-2
Eatonia	G-1
Elrose	G-2
Esterhazy	H-7
Estevan	I-6
Eston	G-2
Foam Lake	F-6
Fort Qu'Appelle	G-6
Glaslyn	D-2
Gravelbourg	H-3
Green Lake	C-3
Grenfell	H-6
Gull Lake	H-2
Hafford	E-3
Hague	E-4
Hanley	F-4
Herbert	H-3
Hudson Bay	E-7
Humboldt	F-5
Indian Head	H-6
Ituna	G-6
Kamsack	F-7
Kelvington	F-6
Kerrobert	F-2
Kindersley	F-2
Kinistino	E-5
La Ronge	B-5
Lafleche	I-3
Langenburg	G-7
Lanigan	F-5
Lashburn	D-2
Leader	G-1
Leoville	D-3
Lloydminster	D-1
Lumsden	G-5
Luseland	F-2

Manitoba
Cities and Towns

Amaranth	H-10
Angusville	H-8
Arborg	G-11
Ashern	G-10
Austin	H-9
Baldur	I-9
Beausejour	H-11
Belmont	I-9
Benito	F-7
Berens River	E-11
Binscarth	H-8
Birch River	E-8
Birtle	H-8
Boissevain	I-9
Bowsman	F-8
Brandon	I-9
Camperville	F-8
Carberry	H-9
Carman	I-10
Cartwright	I-9
Cormorant	C-8
Cranberry Portage	C-7
Crystal City	I-10
Darlingford	I-10
Dauphin	G-9
Deloraine	I-8
Douglas	H-9
Duck Bay	F-8
Elkhorn	H-8
Elm Creek	I-10
Elphinstone	H-9
Emerson	I-11
Erickson	H-9
Eriksdale	G-10
Ethelbert	G-8
Fisher Branch	G-10
Flin Flon	C-7
Gilbert Plains	G-8
Gimli	G-11
Gladstone	H-9
Glenboro	I-9
Glenella	H-9
Grand Rapids	E-9
Grandview	G-8
Gretna	I-11
Gypsumville	F-10
Hamiota	H-8
Hartney	I-8
Holland	I-9
Inwood	H-11
Inglis	H-8
Killarney	I-9
La Broquerie	I-11
Lac du Bonnet	H-12
Langruth	H-10
Lockport	H-11
Lorette	I-11
Lowe Farm	I-10
Lundar	G-10
MacGregor	H-9
Mafeking	E-8
Manigotagan	G-11
Manitou	I-10
Matheson Island	F-11
McCreary	G-9
Melita	I-8
Minitonas	F-8
Miniota	H-8

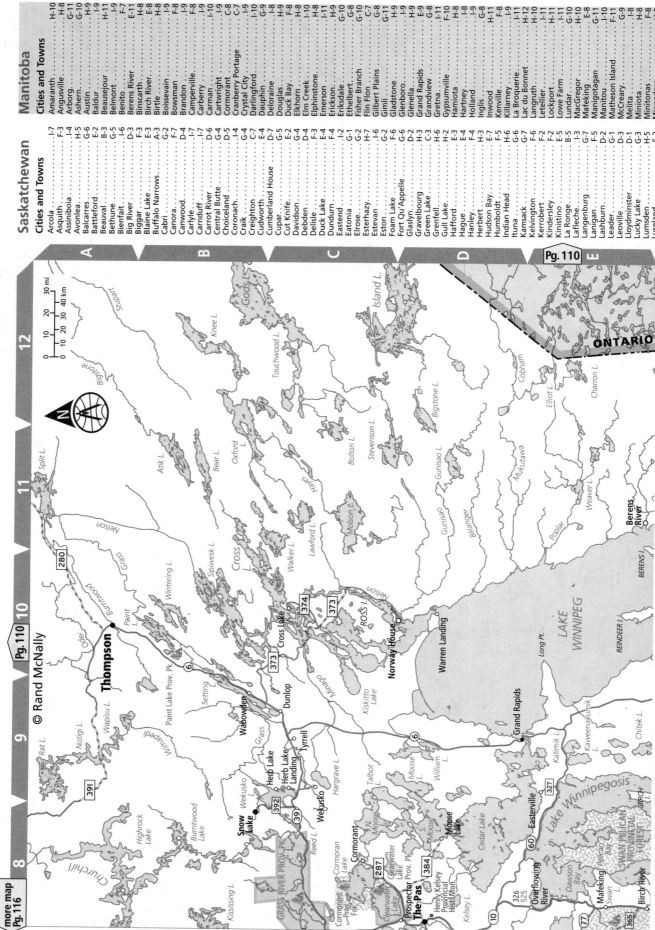

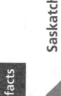

© Rand McNally

NOTE: Maps are not always in alphabetical order.
See Page 1 for map location in this atlas.

Saskatchewan • Manitoba/Eastern   119

Place	Grid
Moose Lake	D-8
Moosehorn	G-10
Morden	I-10
Morris	H-9
Neepawa	H-8
Newdale	I-9
Niverville	I-11
Norway House	D-10
Oak River	H-8
Oakburn	H-8
Oakville	H-10
Ochre River	G-9
Petersfield	H-11
Pierson	I-8
Pilot Mound	I-10
Pine Falls	F-11
Pine River	F-8
Pipestone	I-8
Plum Coulee	I-10
Plumas	H-9
Poplar Point	H-10
Portage la Prairie	H-10
Rathwell	H-12
Reston	I-8
Richer	H-8
Rivers	I-9
Riverton	G-11
Roblin	G-8
Roland	I-10
Rorketon	G-9
Rossburn	H-8
Russell	H-8
Saint Claude	H-10
Saint Jean Baptiste	I-11
Saint Laurent	H-10
Saint Malo	I-11
Saint-Pierre-Jolys	I-11
Sainte Agathe	I-11
Sainte Anne	I-11
Sainte Rose du Lac	G-9
Sanford	I-11
Selkirk	H-11
Shoal Lake	H-8
Sifton	G-8
Snow Lake	B-8
Somerset	I-10
Souris	I-8
Sprague	I-12
Steinbach	I-11
Swan River	F-8
Teulon	H-11
The Pas	D-8
Thompson	A-10
Treherne	I-10
Tyndall	H-11
Victoria Beach	G-11
Virden	I-8
Vita	I-11
Wabowden	B-9
Warren	H-11
Wawanesa	I-9
Whitemouth	H-11
Winkler	I-10
Winnipeg	H-11
Winnipeg Beach	H-11
Winnipegosis	F-9
Woodridge	I-12

Place	Grid
Macklin	E-1
Maidstone	D-2
Maple Creek	H-1
Martensville	F-4
Meadow Lake	C-2
Melfort	E-5
Melville	G-6
Midale	I-6
Milestone	H-5
Montmartre	H-6
Moose Jaw	H-4
Moosomin	H-7
Muenster	F-5
Naicam	E-5
Neilburg	E-1
Nipawin	D-6
Nokomis	G-5
Norquay	F-7
North Battleford	E-2
Outlook	F-3
Oxbow	I-7
Pelican Narrows	B-6
Pense	H-5
Perdue	F-3
Pierceland	C-2
Ponteix	I-3
Porcupine Plain	D-6
Preeceville	E-6
Prince Albert	E-4
Qu'Appelle	H-6
Quill Lake	F-5
Radisson	E-3
Raymore	G-5
Redvers	I-7
Regina	H-5
Regina Beach	G-5
Rocanville	H-7
Rockglen	I-4
Rosetown	F-3
Rosthern	E-4
Rouleau	H-5
Saint Louis	E-4
Saint Walburg	D-2
Sandy Bay	B-7
Saskatoon	F-4
Shaunavon	I-2
Southey	G-5
Spiritwood	D-3
Star City	E-5
Stoughton	I-6
Strasbourg	G-5
Sturgis	E-6
Swift Current	H-3
Theodore	G-6
Tisdale	D-6
Turtleford	D-2
Unity	E-2
Vibank	H-6
Wadena	F-6
Wakaw	E-4
Waldheim	E-4
Watrous	F-4
Watson	F-5
Weyburn	I-6
White Fox	D-6
Whitewood	H-7
Wilkie	E-2
Wolseley	H-6
Wynyard	F-5
Yellow Grass	I-5
Yorkton	G-7

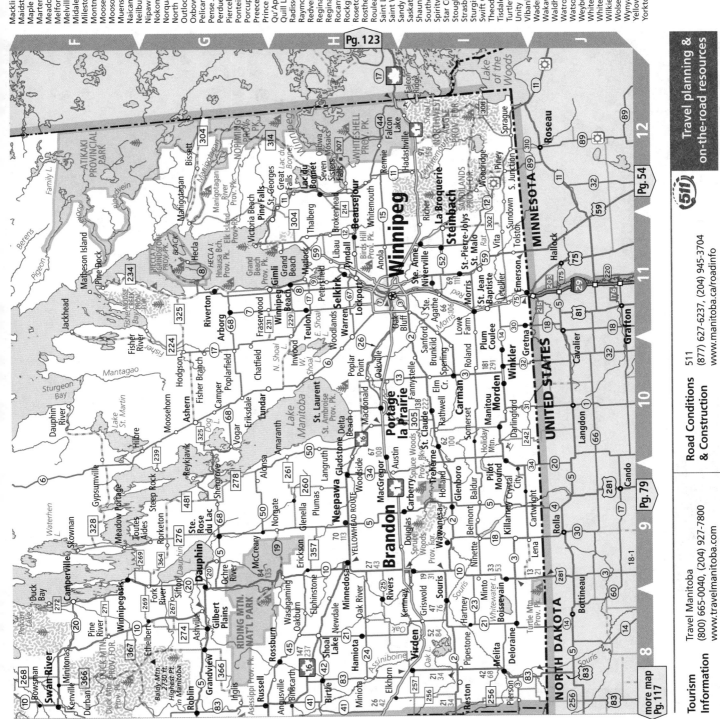

Pg. 123
Pg. 54
Pg. 79
more map Pg. 117

Travel planning & on-the-road resources

Tourism Information
Travel Manitoba
(800) 665-0040, (204) 927-7800
www.travelmanitoba.com

Road Conditions & Construction
511
(877) 627-6237, (204) 945-3704
www.manitoba.ca/roadinfo

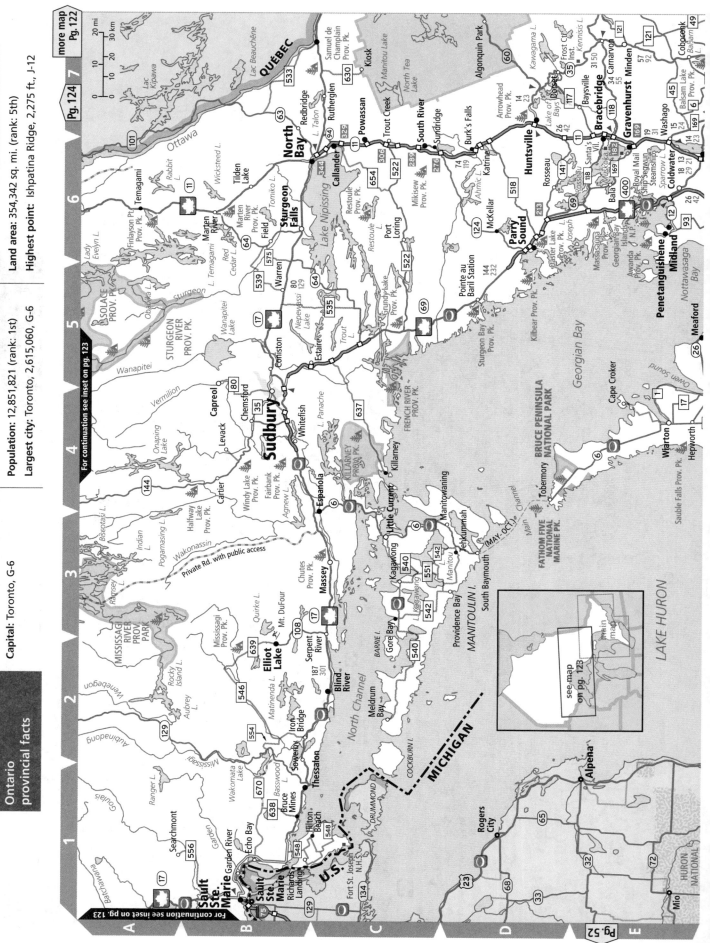

Ontario
provincial facts

Capital: Toronto, G-6

Population: 12,851,821 (rank: 1st)
Largest city: Toronto, 2,615,060, G-6

Land area: 354,342 sq. mi. (rank: 5th)
Highest point: Ishpatina Ridge, 2,275 ft., J-12

For continuation see inset on pg. 123

Pg. 124

QUÉBEC

LAKE HURON

MICHIGAN

U.S.

Pg. 52

see map on pg. 123

For continuation see inset on pg. 123

Ontario/Western   121

NOTE: Maps are not always in alphabetical order.
See Page 1 for map location in this atlas.

© Rand McNally

Road Conditions & Construction
511, (800) 268-4686
Toronto area: (416) 235-4686
www.mto.gov.on.ca/english/traveller

Tourism Information
Ontario Travel
(800) 668-2746
www.ontariotravel.net

Travel planning & on-the-road resources
www.randmcnally.com

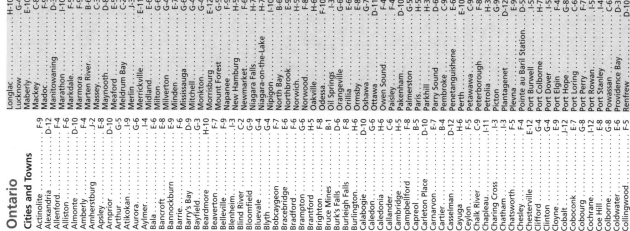

Ontario

Cities and Towns

Name	Grid	Name	Grid
Actinolite	F-9	Longlac	H-10
Alexandria	D-12	Lucknow	G-4
Allenford	F-4	Maberly	E-8
Alliston	D-10	Mackey	C-8
Almonte	F-5	Madoc	F-9
Amberly	F-4	Manitowaning	D-3
Amherstburg	J-2	Marathon	I-10
Apsley	D-10	Markdale	F-5
Arnprior	F-5	Marmora	F-9
Arthur	E-5	Marten River	B-6
Atikokan	I-4	Massey	C-3
Aurora	G-5	Maynooth	D-8
Aylmer	G-6	Meaford	E-5
Bala	E-6	Meldrum Bay	C-2
Bancroft	E-8	Merlin	J-3
Bannockburn	E-9	Merrickville	E-6
Barrie	E-7	Midland	E-11
Barry's Bay	F-6	Milton	E-6
Bayfield	G-3	Milverton	E-8
Beardmore	H-10	Minden	E-9
Beaverton	F-7	Mississauga	F-6
Belleville	F-9	Mitchell	G-4
Blenheim	I-3	Monkton	G-4
Blind River	C-2	Morrisburg	E-12
Bloomfield	G-9	Mount Forest	G-5
Bluevale	G-4	Napanee	H-5
Blyth	G-4	New Hamburg	H-5
Bobcaygeon	F-7	Newmarket	F-6
Bracebridge	E-6	Niagara Falls	H-7
Bradford	E-6	Niagara-on-the-Lake	H-7
Brampton	F-6	Nipigon	I-10
Brantford	G-5	North Bay	B-6
Brighton	F-8	Northbrook	E-9
Bruce Mines	B-1	Norwood	F-6
Burk's Falls	D-6	Oakville	H-5
Burleigh Falls	F-8	Odessa	F-10
Burlington	H-6	Oil Springs	I-3
Calabogie	F-5	Orangeville	G-6
Caledon	F-5	Orillia	E-6
Caledonia	H-6	Ormsby	E-8
Callander	C-9	Oshawa	G-7
Cambridge	F-5	Ottawa	D-11
Campbellford	F-8	Owen Sound	F-4
Capreol	B-5	Paisley	F-4
Carleton Place	F-5	Pakenham	D-10
Carnarvon	E-7	Palmerston	H-5
Cartier	B-4	Paris	H-3
Casselman	D-12	Parkhill	H-3
Cayuga	H-6	Parry Sound	F-8
Ceylon	F-5	Pembroke	E-6
Chapleau	B-4	Penetanguishene	E-10
Charing Cross	I-3	Perth	E-9
Chatham	I-3	Petawawa	F-8
Chatsworth	F-5	Peterborough	H-3
Chesley	F-4	Petrolia	I-3
Chesterville	E-12	Picton	I-12
Clifford	G-4	Plantagenet	D-12
Clinton	G-4	Plevna	E-9
Cloyne	E-9	Pointe au Baril Station	D-5
Cobalt	J-12	Port Burwell	I-5
Coboconk	E-8	Port Colborne	H-7
Cobourg	G-8	Port Dover	H-4
Cochrane	F-7	Port Elgin	F-4
Coe Hill	E-8	Port Hope	G-8
Colborne	F-8	Port Loring	F-7
Coldwater	E-6	Port Perry	F-7
Collingwood	F-5	Port Rowan	I-4
Combermere	F-5	Port Stanley	I-4
Coniston	B-5	Powassan	C-6
		Providence Bay	D-3
		Renfrew	D-10
		Richmond Hill	D-9
		Ridgetown	I-3

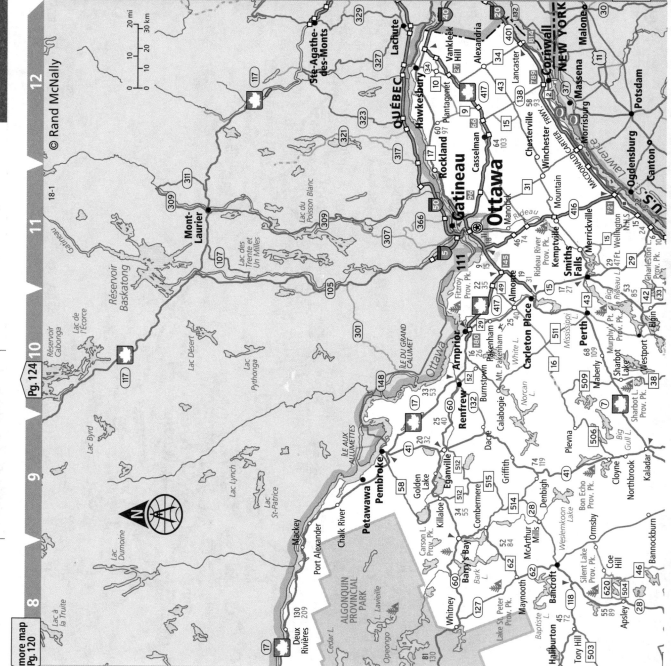

Ontario provincial facts

Capital: Toronto, G-6

Population: 12,851,821 (rank: 1st)
Largest city: Toronto, 2,615,060, G-6

Land area: 354,342 sq. mi. (rank: 5th)
Highest point: Ishpatina Ridge, 2,275 ft., J-12

more map Pg. 120

Pg. 124

Pg. 72

© Rand McNally

NOTE: Maps are not always in alphabetical order.
See Page 1 for map location in this atlas.

Ontario/Eastern   123

Name	Grid	Name	Grid
Rockland	D-11	Cookstown	E-6
Rosseau	D-6	Cornwall	E-12
St. Catharines	H-7	Dacre	D-9
St. Marys	H-4	Denbigh	E-9
St. Thomas	I-4	Deseronto	D-7
Sarnia	I-3	Dorset	I-3
Sault Ste. Marie	B-1	Dresden	H-8
Schomberg	G-6	Dryden	C-8
Seaforth	G-4	Duex-Rivières	F-5
Seeleys Bay	H-6	Dundalk	H-6
Shelburne	F-5	Dunnville	F-5
Sharbot Lake	B-1	Durham	B-1
Simcoe	D-9	Echo Bay	D-9
Smiths Falls	I-5	Eganville	E-10
Smooth Rock Falls	E-11	Elgin	G-5
South Baymouth	I-12	Elliot Lake	I-12
South River	C-6	Elmira	G-6
Southampton	F-4	Englehart	H-10
Sowerby	F-6	Erin	G-3
Stayner	G-7	Espanola	D-9
Stouffville	B-2	Essex	H-3
Stratford	F-7	Estaire	E-6
Strathroy	F-7	Exeter	J-5
Sturgeon Falls	G-5	Fenelon Falls	F-9
Sudbury	B-6	Fergus	F-10
Sunderland	F-7	Field	H-10
Sundridge	H-3	Foleyet	C-3
Sutton	I-5	Forest	H-3
Tavistock	F-9	Fort Erie	H-5
Tecumseh	F-9	Fort Frances	D-12
Terrace Bay	F-10	Foxboro	F-9
Thamesford	I-10	Frankford	F-7
Thamesville	H-10	Gananoque	F-10
Thessalon	G-3	Georgetown	F-4
Thornbury	D-9	Geraldton	B-2
Thornhill	H-3	Goderich	G-5
Thunder Bay	E-6	Golden Lake	F-8
Tilbury	J-5	Gore Bay	C-3
Tillsonburg	F-9	Grand Bend	H-3
Timmins	F-10	Gravenhurst	E-6
Toronto	H-6	Guelph	G-5
Tory Hill	F-4	Haliburton	E-8
Trenton	G-5	Hamilton	H-6
Trout Creek	F-8	Hanover	G-5
Tweed	D-12	Harriston	F-4
Uxbridge	H-11	Havelock	F-8
Upsala	D-7	Hawkesbury	D-12
Vankleek Hill	H-8	Hearst	B-2
Vermilion Bay	H-5	Hepworth	E-4
Verona	B-2	Huntsville	D-7
Walkerton	C-3	Ignace	I-9
Wallacetown	E-9	Ingersoll	H-5
Wallaceburg	I-12	Iron Bridge	B-2
Warren	B-5	Jarvis	E-9
Warwick	F-6	Kagawong	I-12
Wasaga Beach	D-9	Kaladar	E-11
Washago	C-4	Kapuskasing	H-5
Watford	F-4	Kemptville	F-6
Wawa	F-10	Keswick	D-9
Welland	J-2	Killaloe	G-4
Wellington	I-12	Killarney	F-10
Westport	H-5	Kincardine	J-2
Wheatley	F-8	Kingston	I-12
Whitney	D-12	Kingsville	H-5
Wiarton	E-4	Kirkland Lake	E-11
Winchester	F-11	Kitchener	E-11
Windsor	J-2	Lakefield	D-12
Wingham	F-7	Lancaster	I-2
Woodstock	G-4	Lansdowne	J-7
Youngs Point	H-5	Leamington	F-7
		Lindsay	G-4
		Listowel	C-3
		Little Current	H-4
		London	

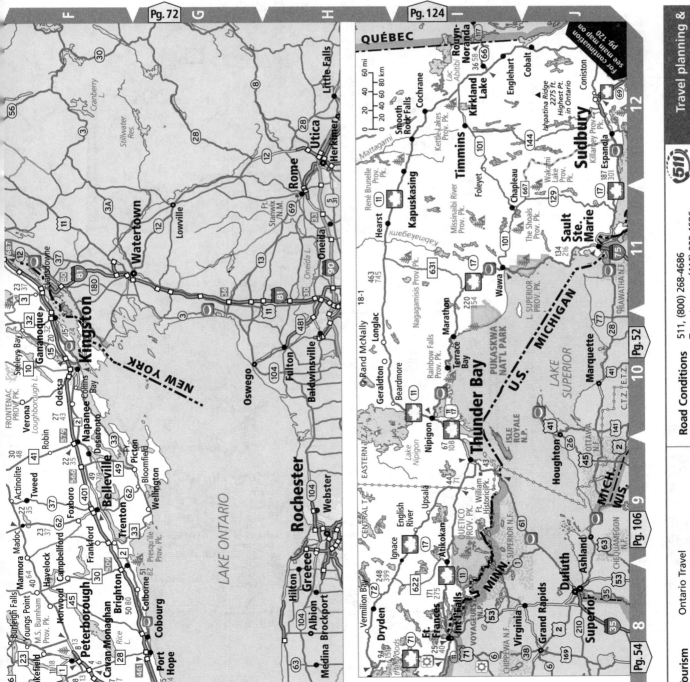

Travel planning & on-the-road resources

511

Road Conditions & Construction
511, (800) 268-4686
Toronto area: (416) 235-4686
www.mto.gov.on.ca/english/traveller

Tourism Information
Ontario Travel
(800) 668-2746
www.ontariotravel.net

Québec

Cities and Towns

Acton Vale	F-4
Alma	B-5
Amos	B-2
Asbestos	F-5
Baie-Comeau	G-8
Baie-St-Paul	C-7
Beauceville	E-6
Bécancour	E-5
Berthierville	E-4
Black Lake	F-6
Bromptonville	F-5
Cap-St-Ignace	D-7
Chandler	G-9
Chicoutimi	B-6
Châteauguay	G-3
Coaticook	G-5
Cowansville	G-4
Dégelis	C-9
Delisle	A-5
Dolbeau-Mistassini	A-5
Donnacona	E-5
Drummondville	F-4
Forestville	A-8
Gaspé	G-9
Gatineau	F-1
Granby	F-4
Grand-Mère	E-4
Havre-St-Pierre	F-9
Joliette	E-3
Jonquière	B-6
La Malbaie	C-7
La Pocatière	C-7
La Sarre	A-2
La Tuque	C-4
Lac-Mégantic	F-6
Lachute	F-2
Laval	F-3
Lebel-sur-Quévillon	A-3
Lévis	D-6
Longueuil	F-3
Louiseville	E-4
Magog	G-5
Malartic	B-2
Maniwaki	C-3
Matane	G-8
Mont-Joli	B-9
Mont-Laurier	E-1
Mont-Tremblant	E-2
Montmagny	D-7
Montréal	F-3
Napierville	G-3
Nicolet	E-4
Notre-Dame-des-Pins	E-6
Plessisville	E-5
Pohénégamook	C-8
Port-Cartier	F-8
Princeville	E-5
Québec	D-6
Repentigny	F-3
Richmond	F-5
Rimouski	B-9
Rivière-du-Loup	C-8
Roberval	B-5
Rouyn-Noranda	B-2
Saguenay	B-6
St-Alexis-des-Monts	E-4
St-Eustache	F-3
St-Félicien	A-5
St-Georges	E-6
St-Henri	D-6
St-Hyacinthe	F-4
St-Jacques	F-3
St-Jean-Port-Joli	D-7
St-Jean-sur-Richelieu	G-4
St-Jérôme	F-3
St-Joseph-de-Beauce	E-6
St-Nicéphore	F-5
St-Pamphile	D-7
St-Raymond	D-5
St-Sauveur	F-3
Ste-Agathe-des-Monts	E-2
Ste-Anne-de-Beaupré	D-6
Ste-Anne-des-Monts	G-8
Ste-Claire	E-6
Ste-Julie	E-5
Ste-Marie	E-6
Salaberry-de-Valleyfield	G-3
Senneterre	B-3
Sept-Îles	F-8
Shawinigan	E-4
Sherbrooke	F-5
Sorel-Tracy	E-4
Témiscaming	C-2
Thetford Mines	E-6
Trois-Pistoles	B-8
Trois-Rivières	E-4
Val-d'Or	B-2
Varennes	F-3
Vaudreuil-Dorion	F-3
Victoriaville	E-5
Warwick	E-5
Waterloo	G-4
Windsor	F-5

Québec provincial facts

Land area: 527,079 sq. mi. (rank: 2nd)
Highest point: Mont d'Iberville, 5,420 ft.
Population: 7,903,001 (rank: 2nd)
Largest city: Montréal, 1,649,519, F-3
Capital: Québec, D-6

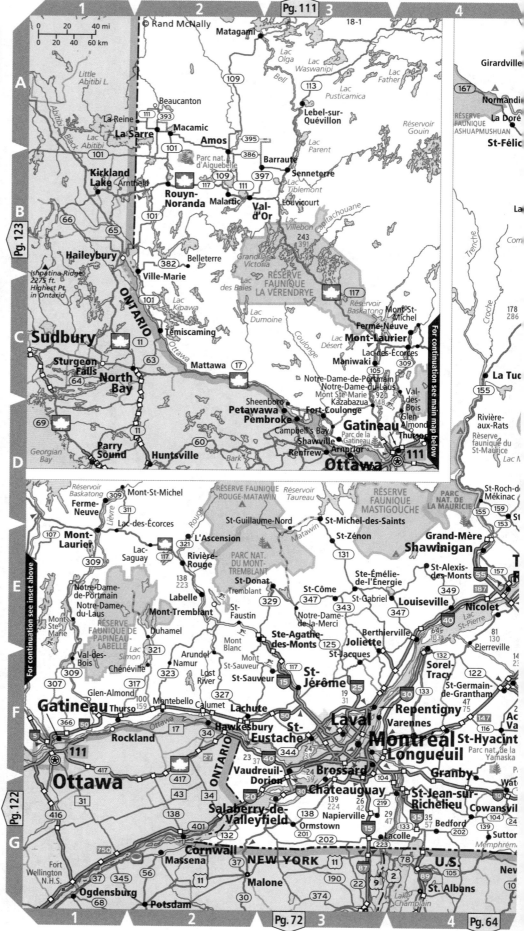

© Rand McNally

Pg. 111
Pg. 123
Pg. 122
Pg. 72
Pg. 64

NOTE: Maps are not always in alphabetical order.
See Page 1 for map location in this atlas.

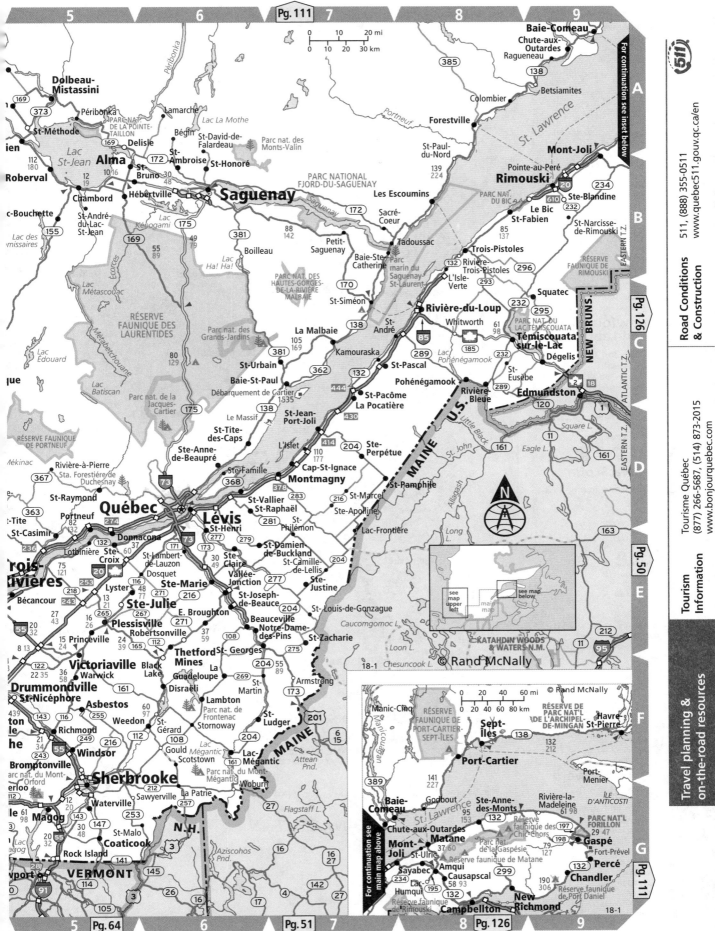

Pg. 111
Pg. 126
Pg. 50
Pg. 64
Pg. 51

© Rand McNally

Road Conditions & Construction

511, (888) 355-0511
www.quebec511.gouv.qc.ca/en

Tourism Information

Tourisme Québec
(877) 266-5687, (514) 873-2015
www.bonjourquebec.com

Travel planning & on-the-road resources

New Brunswick

Cities and Towns

Bathurst C-4
Bouctouche D-5
Campbellton B-3
Cap-Pele D-5
Caraquet B-5
Dalhousie B-4
Dieppe D-5
Edmundston C-2
Fredericton D-3
Grand Falls (Grand Sault) . C-3
Hampton E-4
Memramcook D-5
Minto D-4
Miramichi C-4
Moncton D-5
Oromocto E-4
Perth-Andover C-3
Sackville E-5
St. Andrews E-3
Saint John E-4
St. Stephen E-3
St-Quentin C-3
Salisbury D-5
Shediac D-5
Shippagan B-5
Sussex E-4
Woodstock D-3

Newfoundland and Labrador

Cities and Towns

Bonavista B-9
Channel-Port aux Basques . B-7
Corner Brook B-8
Deer Lake B-8
Gander B-8
Grand Falls-Windsor B-8
Marystown C-8
Mount Pearl B-9
St. John's B-9
Torbay B-9

Nova Scotia

Cities and Towns

Amherst E-5
Antigonish E-7
Bridgewater F-5
Chester F-5
Digby F-4
Glace Bay D-9
Halifax F-6
Hebron G-4
Ingonish D-8
Inverness D-8
Kentville F-5
Liverpool G-5
Lunenburg F-5
Middleton F-5
New Glasgow E-7
New Waterford D-9
Pictou E-7
Port Hawkesbury E-8
Shelburne G-4
Springhill E-5
Sydney D-9
Sydney Mines D-9
Truro E-6
Windsor F-5
Wolfville E-5
Yarmouth G-4

Prince Edward Island

Cities and Towns

Alberton C-5
Charlottetown D-6
Cornwall D-6
Georgetown D-7
Kensington D-6
Montague D-7
Port Borden D-6
Souris D-7
Summerside D-6
Tignish C-6

NEW BRUNSWICK
Population: 751,171 (rank: 8th)
Largest city: Saint John, 70,063, E-4
Land area: 27,587 sq. mi. (rank: 11th)

NEWFOUNDLAND & LABRADOR
Population: 514,536 (rank: 9th)
Largest city: St. John's, 106,172, B-9
Land area: 144,353 sq. mi. (rank: 10th)

NOVA SCOTIA
Population: 921,727 (rank: 7th)
Largest city: Halifax, 390,096, F-6
Land area: 20,594 sq. mi. (rank: 12th)

PRINCE EDWARD ISLAND
Population: 140,204 (rank: 10th)
Largest city: Charlottetown, 34,562, D-6
Land area: 2,185 sq. mi. (rank: 13th)

Provincial facts

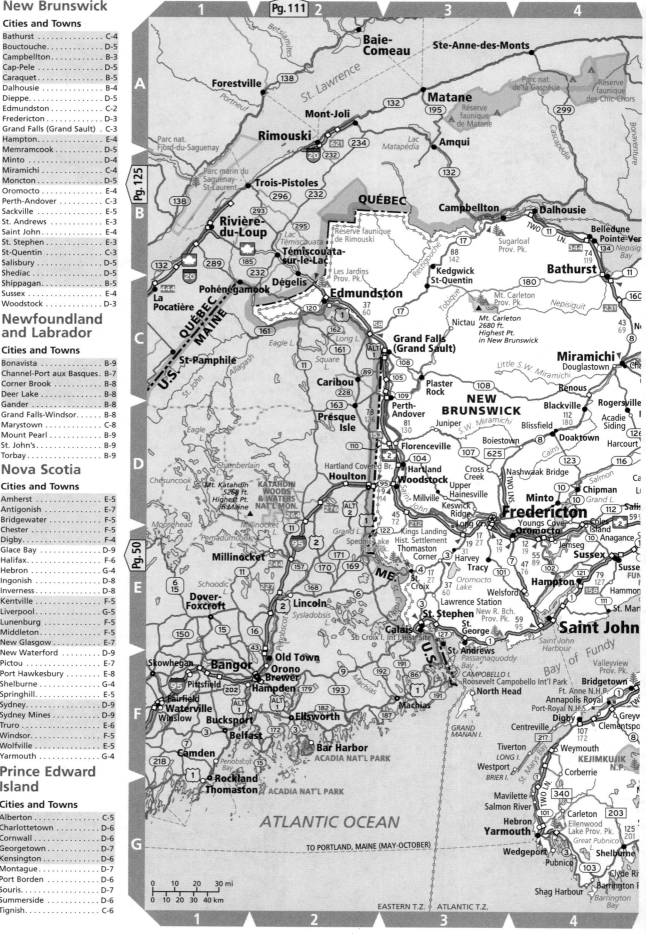

NOTE: Maps are not always in alphabetical order.
See Page 1 for map location in this atlas.

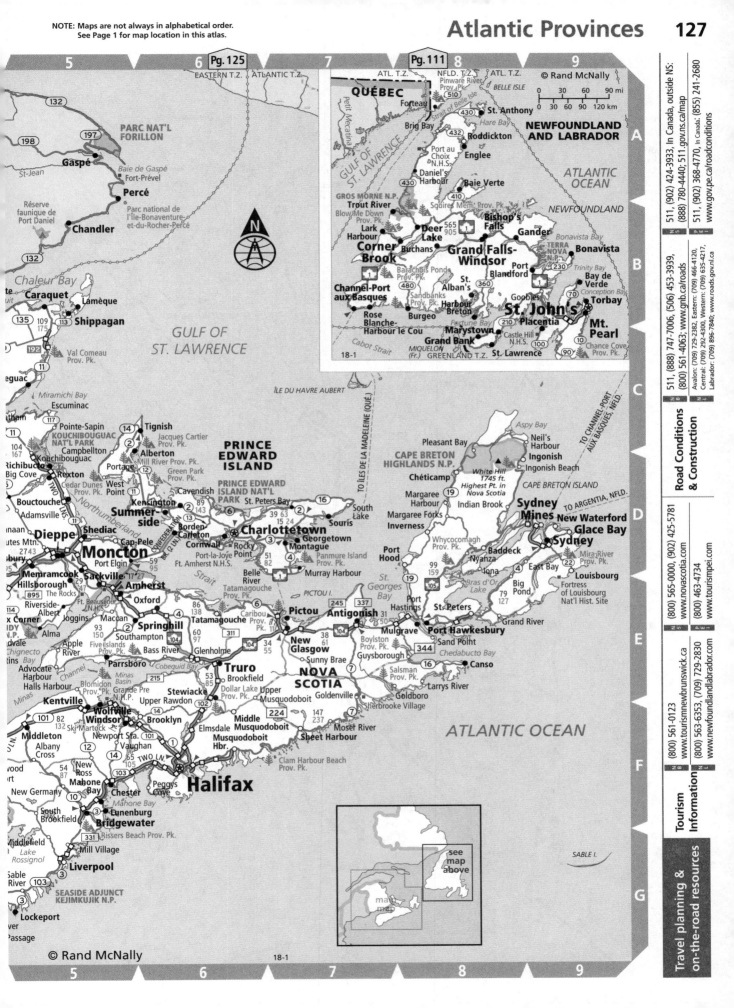

© Rand McNally

Road Conditions & Construction

NS: 511, (902) 424-3933; In Canada, outside NS: (888) 780-4440; 511.gov.ns.ca/map
NB: 511, (888) 747-7006, (506) 453-3939, (800) 561-4063; www.gnb.ca/roads
PE: 511, (902) 368-4770; In Canada: (855) 241-2680 www.gov.pe.ca/roadconditions
NL: Avalon: (709) 729-2382, Eastern: (709) 466-4120, Central: (709) 292-4300, Western: (709) 635-4217, Labrador: (709) 896-7840; www.roads.gov.nl.ca

Tourism Information

NS: (800) 565-0000, (902) 425-5781 www.novascotia.com
PE: (800) 463-4734 www.tourismpei.com
NB: (800) 561-0123 www.tourismnewbrunswick.ca
NL: (800) 563-6353, (709) 729-2830 www.newfoundlandlabrador.ca

Travel planning & on-the-road resources

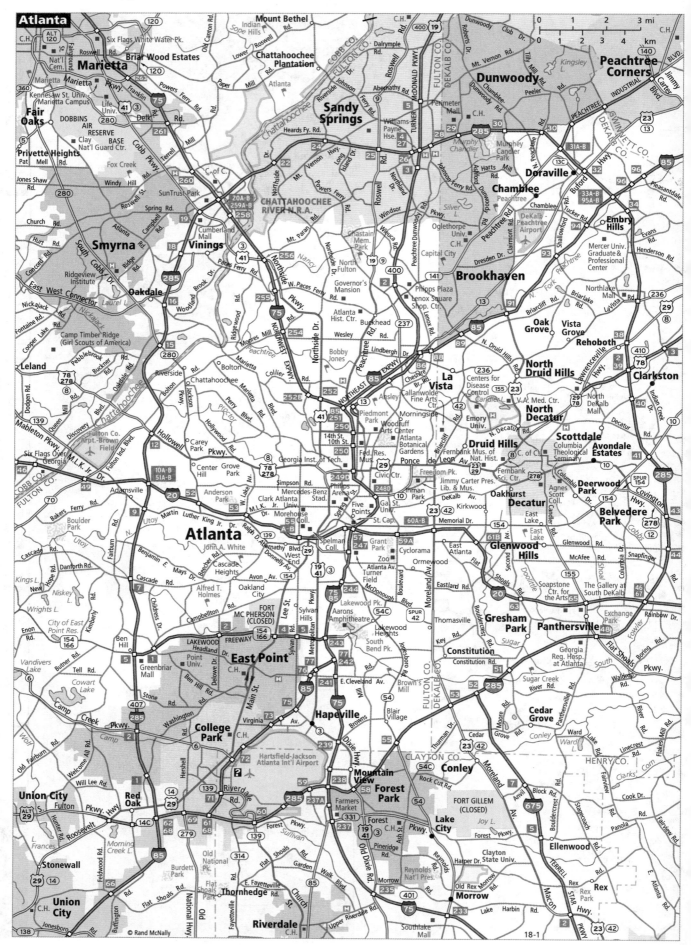

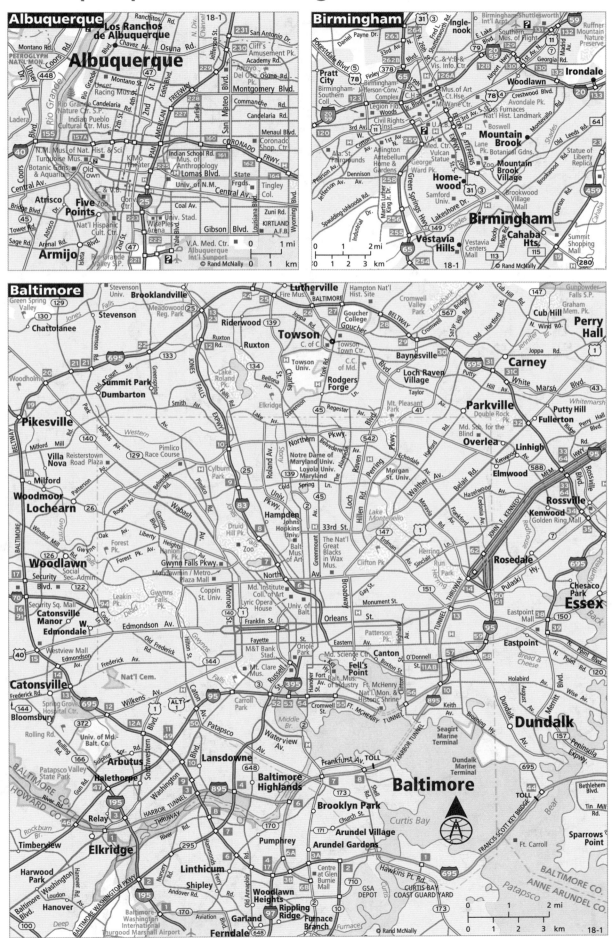

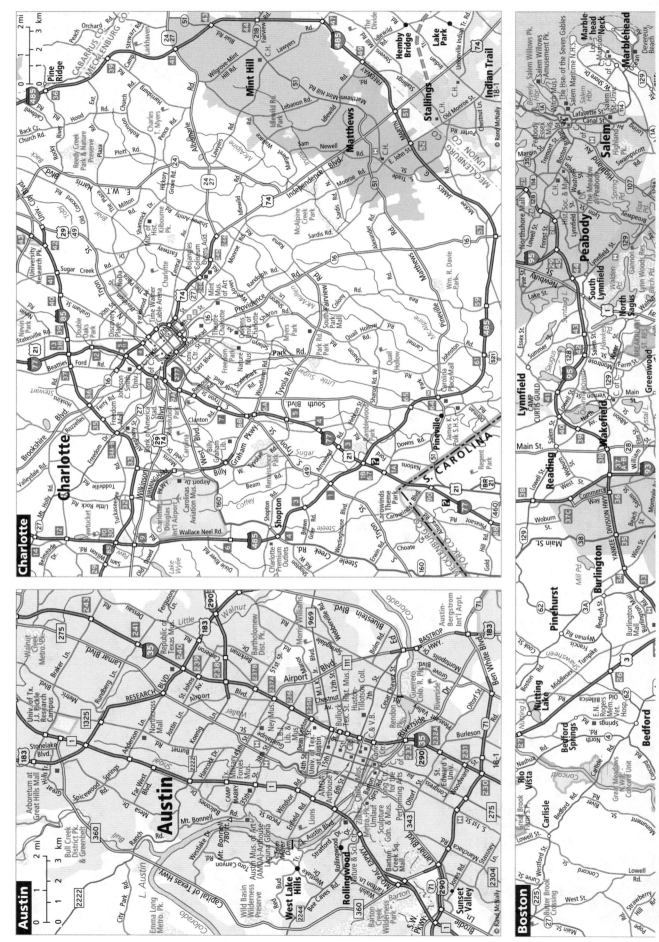

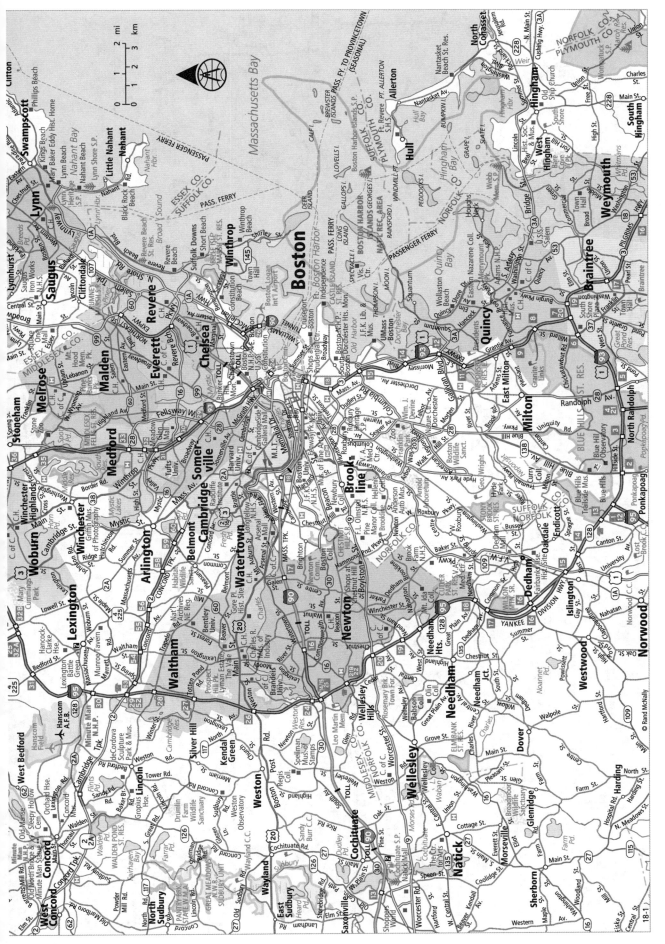

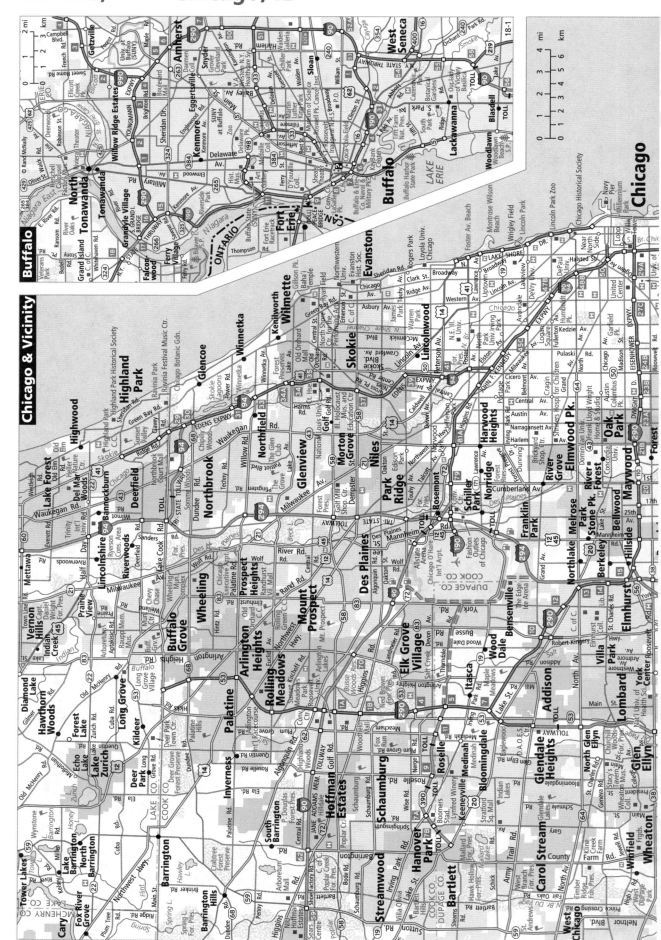

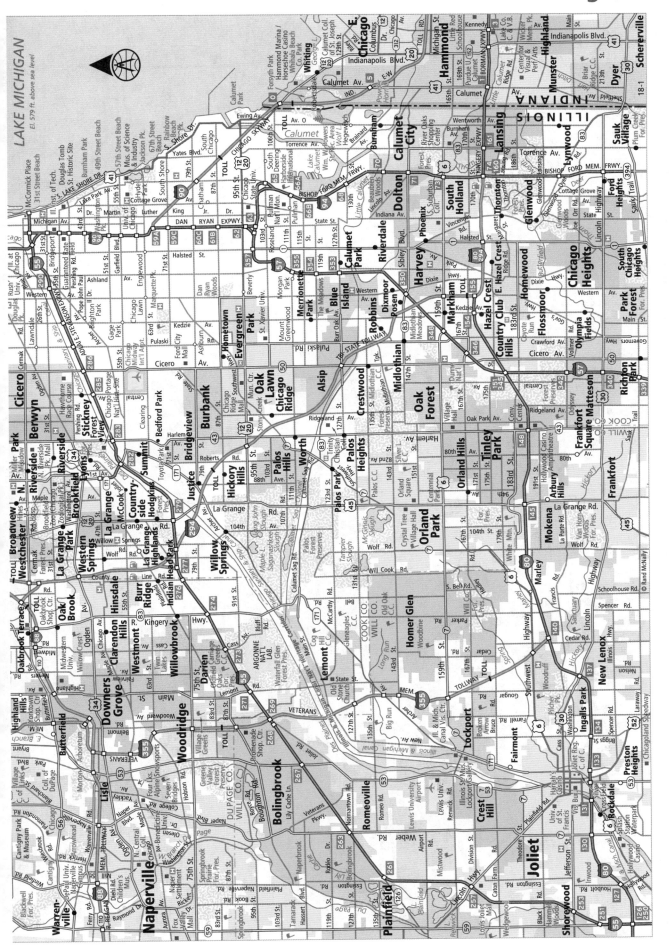

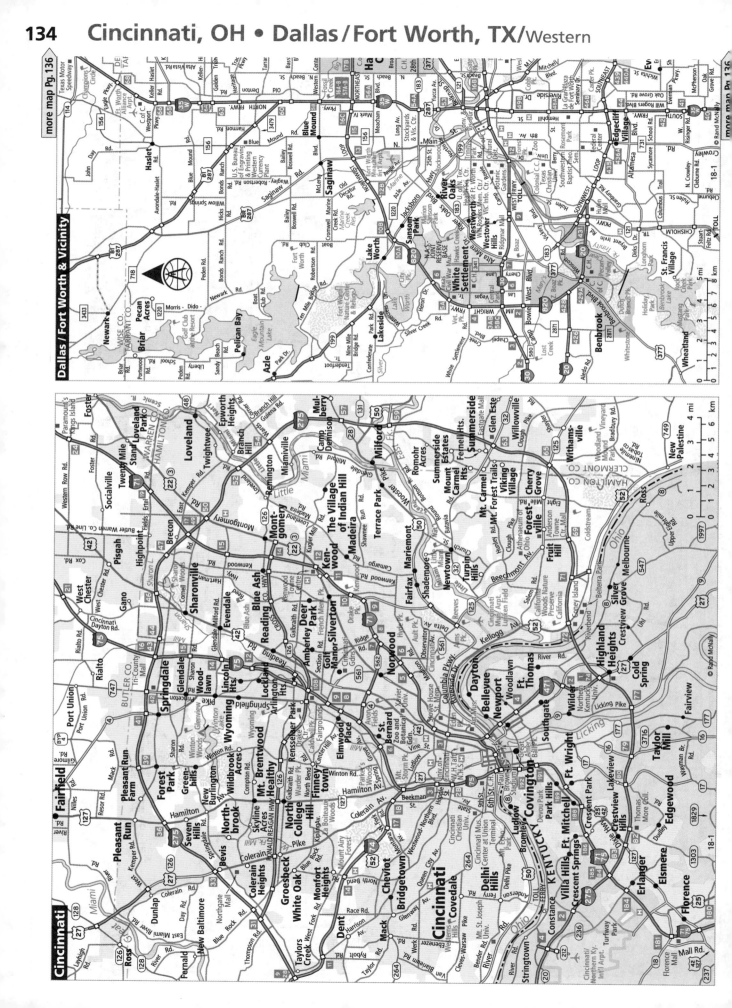

Dallas/Fort Worth & Vicinity

Cincinnati

© Rand McNally

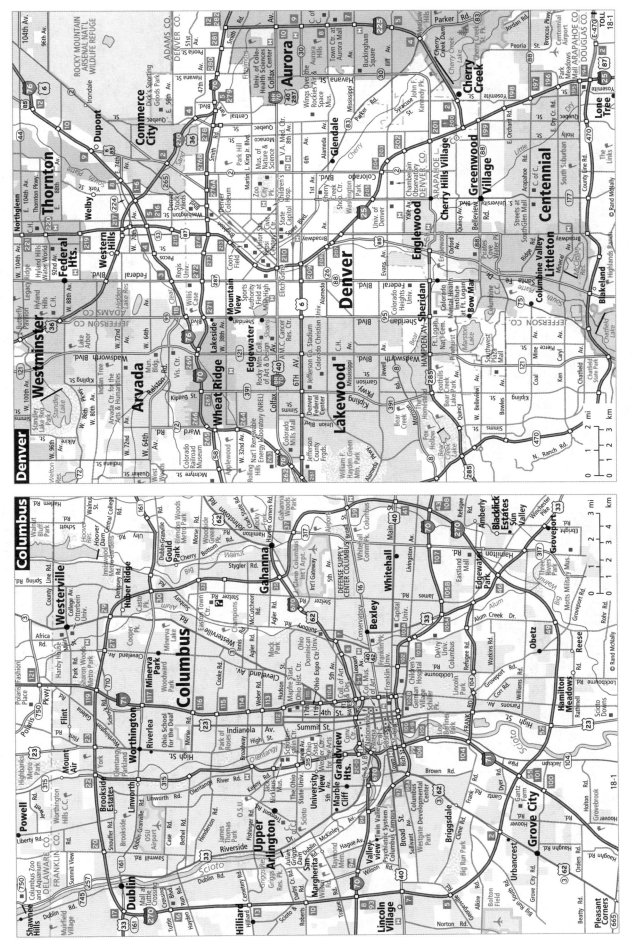

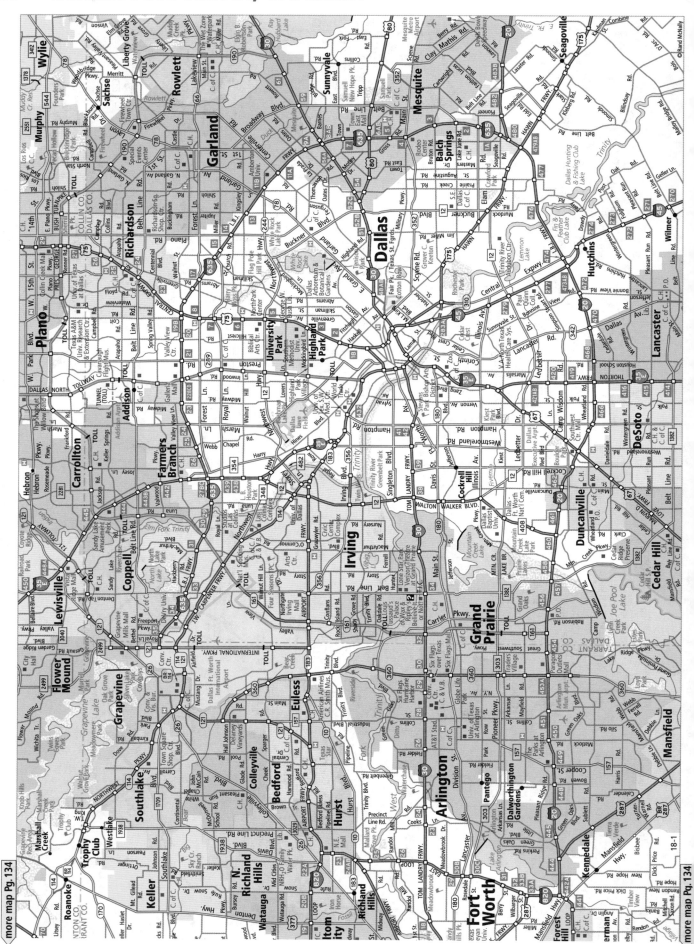

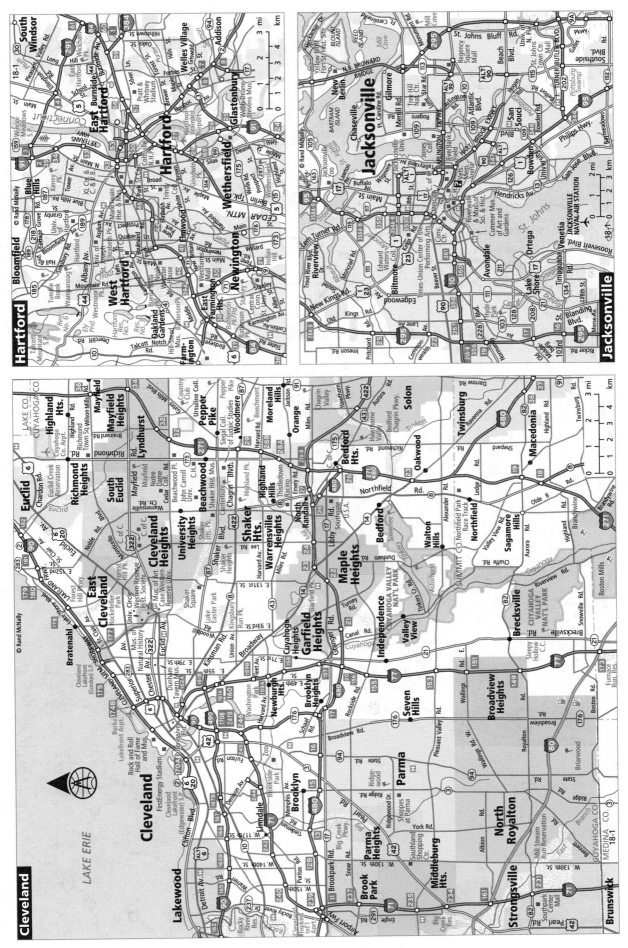

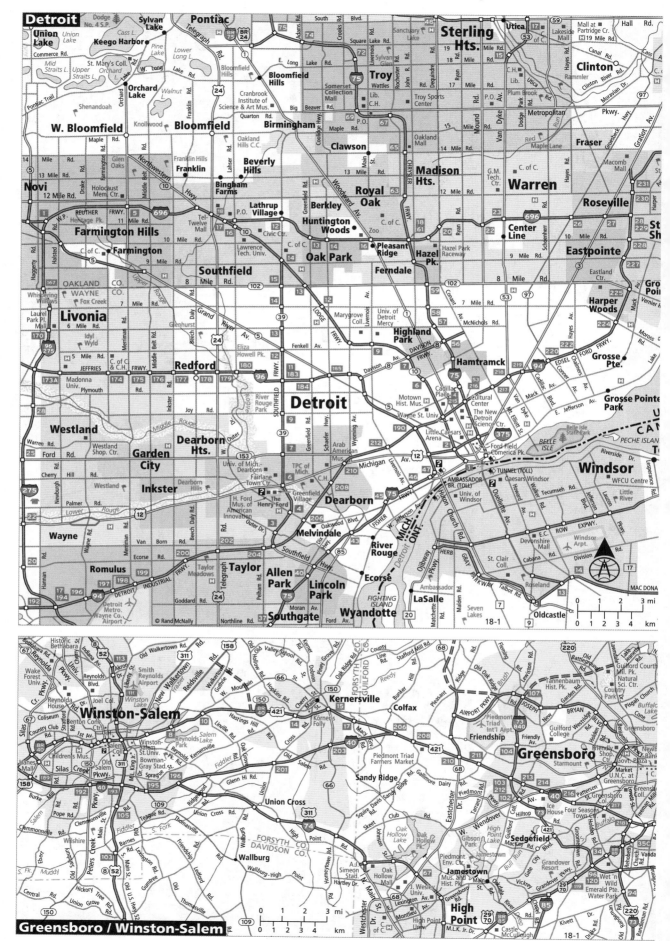

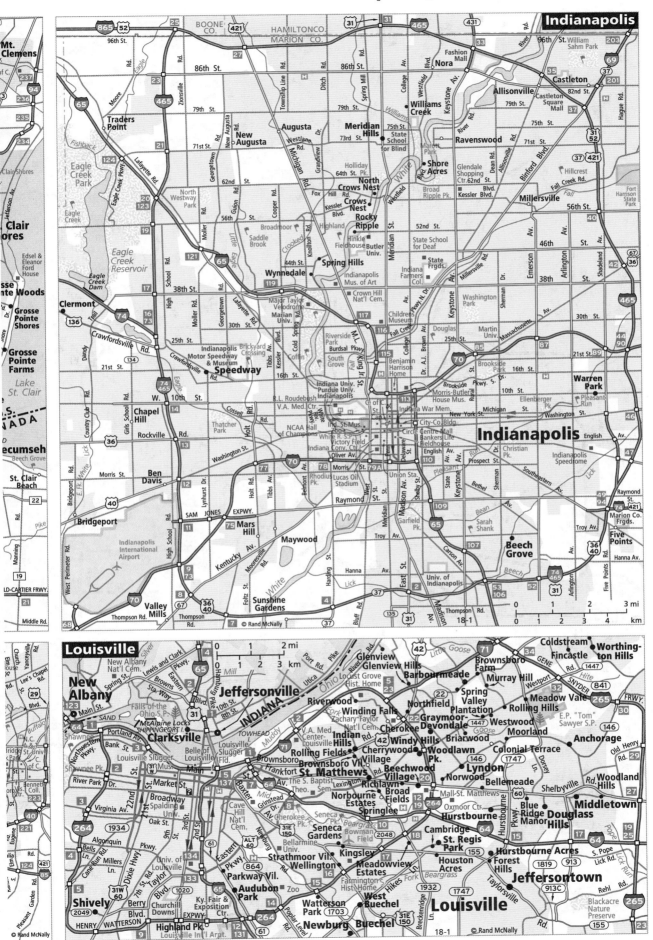

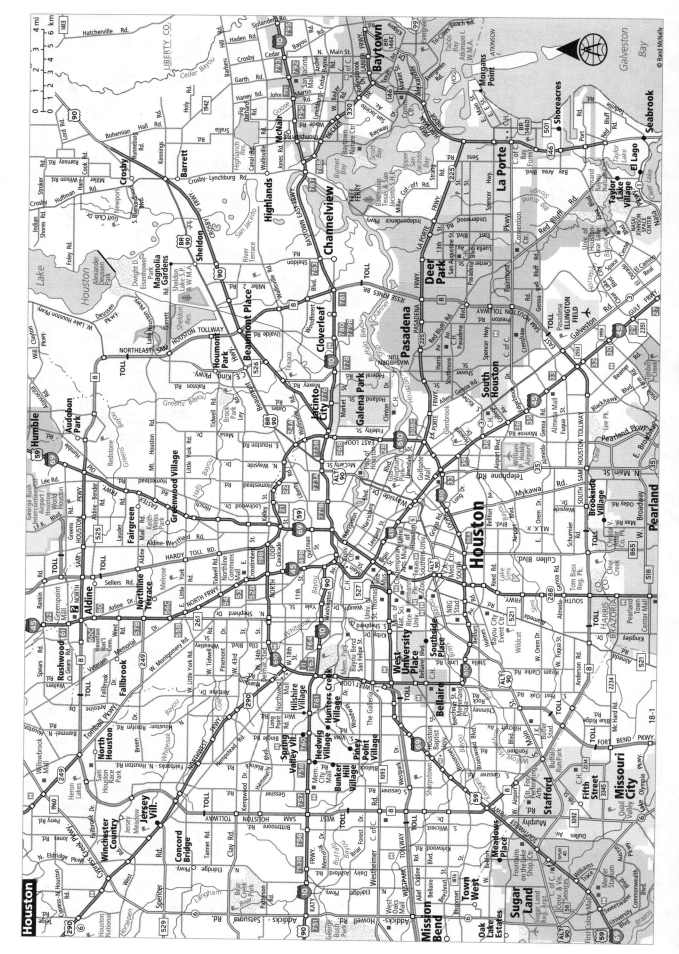

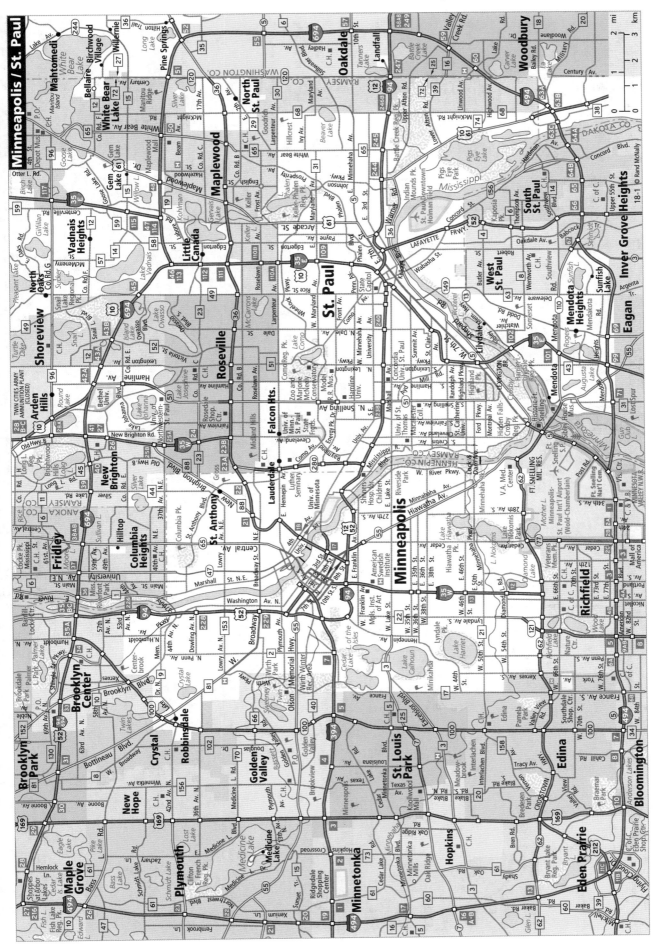

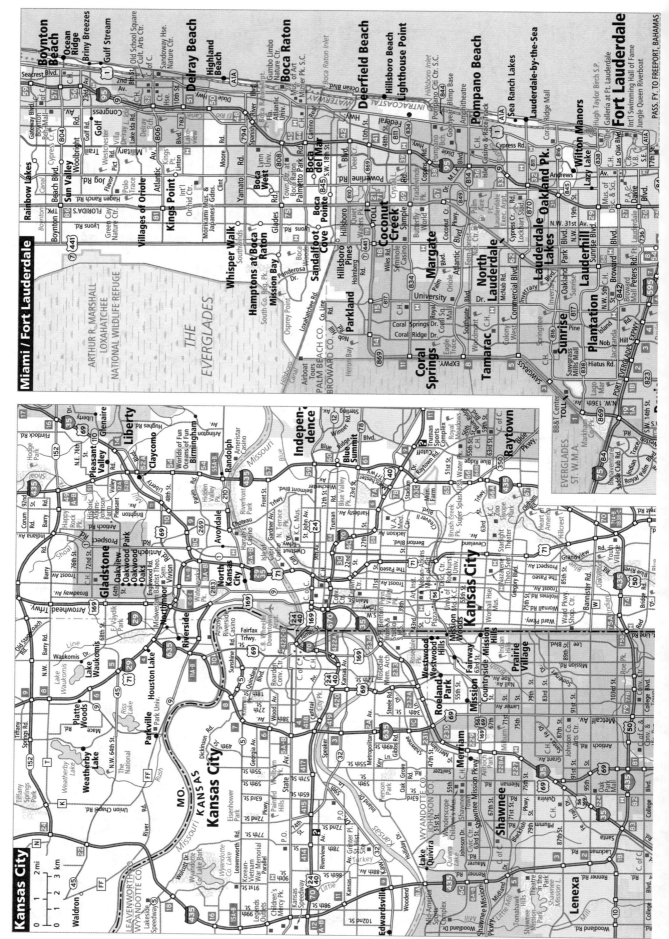

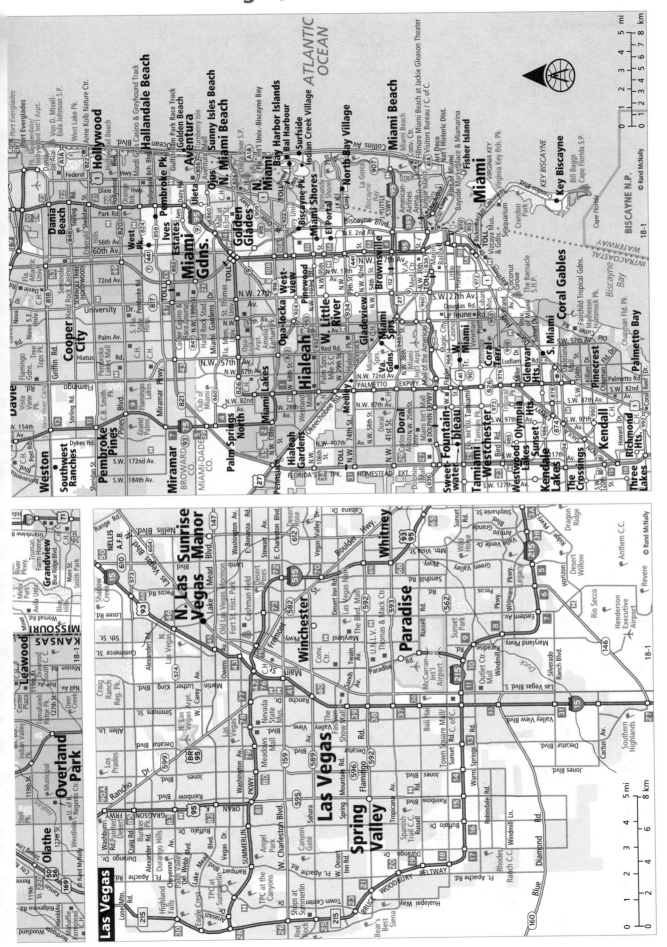

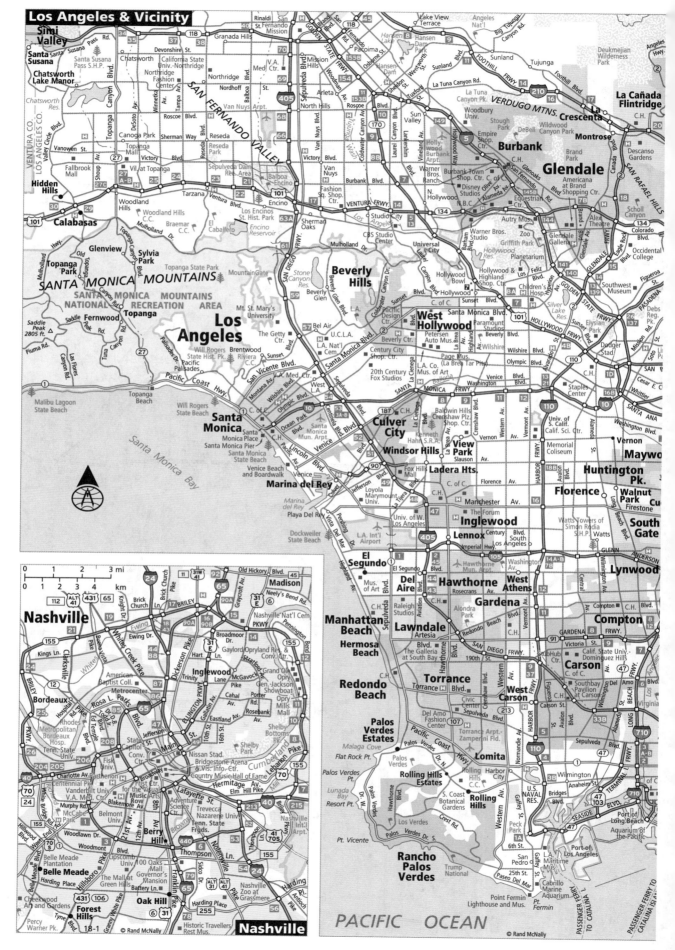

Los Angeles & Vicinity

Nashville

PACIFIC OCEAN

© Rand McNally

18-1

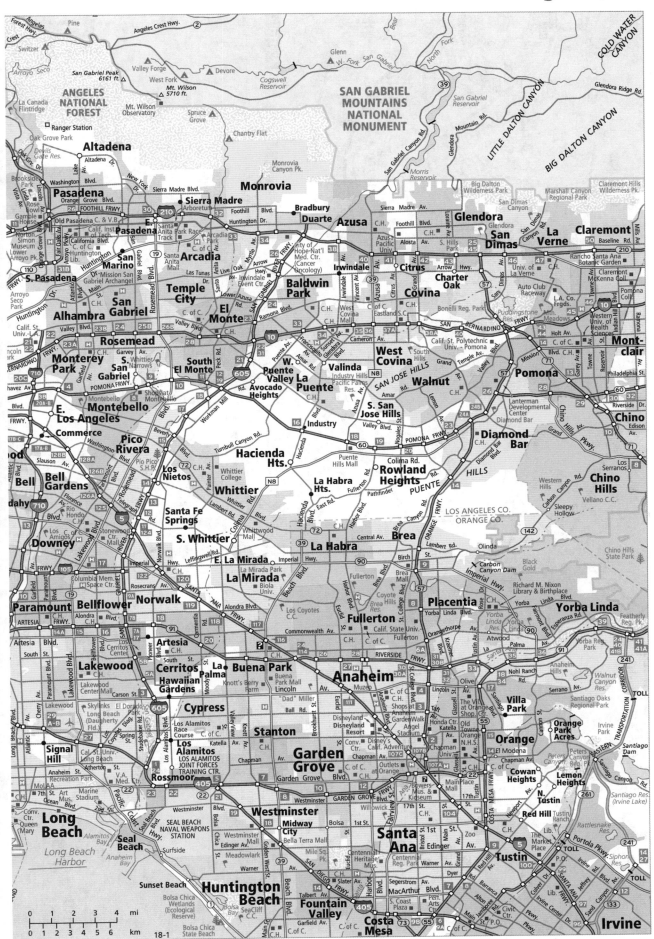

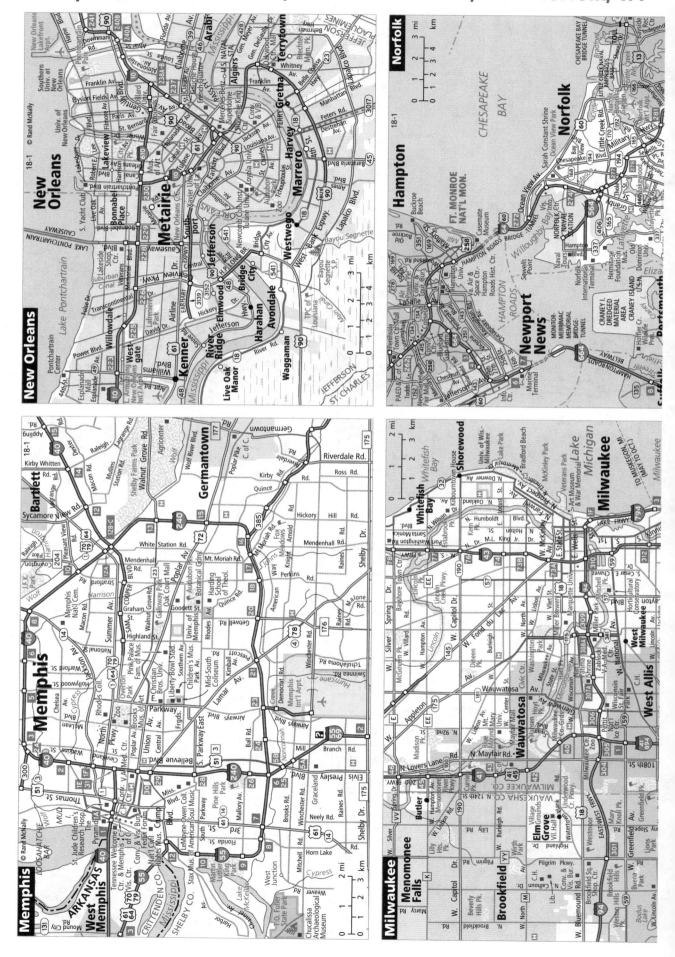

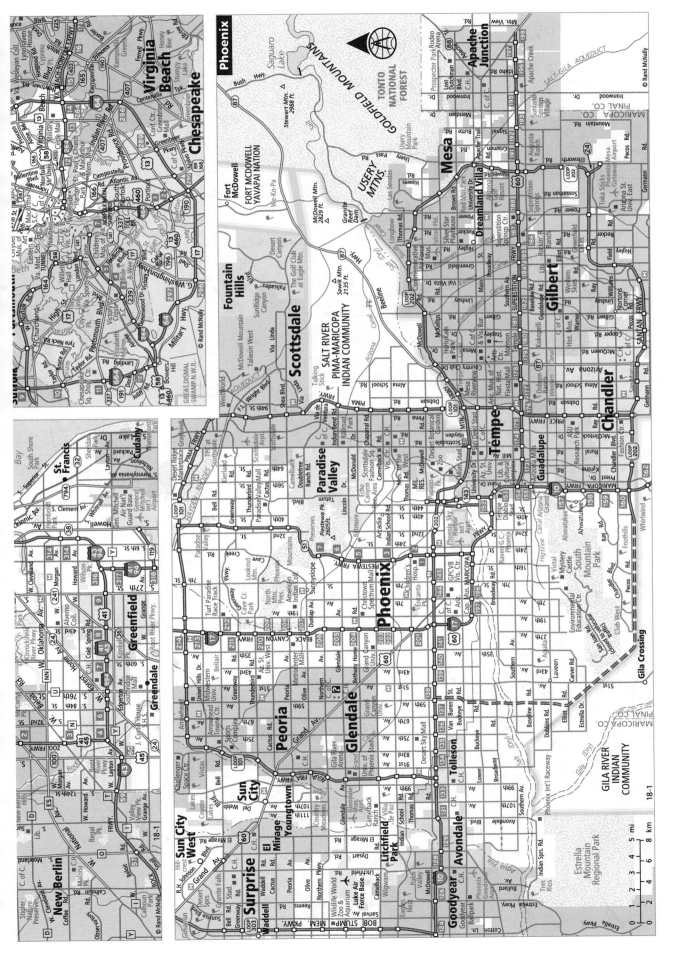

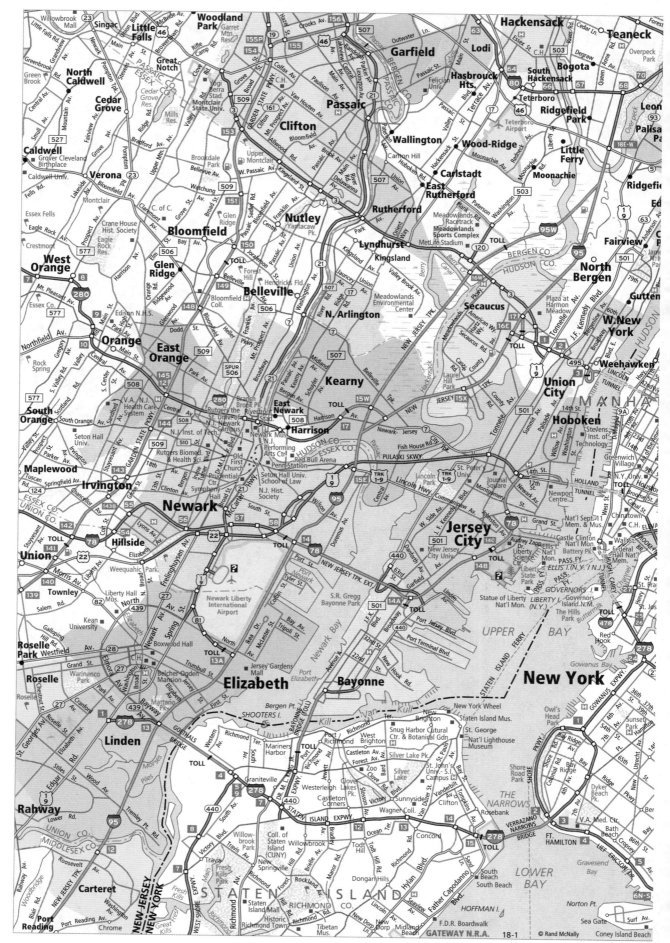

GATEWAY N.R.A.   18-1

New York / Newark & Vicinity

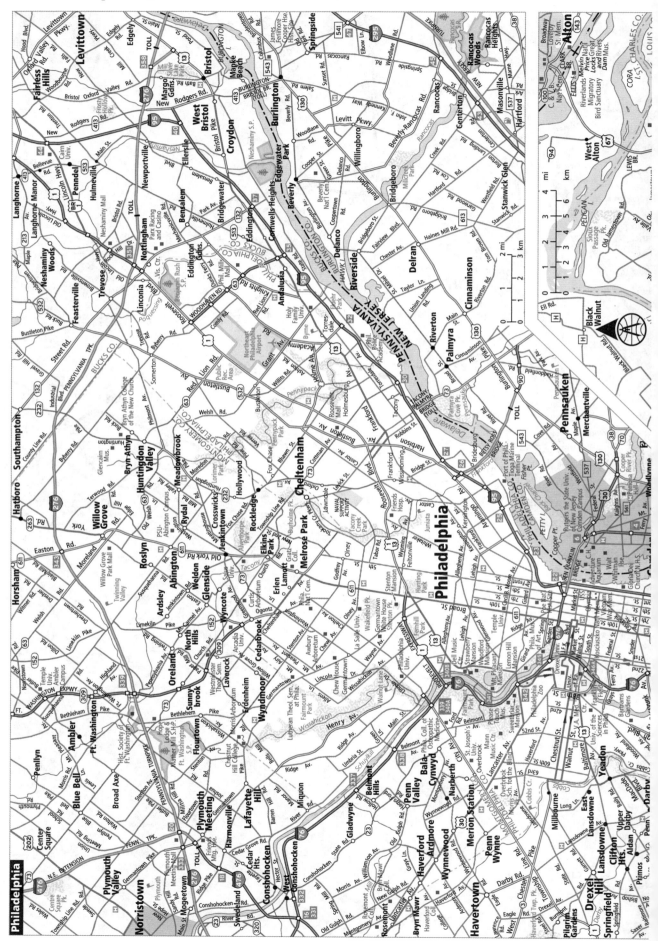

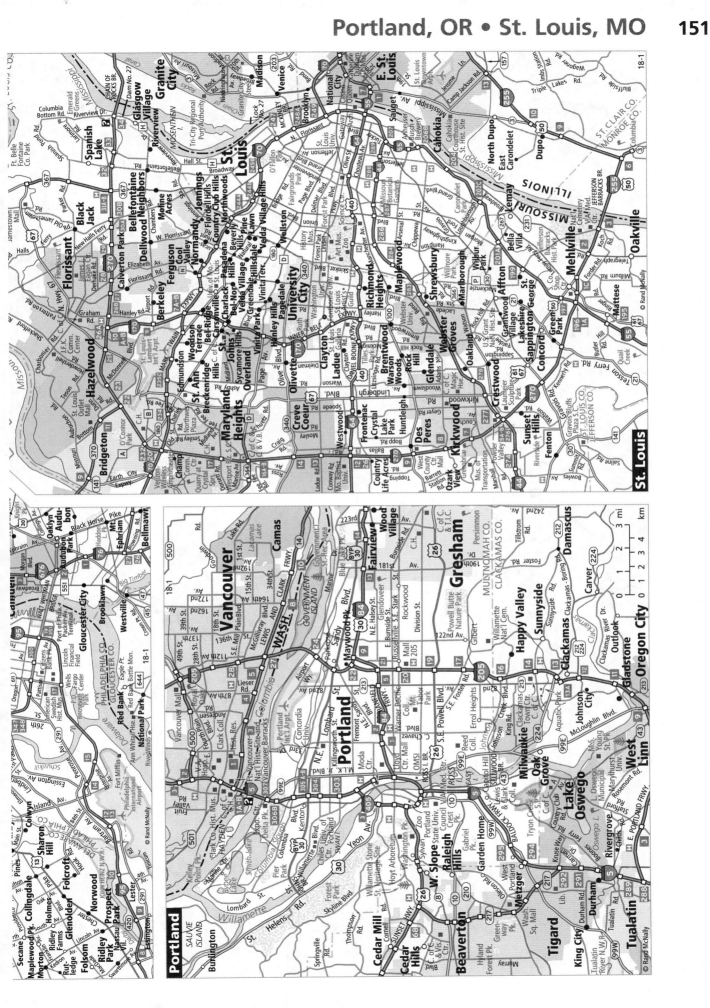

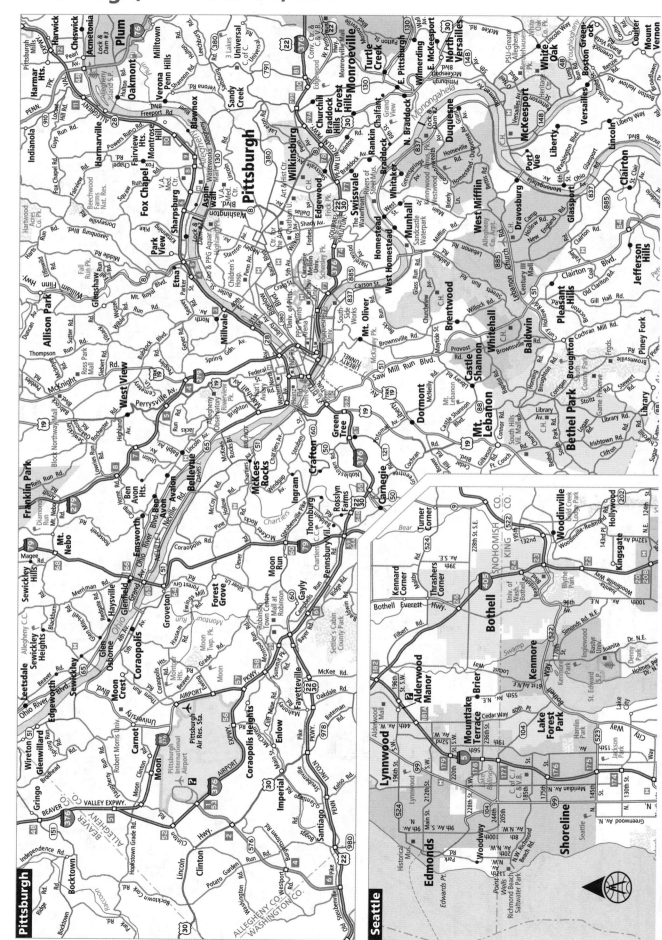

Pittsburgh

Seattle

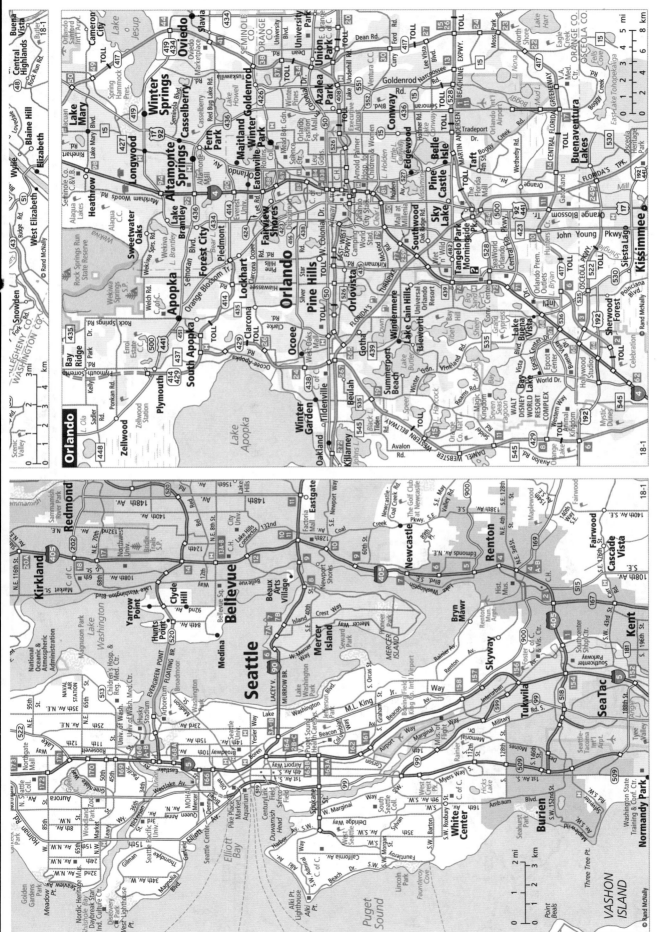

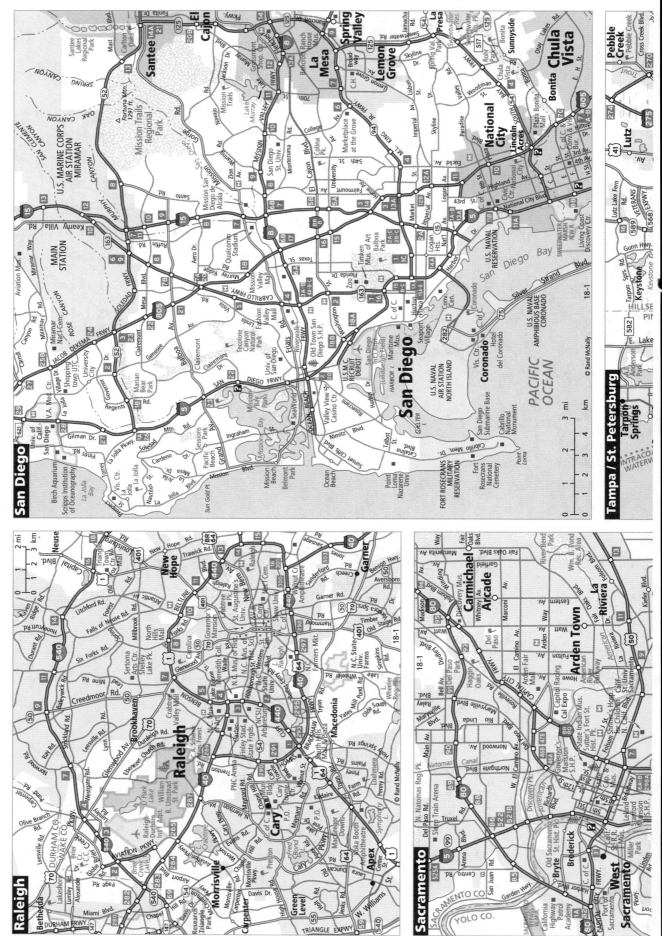

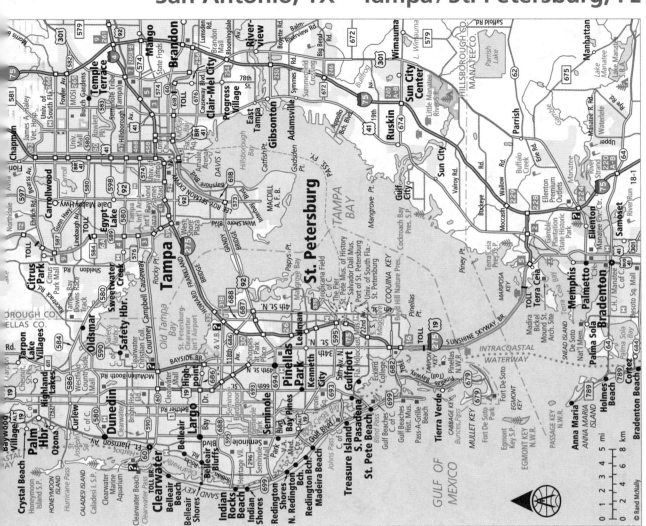

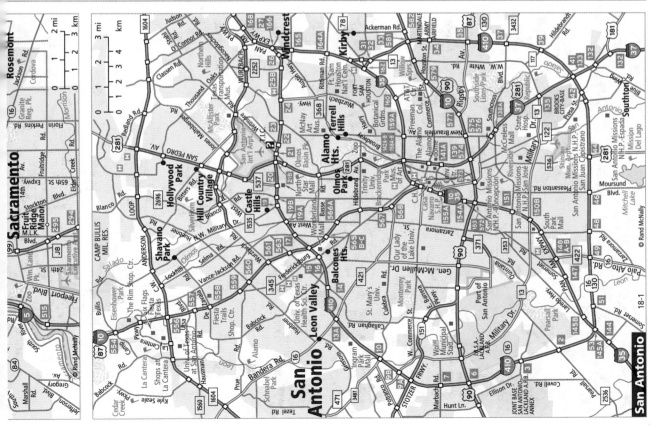

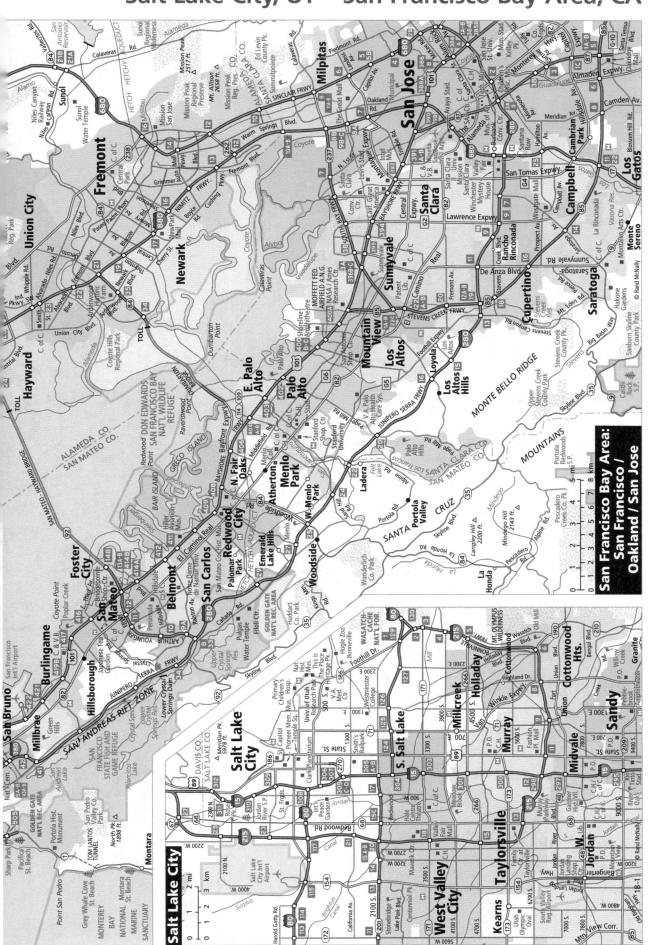

San Francisco Bay Area:
San Francisco /
Oakland / San Jose

Salt Lake City

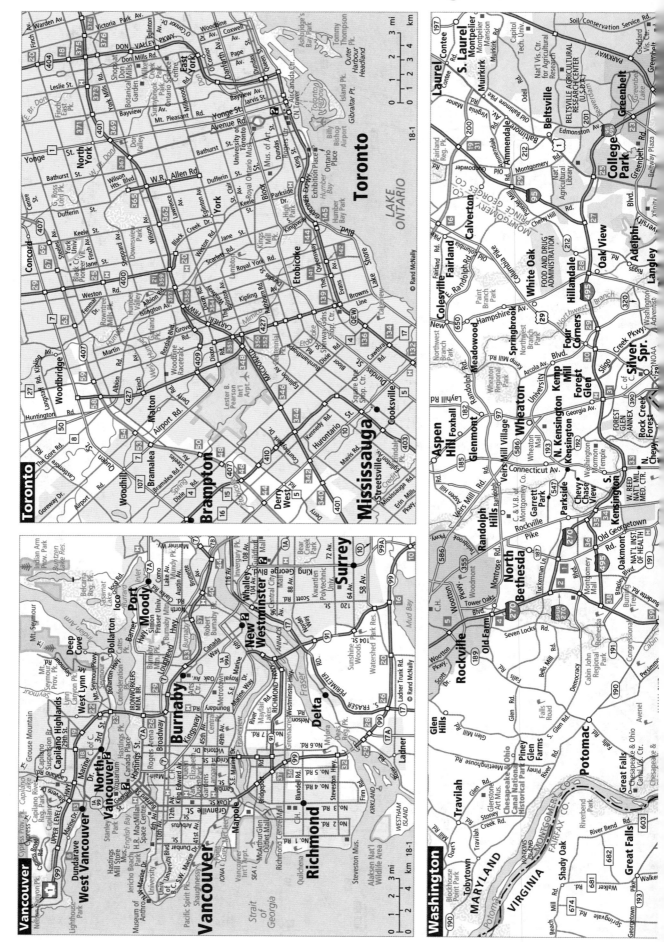

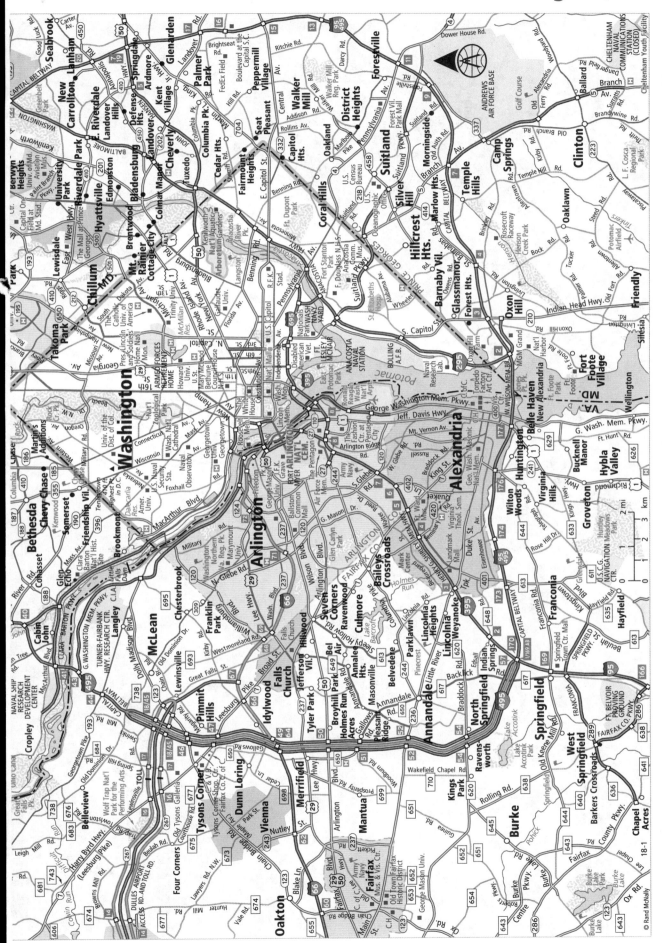

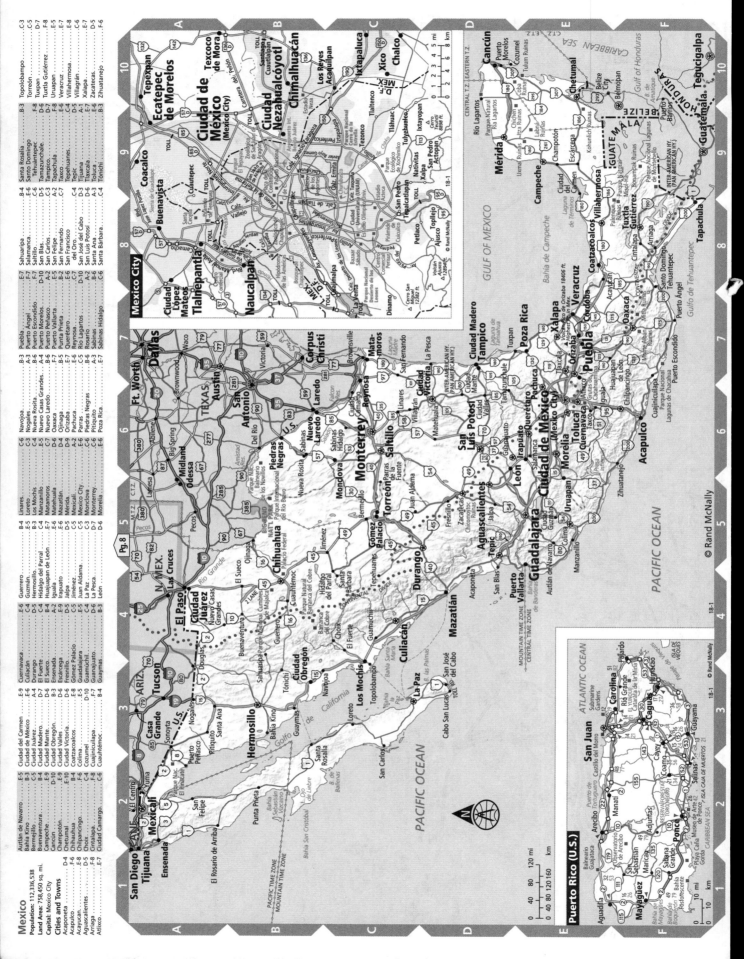